TIPPING POINT

First published by Jacana Media (Pty) Ltd in 2024

10 Orange Street
Sunnyside
Auckland Park 2092
South Africa
+2711 628 3200

www.jacana.co.za

© Individual contributors, 2024

All rights reserved.

ISBN 978-1-4314-3455-8

Cover design by Designer Studio Warburton
Editing by Ali Parry
Proofreading by Lara Jacob
Indexing by Ali Parry
Set in Georgia 10/14.5pt
Printed and bound by ABC Press, Cape Town
Job no. 04135

See a complete list of Jacana titles at www.jacana.co.za

TIPPING POINT

Turmoil or Reform?
South Africa's political economy
after 2024

Edited by Raymond Parsons

Other books authored or edited by Raymond Parsons

The Mbeki Inheritance: South Africa's Economy 1990–2004 (2000)

Parsons' Perspective: Focus on the Economy (2002)

Manuel, Markets and Money: Essays in Appraisal (2004)

Zumanomics: Which Way to Shared Prosperity in South Africa? (2009)

Zumanomics Revisited: The Road from Mangaung to 2030 (2014)

Good Capitalism, Bad Capitalism: The Role of Business in South Africa (2018)

Recession, Recovery and Reform: South Africa after Covid-19 (2020)

Contents

Abbreviations and acronyms ix
About the contributors xv
Overture xxv

1. Unpacking political party dynamics in post-apartheid South Africa
   Anthony Butler 1
2. Coalition politics: Is this the way?
   Ralph Mathekga 15
3. The economy, business and reform
   Cas Coovadia 27
4. Power struggles: Shedding light on South Africa's enduring energy challenges
   Rod Crompton and Bruce Young 37
5. Do geopolitics and trade clash? South Africa's foreign and trade policy options
   Anthoni van Nieuwkerk 57
6. Is Africa open for business?
   Daniel Mminele 71
7. South Africa's financial future: Keeping the debt trap at bay
   Isaah Mhlanga 83
8. Banking on credibility: The central bank and monetary policy after 2024
   Hilary Joffe 95

9. Broadening farm ownership for successful transformation in South African agriculture
   Johann Kirsten and Wandile Sihlobo — 111
10. Can we conquer corruption in South Africa?
    Jan van Romburgh — 123
11. Local government in South Africa after the 2024 election: Will the desirable or probable outcome prevail?
    Erwin Schwella — 133
12. Finding new, bottom-up solutions to grassroots socioeconomic challenges
    Vuyiswa Ramokgopa — 151
13. Strengthening the institutions of public accountability in South Africa
    Dennis Davis — 165
14. South Africa: Grappling with the 'age of uncertainty'
    Raymond Parsons — 181

Coda and recapitulation — 199
Notes and other references — 205
Index — 229

Abbreviations and acronyms

AfCFTA	African Continental Free Trade Area
AGOA	African Growth and Opportunity Act
AGSA	Auditor-General South Africa
AI	artificial intelligence
ANC	African National Congress
ASEAN	Association of Southeast Asian Nations
AsgiSA	Accelerated and Shared Growth Initiative for South Africa
AU	African Union
B-BBEE	broad-based black economic empowerment
BCI	Business Confidence Index
BER	Bureau for Economic Research
BLSA	Business Leadership South Africa
BoE	Bank of England
BoJ	Bank of Japan
BSA	Business for South Africa
BUSA	Business Unity South Africa
CASP	Comprehensive Agricultural Support Programme
CIPC	Companies and Intellectual Property Commission
CO_2	carbon dioxide
CODESA	Convention for a Democratic South Africa
COP	Conference of the Parties

COPE	Congress of the People
DA	Democratic Alliance
DALRRD	Department of Agriculture, Land Reform and Rural Development
DBSA	Development Bank of Southern Africa
DIRCO	Department of International Relations and Cooperation
DTIC	Department of Trade, Industry and Competition
EAF	energy availability factor
ECB	European Central Bank
EFF	Economic Freedom Fighters
EPA	Economic Partnership Agreement
EROEI	energy return on energy invested
ERRP	Economic Reconstruction and Recovery Plan
ESD	enterprise and supplier development
ESI	electricity supply industry
EU	European Union
EV	electric vehicle
FDI	foreign direct investment
Fed	Federal Reserve Bank
FF+	Freedom Front Plus
G3	Group of Three
G7	Group of Seven
G20	Group of 20
G77	Group of 77
GDP	gross domestic product
GEAR	Growth, Employment and Redistribution (strategy)
GFC	global financial crisis
GFCF	gross fixed capital formation
GFECRA	Gold and Foreign Exchange Contingency Reserve Account
GHG	greenhouse gases
GW	gigawatt
HSRC	Human Sciences Research Council
ICE	internal combustion engine

ICT	information and communication technology
IEC	Electoral Commission of South Africa
IFP	Inkatha Freedom Party
IMF	International Monetary Fund
IRENA	International Renewable Energy Agency
IRP	Integrated Resource Plan
JET	Just Energy Transition
JET-IP	Just Energy Transition Investment Plan
JICC	Joint Intelligence Crisis Committee
Jipsa	Joint Initiative on Priority Skills Acquisition
LPG	liquefied petroleum gas
MMP	mixed-member proportional (system)
MPC	Monetary Policy Committee
MTEF	Medium-Term Expenditure Framework
MW	megawatt
NDP	National Development Plan
NDPP	National Director of Public Prosecutions
NECOM	National Energy Crisis Committee
Nedlac	National Economic Development and Labour Council
NERSA	National Energy Regulator of South Africa
NGO	non-governmental organisation
NGP	New Growth Path
NHI	National Health Insurance
NLCC	National Logistics Crisis Committee
NP	National Party
NPA	National Prosecuting Authority
NPC	National Planning Commission
NTCSA	National Transmission Company of South Africa
OECD	Organisation for Economic Co-operation and Development
OPEC	Organization of the Petroleum Exporting Countries
OUTA	Organisation Undoing Tax Abuse
PA	Patriotic Alliance

PAC	Pan Africanist Congress
PIC	Public Investment Corporation
PLAS	Proactive Land Acquisition Strategy
PUI	Policy Uncertainty Index
RDP	Reconstruction and Development Programme
REIPPP	Renewable Energy Independent Power Producer Procurement Programme
RIA	regulatory impact assessment
RMB	Rand Merchant Bank
RPPF	Represented Political Parties Fund
SAA	South African Airways
SABC	South African Broadcasting Corporation
SACCI	South African Chamber of Commerce and Industry
SACU	Southern African Customs Union
SADC	Southern African Development Community
SALGA	South African Local Government Association
SANRAL	South African National Roads Agency
SAPO	South African Post Office
SAPS	South African Police Service
SARB	South African Reserve Bank
SARS	South African Revenue Service
SASAS	South African Social Attitudes Survey
SDGs	Sustainable Development Goals
SIU	Special Investigating Unit
SMME	small, medium and micro enterprise
SOC	state-owned company
SOE	state-owned enterprise
SONA	State of the Nation Address
SRD	social relief of distress (grant)
UAE	United Arab Emirates
UDF	United Democratic Front
UDM	United Democratic Movement
UN	United Nations
UNECA	United Nations Economic Commission for Africa

UNFCCC COP	United Nations Framework Convention on Climate Change Conference of the Parties
UNIDO	United Nations Industrial Development Organization
US	United States
VAT	value-added tax
VUCA	volatile, uncertain, complex and ambiguous
WEF	World Economic Forum
WHO	World Health Organization
WUI	World Uncertainty Index

About the contributors

ANTHONY BUTLER is professor of Political Studies at the University of Cape Town. Previously he was a fellow of Emmanuel College at the University of Cambridge, director of the Politics and Administration programme at Birkbeck College at the University of London and the chair of Political Studies at the University of the Witwatersrand. His research focuses on public policy analysis and contemporary South African government and politics. He is the author of several books, including *The Idea of the ANC* (Ohio University Press), *Contemporary South Africa* (Palgrave Macmillan) and *Cyril Ramaphosa* (James Currey). Anthony is also a regular columnist for *Business Day*. He holds an MA from the University of Oxford and a PhD from the University of Cambridge.

CASSIM (CAS) COOVADIA is the chief executive officer of BUSA (Business Unity South Africa) and the former managing director of BASA (Banking Association South Africa), a position he held for 15 years. During that time, he was instrumental in positioning BASA as a credible voice of the banking industry. He is also the chairperson of the NBI (National Business Initiative), a member of the Council of the University of the Witwatersrand and a board member of CDE (Centre for Development and Enterprise). Cas became actively involved in anti-apartheid politics in the 1980s and was instrumental in the formation of both the Civic Association of Johannesburg and the South African National Civic Organisation of which he was the vice-president. He has considerable experience in, and has written extensively about, housing finance, civil society, local government and the role of civic organisations in governance. He holds a BCom in Accounting from the University College, Durban.

ROD CROMPTON is one of South Africa's leading energy experts, with many years of experience in the formulation of economic policies and regulations for the energy sector. He is currently a visiting adjunct professor at the Wits School of Governance where he established the African Energy Leadership Centre. He is also a non-executive director of Eskom. Previously he was the director of Crompton Consulting, a board member of the National Energy Regulator of South Africa (NERSA), the deputy director-general of the (then) Department of Minerals and Energy, and director of the Minerals and Energy Policy Centre. He was also the general secretary of the Chemical Workers Industrial Union during the anti-apartheid era. Rod is the joint author of the chapter, 'Energy in South Africa', in the *Oxford Handbook of the South African Economy* (Oxford University Press). He holds a PhD in Industrial Strategy from the (then) University of Natal (Durban) and in 2017 was awarded honorary life membership of the South African National Energy Association.

DENNIS DAVIS is one of South Africa's most well-respected legal minds who has spent much of his career challenging the status quo and highlighting the dangers of an unjust society. He began teaching at the University of Cape Town (UCT) in the late 1970s, while simultaneously practising as an advocate specialising in tax law and public law. At that time, he became heavily involved in anti-apartheid activism. For several years during the 1990s, he was the director of the Centre for Applied Legal Studies at the University of the Witwatersrand and a member of the Katz Commission whose recommendations ultimately led to the establishment of the South African Revenue Service (SARS). In 1998, he became a judge of the Cape High Court and in 1999 he was appointed Judge President of the Competition Appeal Court, a position he held until 2020. Although he has now retired from the Bench, he has continued to teach constitutional law and tax law at UCT where he is an Honorary Professor of Law, to host a TV show, 'Judge for Yourself', and to consult to various organisations. During his career, Dennis has handed down several landmark judgments in public and constitutional law and written extensively, including several books, his most recent being *Lawfare: Judging Politics in South Africa*, which he co-authored with Michelle le Roux (Jonathan Ball Publishers). Dennis holds an MPhil from the University of Cambridge and an Honorary Doctorate in Law from UCT.

HILARY JOFFE is editor at large and a columnist at *Business Day*, where she chairs the editorial board. A seasoned journalist, she is best known for her insightful economic and financial analyses, with fiscal and monetary policy being of particular interest to her. She obtained degrees in Economics and Industrial Sociology from the University of the Witwatersrand and an MPhil in Sociology from the University of Oxford. Initially she lectured at the University of Cape Town before embarking on a career in financial journalism. Prior to joining *Business Day*, where she has been for many years, she held positions such as investment editor at *Finance Week*, business editor at the *Weekly Mail*, senior economist at Standard Bank, contributing editor at the *Sunday Times Business Times* and senior adviser at the global consultancy, Brunswick. Hilary left *Business Day* in 2010 to join Eskom as national spokesperson and general manager, returning to journalism in 2013. Over the years she has received many accolades, including being a recipient of the Ruth First Fellowship and a winner of Sanlam awards for excellence in economic journalism.

JOHANN KIRSTEN is the director of the Bureau for Economic Research (BER) at Stellenbosch University. Previously he was professor and head of the Department of Agricultural Economics, Extension and Rural Development at the University of Pretoria, a position he held for nearly 25 years. Having obtained a BSc and BSc Honours in Agricultural Economics from Stellenbosch University, he went on to obtain a master's and then a PhD in Agricultural Economics from the University of Pretoria. Johann is an internationally acclaimed scholar and researcher and enjoys a B2 rating from South Africa's National Research Foundation (NRF), which is a testimony of the breadth and depth of his published works. His main research interests are agricultural policy, agricultural commodity markets, land reform and the economics of origin-based foods.

RALPH MATHEKGA is a political analyst with impressive academic and research credentials acquired both in South Africa and abroad. He is currently a senior expert at the Liechtenstein-based think tank, Geopolitical Intelligence Services (GIS), where he focuses on trade, diplomacy and foreign relations in the SADC (Southern African Development Community) region. His previous positions include senior policy analyst at the National Treasury (Budget Office), political researcher at the Institute for Democracy (Idasa) and political science lecturer at the University of the Western Cape. Over the years he has written over 500 opinion pieces for local and international newspapers and journals and is a regular contributor to international publications such as *The New York Times*, *The Washington Post* and *The Financial Times*. Ralph is the author of *When Zuma Goes*, *Ramaphosa's Turn* and *The ANC's Last Decade* (all published by Tafelberg). He holds a PhD in Political Studies from the University of Johannesburg (UJ) and spent three years at the New School for Social Research in New York where he honed his research skills and contributed to many of their publications.

ISAAH MHLANGA is the chief economist and head of research at Rand Merchant Bank. He leads the RMB markets research team, focusing on macroeconomics, income trends, and currency and credit dynamics in South Africa as well as other developing and developed countries. He is responsible for driving the bank's research-led client strategy in collaboration with sales, trading and the broader teams within RMB. Previously, he was the executive chief economist and exco member at Alexander Forbes Investments and the Investment Committee where he was responsible for macroeconomic strategy. In addition, he has worked as a macroeconomist at ABSA Capital, a senior economist in the National Treasury, an economist at the local office of the International Monetary Fund in Pretoria and a lecturer in mathematical economics and monetary economics at the University of Johannesburg (UJ). He is a columnist for *Business Day* and *The Sunday Times*, focusing on macroeconomics, investment strategy and economic policy issues. Apart from his professional obligations, Isaah is a trustee of the Study Trust and a non-executive board member of the Kutlwanong Centre for Maths, Science and Technology, both non-profit organisations operating in the education sector. He holds an MCom in Financial Economics from UJ.

DANIEL MMINELE was appointed to the boards of the Nedbank Group and Nedbank as an independent non-executive director in May 2023 and as independent chairperson in June 2023. Previous roles include chairperson of Alexander Forbes Group Holdings and Alexander Forbes Investments, chief executive of the ABSA Group and ABSA Bank, and two five-year terms as deputy governor of the South African Reserve Bank where he was responsible for financial markets, international economic relations and policy, and the human and operations cluster. While at the Reserve Bank, he served on the Governors' Executive Committee, the Monetary Policy Committee and the Financial Stability Committee. He also spent some time abroad, working in the banking sector in the UK and Germany. For most of 2022, he headed up the Presidential Climate Finance Task Team, which saw him leading and coordinating the work of the group tasked with giving effect to the Just Energy Transition Partnership and the development of the Just Energy Transition Investment Plan, which was launched in November 2022 at COP27. In 2018, the German president bestowed the Great Order of Merit on Daniel for his work in furthering German–South African relations, and in 2019, he was the recipient of the Lifetime Achiever Award from the Association of Black Securities and Investment Professionals in South Africa.

RAYMOND PARSONS is a prominent South African economist and contributor to public debates on a broad spectrum of issues of critical importance to South Africa's political economy. He is currently a professor at the North-West University Business School. For many years he was a leading figure in the organised business sector, holding positions such as the director-general of SACOB (South African Chamber of Business) and later deputy chief executive of BUSA (Business Unity South Africa). He has also served on the boards of various official bodies, including the South African Reserve Bank and Nedlac (National Economic Development and Labour Council) as well as the council of Nelson Mandela University. He is a frequent guest on televised economic affairs programmes and writes regularly for various online media. He has also written or edited seven books, including *Zumanomics: Which Way to Shared Prosperity in South Africa?*; *Zumanomics Revisited: The Road from Mangaung to 2030*; *Good Capitalism, Bad Capitalism: The Role of Business in South Africa;* and *Recession, Recovery and Reform: South Africa after Covid-19* (all published by Jacana Media). Raymond studied economics at the universities of Cape Town, Oxford and Copenhagen and holds an honorary doctorate from Nelson Mandela University. In 2017, he was awarded honorary life membership of the Economic Society of South Africa (of which he is a past president) in recognition of his contribution to the economics profession.

VUYISWA RAMOKGOPA is an experienced entrepreneur and businessperson with more than 15 years of experience in the commercial and non-profit sectors. She is the co-founder and director of a commercial real estate investment company, AWIP Investments, and the founder of 'Women on the Rise', a voluntary association aimed at giving women more prominence in politics. Previously, she was the chief executive officer of the SA Institute of Black Property Practitioners as well as a member of the Black Business Council National Council and the BRICS Women's Business Alliance Executive Committee. Vuyiswa holds a BCom in Politics, Philosophy and Economics from the University of Cape Town (UCT) and has completed various executive development programmes both in South Africa and abroad. She was among the 2011 Destiny Magazine Top 40 Under 40 and the 2018 Young Independents Top 100, and was a finalist for both the 2018 CNBC Africa All Africa Business Leaders Award and the 2019 Standard Bank Top Women in Business Award.

ERWIN SCHWELLA is the dean of the School of Social Innovation at Hugenote Kollege in South Africa. He is also professor (emeritus) of Public Leadership at Stellenbosch University and at the Law School of Tilburg University in the Netherlands. He has been a visiting academic at several esteemed institutions, such as the Kennedy School of Government at Harvard University, Leiden University, Leuven University and Manchester University. His current research interests include social innovation leadership in governance, institutional capacity building through organisational development, transformation and change management in complex societies, and new forms of accountability in service delivery models. During his lengthy tenure at Stellenbosch University, he facilitated many local governance innovation programmes in municipalities such as Saldanha Bay (fibre to the home), Prince Albert (tourism and agriculture), Mossel Bay (tourism and port and rail development) and Hessequa (water provision). He has also consulted extensively, both locally and internationally, on governance, public administration, public leadership, institution building, and organisational development. Erwin has more than 90 publications and many professional affiliations to his credit. He holds a PhD in Public Administration from Stellenbosch University.

WANDILE SIHLOBO is the chief economist at the Agricultural Business Chamber of South Africa (Agbiz) and a senior lecturer (extraordinary) in the Department of Agricultural Economics at Stellenbosch University. He was appointed to the Presidential Economic Advisory Council in 2019, and reappointed in 2022, and has also served on the Presidential Expert Advisory Panel on Land Reform and Agriculture from 2018. Other appointments include the chairperson of the Agribusiness Working Group of the BRICS Business Council (South Africa), a member of the Council of Statistics of South Africa (StatsSA) and a commissioner at the International Trade Administration Commission of South Africa (ITAC). Wandile is a columnist for *Business Day*, *The Herald* and *Farmers Weekly*, and is the author of two books: *A Country of Two Agricultures: The Disparities, the Challenges, the Solutions* (Tracey McDonald Publishers) and *Finding Common Ground: Land, Equity, and Agriculture* (Pan Macmillan). In 2018, he was named Agriculturalist of the Year by Agricultural Writers SA. He holds an MSc in Agricultural Economics from Stellenbosch University.

ANTHONI VAN NIEUWKERK is professor of International and Diplomacy Studies at the Thabo Mbeki African School of Public and International Affairs at the University of South Africa (Unisa). He is also a visiting research fellow at the Wits School of Governance, and serves on the editorial boards of *African Security*, *Administratio Publica* and the *South African Journal of International Affairs* – all accredited journals. In addition, he coordinates a network of Southern African academics and practitioners and co-edits the biennial *Southern African Security Review*. Anthoni has extensive experience in advising African policymakers and has participated in a number of scenario-mapping initiatives. He has also published widely on African foreign and security policy. In 2023, he co-edited a book on African experiences of countering violent extremism, which was shortlisted by the prestigious Tana High-Level Forum on Security in Africa for its annual book prize. Anthoni holds a PhD in International Relations from Unisa.

JAN VAN ROMBURGH is a professor at the North-West University Business School and a director of Adams and Adams Forensic Investigative Solutions, a company that performs forensic accounting investigations on behalf of public and private institutions. Previously he was the chief director of the North-West University Business School and, prior to that, director of the university's School of Accounting Sciences. In 2006, he was part of the team who designed and introduced the Programme in Forensic Accountancy in the university's School of Accounting Sciences. Jan holds a PhD in Forensic Accounting from the North-West University. He is a member of the Institute of Commercial Forensic Practitioners, Association of Certified Fraud Examiners and Chartered Institute of Management Accountants.

BRUCE YOUNG is a chemical engineering and business development professional with intimate knowledge of the South African and global energy and petrochemical landscapes. He is currently a senior lecturer in the African Energy Leadership Centre at the Wits School of Governance. Prior to taking up this position in 2022, he worked for Sasol for many years where he played a significant role in commercialising several novel processes in the energy and chemicals sectors. He has extensive experience in energy and chemicals technology, corporate strategy, business development, and mergers and acquisitions. A key research interest is understanding the technical, economic and business risks associated with different technology options for the renewable energy transition, and which technologies are most likely to prevail. Bruce holds a PhD in Chemical Engineering from the University of the Witwatersrand. He is also an active member of his local community and chairs a community policing forum.

THE CONDUCTOR
OPENING OF THE 2024 OVERTURE

Overture

'We have not taken the final step of our journey, but the first step on a longer and more difficult road' – Nelson Mandela[1]

'It is not possible to remain stationary. We can only choose between two possibilities: moving backwards or moving forwards'– Erich Fromm[2]

Why are so many South Africans seized with, or concerned about, the upcoming general election this year? After all, this country has had regular 'free and fair' general elections since 1994. This year also happens to be one in which elections are being held in over 40 democracies around the world – a record number. What is it about the dynamics of the 2024 election in South Africa that is generating both heightened risks and opportunities, under a big cloud of uncertainty? What are the alternative political economy scenarios that might materialise? Is social stability at risk? What forces will shape the outcomes? What is the end game? And what are the special features of the political campaigning and party manifestos that the electorate needs to navigate?

These questions are the points of departure for *Tipping Point – Turmoil or Reform?* It is common cause that South Africa's 2024 general election is indeed the most important one since 1994 and will be a watershed political event and experience. All the evidence points to a distinct breaking (to a greater or lesser extent) of the mould in which South African politics has traditionally been cast.

The wide range of persuasive outcomes of the election being offered by the political pundits underscores the level of uncertainty that accompanies the current set of circumstances.

Against this background, a more fluid and volatile political situation has inevitably emerged, with its associated risks and opportunities. And eligible voters ought to be fully engaged if they wish to influence the course of events. Likewise, this book hopes 'to influence the course of events' by assembling a cross-section of expert contributors to unpack several of the political and economic factors that will shape South Africa's debate, both during and after the election.

A series of political and economic developments in recent years have brought South Africa to a decisive juncture or a 'tipping point'. For reasons well captured in the book's 14 chapters, the pending election and its possible outcomes have sparked much interest and debate, both within and outside the country. The contents of the 2024 SONA and 2024/25 Budget also reinforced the critical challenges outlined in these pages and the need to find urgent solutions. Many view this as a defining moment for South Africa, which will irrevocably alter its future – for better or for worse.

That the 2024 election is seen as a high-stakes event for South Africa is evident from the effort that political leaders and parties have put into persuading eligible citizens to register as voters, with the power to shift the needle in the direction of their desired political outcome. Yet citizens should not just exercise their right to vote; they should also be as well informed as possible when they make their electoral choices regarding economic reform, accountability, transformation and many other issues. A vibrant and effective democracy depends, in the first place, on citizens being willing and able to participate in the voting process, armed with a basic grasp of the major issues at stake.

This book will help the electorate to see the big picture in this significant election year and how several major and pressing issues intersect in South Africa's political economy. The insights shared in the different chapters will be a valuable supplement to what voters are hearing from political campaigners and other sources and will hopefully help voters to make more informed choices. But the value in the book extends well beyond being a source of voter information. Once the immediate outcome of the 2024 election is known, the real work begins – tackling the immense challenges of unemployment, poverty and inequality with renewed commitment and rigour.

While the virtues of democracy in general and South Africa's Constitution in particular are often rightly lauded, a *successful* democracy is one that delivers the economic benefits that many citizens have come to expect. A bigger, stronger and better economy is an indispensable bulwark of democracy in South Africa. In the final analysis, *shared* economic prosperity remains the only secure guarantee of a democratic order in this country.

In this regard, a few questions come to mind – all pivotal questions that this book attempts to answer: In what ways might a post-election change in political leadership benefit South Africa? Who and what will prevail? What are the prospects of the election outcomes necessitating the formation of a coalition government? How stable would such an arrangement be? What would be the implications of possible provincial coalition governments in Gauteng, KwaZulu-Natal and the Western Cape?

What (fundamentally) is the role of politicians? Basically, good leadership is what it is all about. As Henry Kissinger broadly put it:

> Any society, whatever its political system, is perpetually in transit between a past that forms its memory and a vision of the future that inspires its evolution. Along this route, leadership is indispensable: decisions must be made, trust earned, promises kept, a way forward proposed. Within human institutions – states, religions, armies, companies, schools – leadership is needed to help people reach from where they are to where they have never been and, sometimes, can scarcely imagine going. Without leadership, institutions drift, and nations court growing irrelevance and, ultimately, disaster.[3]

The shifting *realpolitik* landscape in South Africa in 2024 and the future national agenda will inevitably present daunting new tests for leadership at several levels of governance.

Winston Churchill once said, referring to a prominent British leader at the turn of the 20th century, that 'he was one who made the weather' by shaping the political agenda at a time when the British Empire was at the pinnacle of its power.[4] So, as South Africa goes to the polls amid innumerable socioeconomic challenges, who will best 'make the weather' politically and what are the factors that will decide this? To paraphrase Lenin, what now needs to be done?

In the face of the new dynamics surrounding the coming election, the various chapters in this book flag several key items appearing on the national agenda and offer impressions of South Africa's future, often with provisos attached. The analyses and forecasts centre on both the public and private sectors, and a sense of urgency pervades the authors' respective contributions. Together, the chapters identify realistic ways in which a future government can make a difference, where the private sector can play a bigger role in finding and implementing solutions, and where – through intensified collaboration between civil society and the public and private sectors – South Africa can assume the mantle of a *delivery state*.

The book recognises that tackling South Africa's serious socioeconomic challenges remains a continuing process. As the country appears to solve some problems, others develop – frequently out of earlier solutions, especially where timely actions were not taken. Eskom is a prime example. We would naturally prefer to see strong solutions being applied to serious or pressing problems. But in a world of elevated domestic policy uncertainty and frequent external geopolitical 'shocks', we must temper our expectations. Global and domestic headwinds need to be skilfully navigated, economic buffers created and resilience built. Moreover, even the best solutions might provide only a temporary reprieve, although their importance should not be underestimated, particularly if they help to buy time while we look for longer-term, more sustainable answers.

Pragmatists recognise this reality. It was echoed in the call by political economist Peter Attard Montalto for 'hard work and calm patience for the long road ahead'.[5] Outlining the dynamics and complexities of the reform agenda facing South Africa, he argued that we are going to require nerves of steel and great patience to get certain key changes implemented. He acknowledged that 'patience and a little optimism through the madness doesn't ignore that there are deep risks and negative outcomes still being produced. Yet when you leave reforms this late, there is little choice'. Looking to the post-2024 election period, Montalto concluded: 'There is no low-hanging fruit, only hard work. Any party that is selling easy fixes is deluding the voters.'

The ensuing chapters describe many of the flaws and dysfunctionalities in the institutions and mechanisms through which South Africa has been attempting to address its accumulated challenges over the years. And like the waves on a beach, these challenges will continue to come. State capture and corruption, for example, have been widespread and systemic. How do we eradicate them? Many chapters suggest solutions to several of South Africa's most persistent problems, which have been gnawing away at the country for years.

There is much global evidence that the establishment or reform of institutions in a country is as much a political problem as it is a technocratic problem. If political actors in South Africa are not demanding reform, then successfully rehabilitating failing institutions may well remain a pipe dream. How viable, then, are the institutions in South Africa that should be leading the way in practising good governance and delivering a job-rich economy in future? What reforms and other remedies are urgently needed to make them more effective after the election, and what political outcomes are required to underpin and reinforce the process? What are the tailwinds that will push South Africa forward and what will propel them?

The very real dilemma that South Africa faces is that without strong institutions and generous helpings of political will, the right policies will *not* be adopted, and implementation attempts will fail. South Africa needs an action-oriented national agenda that allows the tailwinds to prevail over the headwinds and, in turn, helps to tip the balance of the political economy in the direction of reform rather than turmoil.

Finally, we need to recognise that even the 'right' institutional reforms will deliver desirable and valuable outcomes only if we (voters, consumers, businesspeople or workers) *decide* what is desirable and valuable. How we think about economics, politics, business and related issues shapes the quality of the strategic choices that we make. This suggests that South Africa has a range of possible futures. The National Development Plan (NDP) emphasised the role of 'active citizenry' in arriving at solutions, a topic that is covered in one of the chapters. The test of the 2024 election and whether it delivers the desired outcomes will therefore clearly depend on the ability of the people to choose and act wisely in challenging circumstances.

We hope that, in its own way, *Tipping Point* will encourage and empower its readers to make informed choices. Some readers may wish to read all the chapters in sequence; others may select those chapters that are particularly interesting or accessible – or potentially controversial! A 'coda and recapitulation' section captures the highlights of each chapter. And while every effort has been made to minimise repetition, it is inevitable that certain chapters will overlap to some extent, although this is not necessarily a bad thing. It not only accommodates different views but also emphasises the extent to which major economic and political variables, which will help shape South Africa's political economy in the years ahead, are interdependent.

A book of this nature and scale is inevitably a collaborative effort at several levels, and I am indebted to many people. First, my deep appreciation goes to the other 13 esteemed authors, without whose expert and knowledgeable inputs – so generously shared despite the competing demands on their time – the book would not have come to life. Then Ali Parry has been indispensable in doing most of the heavy lifting of the editorial load, and I am most appreciative of her usual excellent professional assistance throughout the project.

My fulsome thanks also go to the Jacana Media team, under the inspired leadership of Bridget Impey, who have so ably taken the book to publication in the face of tight timeframes brought about by the looming 2024 election. In addition, I am grateful to Lodewalt Venter, my research assistant, for lending a hand, with his characteristic diligence, in bringing the book to fruition.

The usual *caveat* applies, in that the views I have expressed here are personal and do not necessarily represent those of any organisation or institution with which I am associated. Likewise, all the authors who have contributed to the book are responsible only for their own views, and not for those of other contributors.

Raymond Parsons
North-West University Business School
March 2024

ONE

Unpacking political party dynamics in post-apartheid South Africa

Anthony Butler

Introduction

Opposition parties play a crucial role in any democracy.[1] Their ability to challenge the power of government is especially important when political life has been dominated by a single party.[2] This chapter explores the key features of South Africa's party landscape since 1994 and registers the implications of the extended dominance of a single party, the African National Congress (ANC), at national level. One-party dominance has posed many hazards but also brought advantages during a difficult period of political transition. South Africa's party system has considerable strengths relative to many other middle-income countries and new democracies.

The chapter then moves on to the dominant ANC and details its failings as a party of government. Despite the many advantages that incumbents enjoy, the ANC's performance has recently been so poor that one might reasonably expect its eviction from office as soon as 2024. Opposition parties have hitherto failed to challenge the ANC successfully, however, and so the chapter goes on to explore five possible explanations for their failure to capitalise on the governing party's disarray. It concludes by considering how parties contending for national power can improve their prospects of successfully displacing the incumbent party.

The role of opposition parties in a democracy

The function of opposition parties is to counterbalance the power of the governing party or coalition, scrutinising the actions, policies and decisions of the government and interrogating whether they are in the best interests of the people.[3] By doing so, they can help prevent power abuses, corruption and authoritarianism. Opposition parties are also responsible for presenting alternative policies and solutions. This allows voters to make informed choices and ensures that there are healthy debates about the potential courses of action for government.

The role of political parties is especially pronounced in a parliamentary system like South Africa's, which is characterised by a fusion of the executive and legislative branches. Opposition representatives should conduct in-depth investigations and influence proposed legislation in parliamentary committees. Criticism and debates in the legislature's chamber can help shape public policy and legislation through a process of negotiation and compromise. By raising questions, demanding transparency and conducting investigations, opposition parties help to ensure that the government operates in an open and accountable manner.[4]

South Africa's opposition parties have performed these roles quite successfully over the past three decades. However, they have been less successful at developing credible policies, grooming leaders and preparing for the possibility of governing. This failure is both a cause and a consequence of the predominance of the governing ANC across the entire democratic period. As Hideo Otake has logically observed, 'to ask why a single party enjoys long-term dominance over a nation's government is to ask why no opposition party or coalition was able to defeat it'.[5]

South Africa's dominant-party system

A dominant-party system is usually defined as consecutive electoral wins in a representative democracy over a period of 20 years or more. Scholars of dominant-party systems insist that they differ from authoritarian regimes because the repeated re-election of the dominant party is not accompanied by bone-crushing repression. Political association, electoral competition and significant media freedom are all permitted.[6]

Much political analysis over the past three decades has focused on the implications of such one-party dominance for the future of South Africa.[7] Dominance evidently has an uneasy relationship with democratic politics because the vitality of opposition is central to democracy. The lack of credible opposition parties is, on one famous account, 'evidence, if not conclusive proof, of the absence of democracy'.[8] In some evident democracies, such as Sweden and Japan in the second half of the 20th century, a majority of voters kept choosing the same party over and over again.[9] In many less clear-cut cases of democracy – countries one might describe today as 'hybrid regimes'[10] – meaningful elections took place, relatively few journalists were jailed and crude election rigging was avoided, yet the same party won again and again over a period of more than two decades.[11]

In trying to define the phenomenon, political scientists have pointed to other aspects of dominance. Duverger famously argued that a dominant party is 'identified with an epoch', its ideas dominating policy debate and its dominant position acknowledged by citizens and elites alike.[12] The core doctrines and policies of the dominant party become a 'common practice' or shared blueprint, so creating an intellectual path dependency that cannot be directly countered.[13] Since 1994, the ANC has offered a clear-cut case of one-party dominance in a broadly democratic political system, given its share of the vote in consecutive elections, its dominance of policy debates and its influence over narratives of historical change.

The ANC's dominance since 1994 has been viewed positively and negatively. Some analysts have argued that only an extended period of political stability could establish preconditions for the entrenchment of democracy. South Africa has faced major developmental challenges in a context of inequality, poverty and social division. During the first decade of democracy, in particular, political competition was structured around historical – and therefore often ethnic or racial – affiliations, with no compelling policy differences setting government against opposition.[14] For this reason, adversarial opposition, such as the Democratic Alliance's (DA) campaign on a 'fight back' manifesto in 1999, was inevitably interpreted in polarising racial terms. A threat to ANC dominance in such circumstances might threaten political stability and undermine the creation of legitimate political institutions.

Figure 1.1: Selected parties' vote share in national elections, 1994–2019

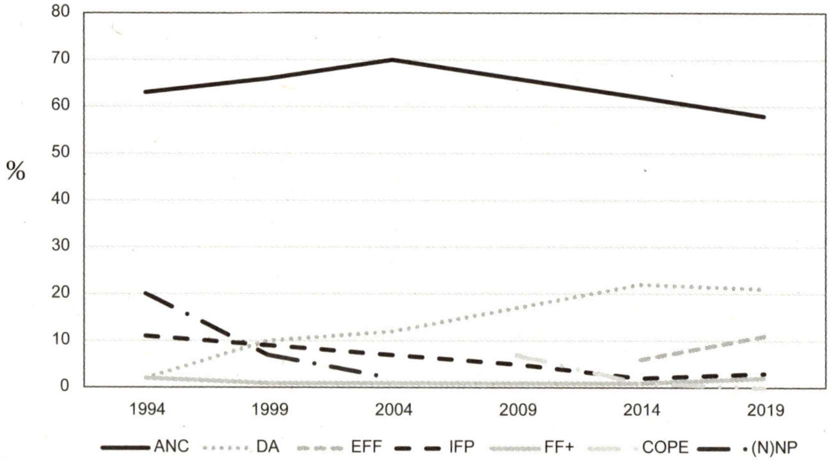

[Line chart showing vote share percentages from 1994 to 2019 for parties: ANC, DA, EFF, IFP, FF+, COPE, (N)NP. ANC remains dominant, ranging from about 62% in 1994, peaking near 70% in 2004, declining to about 57% in 2019.]

Source: Adapted from Schulz-Herzenberg[15]

Meanwhile, the ANC's self-conception as a non-racial national liberation movement helped it to contain conflict, defuse racial or ethnic polarisation, manage high levels of inequality and subdue potentially anti-democratic leaders.[16]

Political violence was drastically curtailed, and the territorial conflict that characterised the 1994 elections was significantly reduced. The ANC forged integrated programmes of government that helped contain social conflict and stabilise the democratic settlement. The invulnerability that the party enjoyed allowed it to enforce unpopular but necessary fiscal policies. The ANC also discouraged racial and ethnic conflict that many believed would shake post-apartheid society.[17] The ANC's system of alliances allowed diverse class and ideological interests to be represented, and its relatively decentralised candidate-selection processes and democratic internal elections have ensured that local and provincial elites have felt represented within subnational governments.[18]

In contrast to such positive assessments, critics have argued that ANC dominance is dangerous and threatens to create new post-apartheid authoritarianism. 'Democracy', according to Giliomee and Simkins' landmark study, 'rests on countervailing power able to check tendencies towards authoritarian domination'.[19] The best counter, they argue, is 'the presence of a strong opposition party that can guard against the erosion of the autonomy of democratic institutions and ... replace a governing party that has outstayed its welcome'. Such sceptics argue that the ANC has represented itself as the state. Ultimately, they claim the ANC's 'sheer preponderance of political power' would allow it to rule unilaterally and abuse 'the advantages of incumbency and the state media to get re-elected time and again'.[20]

These positive and negative reflections on ANC dominance are both highly persuasive – and they are in most respects compatible with each another.[21] Single-party dominance was indeed essential during democracy's first two decades, but it has become increasingly damaging. South Africa's democracy was not initially robust enough to cope with conflict, and stability was required to build legitimate and trusted institutions. The longer the ANC remained dominant, however, the more state–party integration, unchecked patronage politics, growing corruption, opposition de-legitimation and the abuse of incumbency damaged political and economic institutions.

The extended period of ANC electoral dominance entrenched the legitimacy of democratic institutions, by making them more racially representative and aligning them to a constitutional order. Meanwhile, opposition parties that lacked the capacity to govern a complex and divided society have gradually acquired such capacity. The progressive attrition of ANC support and the growth in opposition-party experience in provincial and local government have built up the capacity of political leaders outside the ANC to offer a realistic alternative.

South Africa's party system has one other great attribute: the surprising strength of two of its opposition parties. There was great fluidity in the party system across the 1990s and 2000s, with the National Party (NP) broken up, the Inkatha Freedom Party (IFP) declining, and smaller parties, such as the United Democratic Movement (UDM), the Congress of the People (COPE), the Freedom Front Plus (FF+) and the Pan Africanist Congress (PAC) waxing and waning. They have been joined by a range of newer parties, encouraged by a proportional electoral system, most recently the FF+, Action SA, the Patriotic Alliance (PA) and many others. Even the smaller parties typically have firm, if narrow, policy platforms and offer a meaningful outlet for citizen energies.

Amid this energy and flux, the party system has crystallised to some degree, with the DA and the Economic Freedom Fighters (EFF) turning into substantial and well-organised parties with stable and significant bases of support among electors. The DA has faced major challenges in trying to expand its support base, but it has retained and recently reasserted its character as a 'liberal' party with a coherent policy platform. It has a constitution that guides its activities between elections, including the key internal processes of selection of leaders, selection of candidates and formulation of policy positions which can be presented to citizens at election time. It has access to the financial resources needed to campaign nationally, its annual R30 million from the Represented Political Parties Fund (RPPF) supplemented by significant donations from wealthy individuals and their companies.[22] These and other funding sources have allowed the DA to build formidable research, policymaking and campaigning teams. The DA also suffers from some serious limitations, of course, with its capacity and attention heavily concentrated in the Western Cape, its organisation primarily urban and its support base – with roughly equal shares of white, coloured and black voters – bearing testimony to its failure to make a real breakthrough with the black electorate. It has also lost a swathe of prominent black leaders in recent years.[23]

The EFF, the second-largest opposition party, also has great strengths. It proclaims an anachronistic revolutionary ideology, embraces a wide range of radical intellectual positions, and advances dramatic policy proposals regarding nationalisation without compensation and state-driven job-creation programmes. It has put youth unemployment on the political agenda and maintains a principled policy on intra-African migration. Building on its breakthrough 2014 election result, it has expanded on its initially northern and disproportionately Sotho-speaking power base, most notably in KwaZulu-Natal and among more highly educated electorates. By 2019, it was enjoying increased support in every province, and its share of the vote rose again to more than 10% in the 2021 local government elections.

The EFF has a competent organisational machinery, and it appears to be relatively well funded. It receives around R20 million annually from the RPPF, but no significant donations to the party, above the R100 000 declaration, have been recorded.[24] There have been accusations of monies received from illicit tobacco companies, siphoning of bank savings and tender kickbacks, but these do not seem to differentiate it significantly in electors' eyes from parties such as the ANC. The party also faces conundrums in respect of its leadership style. In late 2023, the EFF's Central Command Team removed more than 200 public representatives by fiat because of their alleged failure to meet unrealistic mobilisation goals for the party's 10th anniversary celebrations. The EFF has roughly 50 members of parliament, the same number of provincial legislators and about 1 000 councillors – almost all of whom fear arbitrary removal.

South Africa is fortunate to have such credible, even if flawed, opposition parties and a reasonably stable party system. The country stands in strong contrast to most middle-income countries where power is more often personalised, party politics is fragmented, unstable and transactional, and voter loyalty is fleeting. South Africa's opposition parties provide coherent and robust opposition to the governing party. They have taken some control of government at provincial and municipal levels, and they have accumulated experience that prepares them, to some degree, for national government. They offer electors real choices at election time between identifiable leadership teams, accountable candidates and clear policy programmes. The presence of credible parties is important during a period of possible transition from a dominant-party system to a more complex multiparty system, especially since such transitions typically occur alongside economic and sociopolitical crisis.

A realistic expectation of ANC defeat

While these parties have stabilised, the ANC has suffered governance crises that have undermined its former electoral invulnerability. South Africa faces prolonged economic stagnation and deep structural unemployment.[25] There has been a visible decline in the quality of infrastructure, with failure accumulating across hospitals, schools, roads, bulk water and sanitation systems, rail services and solid waste management facilities.[26] Economic stagnation has been accompanied by the rise of illicit economic activity, which is further eroding the country's tax base. Service delivery crises in municipalities have worsened, and skills shortages, exploding municipal debt and corruption at local level make their resolution difficult.

Violence and crime are accelerating alarmingly. Episodic xenophobic violence and a massive breakdown of public order in KwaZulu-Natal in July 2021 have deepened perceptions of a state in crisis. Worse still, from an electoral perspective, a major commission of inquiry into corruption, led by Chief Justice Zondo, placed much of the responsibility for the period of 'state capture' on the shoulders of senior members of the ANC.[27] There is pervasive exploitation of the liberation movement as a stepping stone to public positions that can be abused for personal gain. The movement's political rhetoric is still infused with references to struggle icons, historical doctrines and political ideals, but the central dynamic of the movement's politics is now the pursuit of resources by organised political factions.

The decline of key parastatals, notably the electricity parastatal Eskom and the state transport monolith Transnet, partly explains South Africa's growth and fiscal crises, with rotational electricity blackouts, logistical dysfunction, and the failure of air, postal and other state-owned entities throttling growth, undermining tax revenues and imposing the burden of escalating Treasury bailouts.[28] Rotational electricity blackouts have become a symbol of the dysfunction of the governing party, its corruption and its failure to manage and maintain public assets. These interlinked crises were manifested increasingly across the two terms of President Jacob Zuma between 2009 and 2018. Little wonder, then, that by the time of the 2019 national and provincial elections, voter identification with the ANC had fallen to just 29%, from 52% in 2006.[29]

In the 2024 election, the ANC's capacity to maintain support will come under additional pressure because of the country's unprecedented fiscal crisis. To avert a collapse in the country's finances, the National Treasury has told big-spending departments that no new resources will be allocated to them in 2024. While the ANC will try to maintain social spending and avoid a wave of job reductions in the public service, it is not clear to what degree it can do so. Incumbency advantages will be unusually constrained in the run-up to the elections.[30]

In such circumstances, opposition parties might normally be confident of victory in national and provincial government elections. Recent scholarship, however, points to the failure of opposition parties to capitalise on the opportunity that a languishing ANC presents. These parties need to go beyond merely holding the government to account and formulating an alternative set of policies. They need to energise activists and mobilise voters – not merely to fight, but also to win. Significant doubts remain about their ability to do so.

Non-voters and opposition impotence

Why have opposition parties so far failed to capitalise on the opportunities that a languishing ANC presents?[31] Fewer than a quarter of potential voters think the ANC is doing a good job of running the country. The trouble is that disaffected ANC supporters are not 'switching' their votes to other parties. Instead, they are 'exiting' the electoral process altogether.

The decline in voting is striking. The proportion of eligible electors who registered and then turned out to vote fell from 86% in 1994 to 49% in 2019. The percentage of the voting age population who voted for the ANC was 54% in 1999, 39% in 2009 and just 28% in 2019. Worse still, even former opposition party loyalists are staying home on election day. The swelling ranks of non-voters now comprise more than half the potential electorate.[32] The key puzzle of opposition politics, and the main strategic conundrum for opposition parties, is why potential voters are exiting in such large numbers – and what to do about it.

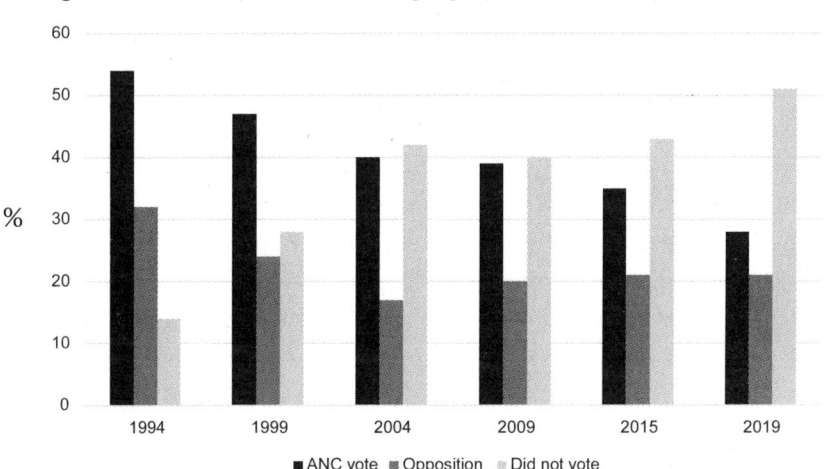

Figure 1.2: Participation of voting age population, 1994–2019

Source: Adapted from Schulz-Herzenberg and Mattes[33]

Why opposition parties do not attract ANC deserters

Support for the ANC has dropped sharply, but most disaffected former ANC supporters do not believe available opposition parties would do a better job in government. Neither do many think the opposition would look after the interests of all the people, and few find any opposition leader more appealing than Cyril Ramaphosa.[34] There are several plausible explanations for the failure of opposition parties to sweep up these former ANC loyalists and so capitalise on the ANC's predicament.

First, the ANC has a legacy of achievements from its first two decades of government, whereas opposition parties mostly do not. These include addressing legacy backlogs inherited after apartheid, including increasing access to sanitation, drinking water, electricity and transport,[35] and forging some excellent institutions, such as the National Treasury, the South African Revenue Service (SARS), the South African National Roads Agency Limited (SANRAL), the information and communication technologies (ICT) network and the country's airports. In terms of government effectiveness, regulatory quality and the rule of law, the country is unquestionably a mess – but it remains in the middle of the pack of middle-income countries.[36] While the electorate is losing confidence in the ANC's ability to deliver such gains at some stage, this has not brought with it any confidence that opposition parties would do any better. Recent obstacles to the effectiveness of unstable opposition coalitions in metropolitan authorities may have deepened this perception.

There are also barriers that result from eligible electors' perceptions of political parties. Racial and other identities play a role in explaining how people vote, alongside voters' lived experience under apartheid, residual loyalty to the liberation movement, white and coloured mistrust of the ANC, and socioeconomic factors.[37] The three biggest parties all enjoy multi-racial support. All three have some pull in urban centres, peri-urban townships and informal settlements. Simple 'racial census' analysis of voting behaviour is unpersuasive, with black and white votes now being cast in quite variegated ways.[38]

Nonetheless, opposition parties still face challenges regarding citizen perceptions. As Schulz-Herzenberg and Mattes observe, voters depend on 'low-cost informational cues' – images or 'party attributes'

– to identify parties that will best represent their interests. Given the history of South Africa, the racial and ethnic identities of party leaders and candidates inevitably shape the mental images and cues that electors use to assess parties' likely policy stances. Moreover, perceptions of party attributes 'are likely to be less ephemeral and more stable than voter evaluations of government performance, candidates, or policy positions'.[39] This poses a challenge for the DA, which struggles to shake off perceptions that it is a 'white' party, and for the EFF, which battles when appealing to older and more conservative voters, and women.

Another factor is the presence of 'incumbency advantages', which flow to the party of government through its occupation of government positions and control of government budgets. Such advantages include visibility, the ability to claim credit for policy successes and government programmes, access to the media and the public broadcaster, and access to the administrative capacity of the state to campaign. Greene has observed that dominant parties enjoy 'hyper-incumbency advantages', most notably the ability to divert resources from state-owned enterprises to the party, its allies, its donors and its activists.[40] A dominant party may lose access to such resources during an economic crisis and so lose the ability to tilt the electoral playing field in its favour. Nonetheless, such hyper-incumbency advantages are lost rather than transferred; opposition parties do not gain access to them until they are elected.

A powerful ideal of unity may also play a role in undermining the opposition. Such an ideal is embraced by the ANC at election time when party Marxists and modernists embrace religious and traditional leaders as part of a broadly inclusive, if contradictory, campaign. It is sometimes suggested that an African communalistic ethic or widespread Christian practice may partly explain unease about confrontational opposition in African societies. In fact, this sentiment is found far more widely. 'Healthy democratic competition' always resembles the partisan pursuit of sectional interests and values at the expense of communal cohesion. Indeed, party politics has been regarded in just this way – as a divisive problem – across most of the political history of Christian societies. Cabals, factions and political parties have been viewed as threats to the 'one perfect body' to which a Christian people should aspire. It is a small step from the celebration of an indivisible community to the perception that opposition leaders are promoters of disharmony.[41]

Finally, and most importantly, opposition parties are deformed by their emergence in a dominant-party system. As Greene has observed, office-seeking politicians have little incentive to join a party when they know it is going to lose. In the absence of any prospect of gaining office, opposition parties must attract potential candidates and activists by appealing to their distinctive values, identities and policy preferences.[42] This results in the party adopting 'non-centrist policies' and embracing activists and supporters whose preferences are out of step with most voters.

Once supporters are recruited on the basis of marginal values and policies, it is difficult for the leadership to move the party to the political centre, especially if they are fearful of losing the loyalist core.[43] In this situation, party leaders fear they cannot 'win the election without losing the party'.[44] The DA's failed 'catch-all' strategy under Mmusi Maimane and its reversion to a 'liberal' position are one illustration of this trap; the EFF's inability to align its activist-friendly policy proposals with the preferences of a relatively conservative broader electorate are another.

One further implication of Greene's analysis concerns the politics of coalitions. The ideological differences between opposition parties that have been forged in a dominant-party system may be too great – and their activists' positions too marginal and entrenched – for them to successfully cooperate in a coalition framework.

Conclusion: What can opposition parties do?

It is tempting to simply blame opposition parties for failing to capitalise on disillusion with the ANC. As we have seen, however, there are reasons why opposition parties in dominant-party systems have often proved disappointing. They find it hard to demonstrate competence to govern; their perceived 'party attributes' are unfavourable and hard to shake off; they lack incumbency advantages; and robust opposition lacks legitimacy. Most importantly, the legacies from their development in a one-party-dominant system include an inability to move to the programmatic centre and an aversion to forming coalitions with other opposition parties that are just as marginalised as they are.

To win, opposition leaders will need to get voters to the polls. This means counteracting the effects of dominant-party politics on their own parties' ideas, policies and modes of organisation. Given that their focus has been skewed towards ideologically marginal and minority constituencies, their party infrastructure and campaign resources need to engage potential voters in regions and populations quite alien to current party activists. Rather than relying on familiar rallies in urban areas, they should reach new elector segments outside the cities and present a vision for the future relevant to them. Where organisational resources are absent, they need partners among civil society organisations, mobile campaigns and bus rallies, and targeted digital strategies.

Second, parties need to advance potential election-winning policies that lay claim to the political centre ground, even if these are unappealing to their own activists. This means focusing on issues of concern to most voters: unemployment, housing on peri-urban land, crime as it is experienced by potential (and not just current) supporters, and the public healthcare that disaffected ANC voters receive. Opposition parties know this intellectually – the DA's proposed universal health coverage and cash transfers for the poor are designed to appeal to ANC deserters who find national health insurance and a basic income grant attractive. Urban housing policies partly challenge the interests of the party's middle-class support base. The trouble is that activists are rarely engaged in promoting such policies energetically, and party leaders fail to lead from the front by making them central to their campaign efforts.

Third, parties cannot win on their own; they require partnerships with civil society organisations if they are to link up with hard-to-reach segments of the population. For historical reasons, non-governmental organisations, trade unions and traditional leaders often have frosty relationships with opposition parties, and this history needs to be addressed and overcome. Coalitions, meanwhile, must be reconceived as broad and inclusive, organised around issues rather than positions and cemented by concrete policy proposals.[45]

Fourth, the integrity of elections should be a focus and a mobilising activity. As Nic Cheeseman and Brian Klaas have reminded us, election rigging is one of the political world's growth industries.[46] Civil society organisations and opposition parties divided by ideology can unite around the need to provide protection against internal and external interference in elections, the vulnerabilities created by new digital technologies, unequal access to the public broadcaster, narrative-shaping bot armies, the security of campaign networks, and biased or selective rule enforcement by electoral commissions.

South Africa's opposition parties, as we have observed, are capable and well organised. They have no doubt considered all these strategies, and more. What they lack may well be a sufficient degree of self-consciousness, and what they need may be some judicious political psychotherapy. After all, the key opposition parties have chosen, or at least retained, polarising political leaders who cannot speak to the centre ground of the South African electorate. They tick the policy boxes that look vote-enhancing on paper, but they do not speak to them with enthusiasm or credibility. Rather than trying to understand the disillusion and anger of ANC deserters, they continue to speak to their own entrenched concerns and values. Behind the bluster that sometimes dominates their campaigns, there remains a palpable sense of self-doubt about whether they can secure a victory – or even whether they really want one. The one thing we have learnt from the history of our dominant-party system is that citizens will not vote in sufficient numbers for parties that do not believe that they can win.

TWO

Coalition politics: Is this the way?

Ralph Mathekga

The electoral system and newer democracies

South Africa's experience with democracy is still in a formative stage, with only six elections having been held since the advent of democracy in 1994. The same can be said of the local government system, with the first elections having taken place in 1996. Despite this relatively short experience with democratic competitive politics, South Africa's political system is evolving significantly, revealing a trend towards political dynamism amid increasing political competition. This partially derives from the proportional electoral system, which essentially allows even smaller political parties to gain representation in Parliament.

Compared to other electoral systems (such as the presidential system), the proportional electoral system has a lower threshold for political parties when it comes to attaining representation in Parliament. This tends to encourage the formation or proliferation of new political parties due to the real potential for gaining seats in the legislature. The proportional electoral system is lauded for not wasting votes, as even the smallest political party may gain representation in the legislature. The idea behind this system is that 'the distribution of views among those who are elected to representative bodies should resemble the distribution of views in the electorate.'[1]

There are variations in the proportional electoral system. Moreover, the way the system is applied and the results it produces differ between countries, depending on their history and political culture. South Africa has adopted what in practical terms is a party proportional electoral system, where voters elect a political party, which then decides on individual representatives based on a closed party-lists system. The system is actually more complex than is suggested here.[2] However, the underlying idea is that the proportional electoral system leans more towards multipartyism than can be said of other electoral systems. The presidential system in the United States (US) provides an interesting contrast to the proportional electoral system. The US elections have become a contest between the Democratic Party and the Republican Party. The presidential system generally leads to a two-party system, while the proportional electoral system tends to result in multiparty competition and ultimately coalition governments.

Why the electoral system matters

Should South Africa brace itself for a permanent state of coalition governments, with its perceived instabilities, in the national and provincial spheres of government? Arriving at an answer to this question requires an examination of the electoral system that is in place, which will reveal the different forms of government that are possible. Despite the dominance of a single political party, the African National Congress (ANC), the proportional electoral system fundamentally favours those forms of government that involve power sharing. Thus, coalition governments are inevitable. South Africa is no exception in this regard. Coalition governments in the country are not accidental; they are part of the logic of the system.

There are two reasons why South Africa will undoubtedly experience coalition governments at the national level: the electoral system fundamentally leans towards power sharing in governance, and the electoral system was deliberately decided on. The proportional electoral system applied in South Africa – which was adopted from the English tradition – was agreed upon during the multiparty negotiations for democracy. It is important to consider what the intentions of the founders of South Africa's democracy were when they decided on the proportional electoral system. For example, did they envisage coalition arrangements as a political solution in the medium to longer term?

The way one approaches the above question will be influenced by how one views coalition arrangements at the national level in South Africa. If one takes it for granted that the proportional electoral system is geared for power sharing in government, then it follows that coalitions should not be viewed with suspicion. Coalitions are not a symptom of a failing political system in the country; rather, they are part of the evolution of the political system.

However, there is a tendency to view coalitions as transitory; a temporary lapse that will be corrected. This view reflects the general anxiety about coalitions in South Africa, which has permeated the public discourse in the build-up to the 2024 election.[3] Given their experience of crumbling coalition governments in metropolitical municipalities in Gauteng (City of Johannesburg and City of Tshwane) and in other municipalities where there were no outright winners, South Africans are increasingly viewing the prospects of a coalition government at the national level as a step towards political instability.

South Africa's anxiety about coalitions as the 2024 election approaches

As South Africa gears up for the 2024 general election, there are concerns regarding the prospects of a stable government if no political party gains the required outright majority (50+1 per cent) to constitute a government. While many subscribe to the idea of coalitions improving accountability in the system, there are also deep doubts about their sustainability. Moreover, the implosion of coalition governments across metros signals to voters that coalition governments do not result in improved service delivery. Yet South Africa does not have any experience of sustained attempts to build coalition governments. Therefore, a possible hasty abandonment of the idea of coalition governments would be worrying, as the country does not have any lessons on which it can reliably draw to justify even mild resistance to the coalition system.

The criticisms levelled at coalition arrangements in South Africa are the result of the prevalence of a dominant-party system over many years and several different regimes. They suggest a general fixation with a two-party system or a dominant-party system and are not born out of experience of genuine efforts to build and sustain coalition governments based on the principle of power sharing. The two-party system, where political power alternates between two political parties (as in the US), is widely accepted as an indication of political maturity and stability. By contrast, the proportional electoral system, with its multiparty representation and amenability towards coalitions, is seen to reflect the intractable differences in society.

Anthony Downs argues in *An Economic Theory of Political Action in a Democracy* that in a system where two political parties dominate and emerge within a political space, '... the two parties move closer together, they become more moderate and less extreme in policy in an effort to win the crucial middle-of-the-road voters'.[4] The idea of multiple political parties, including stronger small parties that may have only a single seat, being represented in the legislature and having realistic prospects of forming part of a coalition government is an irritation that has resulted in the drive to regulate the coalition system as it applies to municipalities. Owing to a slew of collapsing coalition governments in various municipalities, including some metros, following the much-contested 2021 municipal elections, voters have been left unconvinced about the ability of political parties to maintain stable and effective coalition arrangements. Regulations to establish the threshold for parties to participate in coalitions has been mooted with a view to resolving the political impasse or instabilities surrounding coalitions, which have often vividly played out at the municipal level.

South Africa's policy discourse is fraught with suspicion about the reality of coalition governments, despite widespread acceptance of the principle that power sharing should be an integral part of South Africa's political system. South Africa's Constitution notably refers to multiparty democracy as one of the pillars of democracy. Indeed, the idea of multiparty democracy was entrenched in the Constitution as one of the concessions that the ANC made to the National Party during the negotiations underpinning the transition to democracy.

The interim Constitution of South Africa (1993 Constitution) states, as one of its binding principles, that 'there shall be representative government embracing multiparty democracy'.[5] The multiparty approach was chosen to avoid a 'winner-takes-all' outcome where the political party that won the first democratic elections would thereafter dominate the system, potentially undermining competitive politics. The proportional electoral system was an institution of choice to ensure that power sharing was possible among political parties. The principle of multiparty democracy was not lost in the interim Constitution, which paved the way for the transition to the first democratic elections in 1994. The principle was then carried into the final Constitution adopted in 1996.

The 1996 Constitution states that South Africa is founded on values such as a 'multiparty system of democratic government'.[6] It is therefore clear that the idea of multiparty democracy was not merely a once-off concession that applied only during the transition. While this principle might have originally been aimed at allaying fears of a winner-takes-all result, as provided for in the interim Constitution, it was intended that in the final 1996 Constitution the ideal of multiparty democracy should prevail as part and parcel of the democratic system in South Africa. Taking this route would necessitate remaining cognisant of the country's history and opting for the system that embraces diversity and multiple identities – as evidenced in coalition arrangements, for example.

With reference to South Africa's transition, it has been argued that a multiparty system was meant to apply only to the transition period itself and not remain a feature of the political system on a long-term basis. This, though, undermines the basic tenet of the impact that multiparty participation has on policymaking in the South African context, or in a diverse society. As coalitions are vehicles for decision making, where more than two parties are involved in the process, they are essentially consultative and should therefore yield more accountability. Coalition arrangements are not an aberration of multipartyism; they complement the system and have the potential to steer societies towards consensus-driven politics.

Multiparty democracy: Towards consensus-driven politics

To understand how South Africa's political system would evolve in the post-apartheid dispensation, it is important to begin by describing some of the underlying features of the transition from apartheid to democracy. South Africa has a long history of a dominant-party system, dating back to colonialism and later apartheid, which is often referred to as 'colonialism of a special type'. South Africa experienced more than 300 years of white domination, upon which the apartheid system was built. The sustained domination of one racial group by another implied that South Africa's transition would require not only changes in policies and legal instruments, but also considerable ideological, cultural, institutional and social transformation. Therefore, the question that needs to be asked is: what are the conditions for such extensive transformation? To pursue the level and depth of transformation that is required in South Africa, certain institutional arrangements need to be in place. Such institutional apparatus could then possibly provide a platform for the necessary extensive transformation to take place.

Given its long history of political, social and cultural domination, South Africa can be regarded as a country that lacks the culture of political and social tolerance. Makinda referred to the challenge of attempting to introduce Western-style democracy in Africa, as it created problems both for leaders and voters who had no experience of operating in open, competitive political systems.[7] This is particularly pronounced in the case of South Africa because of the intensity and systemic nature of the apartheid regime, which perfected some of the colonial habits of arranging society – notably the idea of 'separate development'. This resulted in the 'marginalisation of certain ethnic [and racial] groups to generate deeply felt antagonisms'.[8] There are certain basic requirements that need to be in place for democracy to work, and South Africa's history is such that it lacks those attributes and may even be endowed with the opposite attributes.

If one begins from the presumption that the South Africa that adopted a democratic dispensation in 1994 is essentially characterised by a deficit in those attributes that are accepted as preconditions for a successful transition to democracy, then it is important to consider how such attributes can be deliberately attained. The concept of a multiparty approach being an essential feature of a successful transition needs to be explored in depth. If pursued meaningfully, as is explained below, multiparty cooperation can potentially provide a 'catch-up' opportunity for South Africa to further accelerate its democratic transition. However, it is necessary to first outline what multiparty democracy entails and how it can be useful in mediating a tense policy-implementation atmosphere in South Africa in this third decade of democracy.

Recognising the historical facts surrounding conflict in society

Quite often, a multiparty democracy is regarded as a transition phase, a conflict-management system for countries that are latecomers to the process of democratisation. It entails some form of power sharing among different political parties to avoid a winner-takes-all approach. A multiparty democracy is not viewed as a manifestation of mature politics where differences in society will have coalesced. Where there are multiple cleavages shaping political representation in society, the best way to represent these varying positions has always been through a multiparty arrangement.

It has been argued that a mature political system is often characterised by a two-party system in which two political parties largely define the cleavages and offer representation along those lines within society. A multiparty system, in turn, is seen as the transition phase towards the two-party system. It is due to this understanding of multiparty democracy that newly democratised countries tend to hastily discard a multiparty system in favour of a shift towards a two-party system.

What tends to influence people's outlook on the multiparty system in the field of political science is the reality that countries that recommend this system are often on the brink of conflict, or at least have a long history of conflict. South Africa is one of the countries that was prone to political conflict in the period leading up to the end of apartheid in the early 1990s. At the time, South Africa was more appropriately characterised as a country with deep ethnic and racial divisions whose expression and representation in an open democratic system were made possible only through a multiparty arrangement.

It was clear during the Convention for a Democratic South Africa (CODESA) negotiations that one of the conditions for a successful transition and the formation of a democratic government was the adoption of an electoral system in which even the smallest political party would be able to secure representation in Parliament. This was a way to forge tolerance and cooperation among political parties that were completely devoid of such culture due to the impact of colonialism and later apartheid. The conflict that engulfed South Africa during the negotiation process, including violence in the townships, necessitated commitment to multiparty democracy as a way of breaking the deadlock. A government of national unity was subsequently adopted as the first multiparty arrangement in post-apartheid South Africa.

The fact that the parties who were involved in the CODESA negotiations saw the multiparty arrangement as a conflict-aversion strategy meant that the system would be treated as a temporary political arrangement – a short-term measure for a country on the brink of a violent descent into chaos. It also meant that there would be less genuine commitment to a multiparty system as a necessary mechanism to ensure a successful shift from a historically entrenched one-party-dominant system to an open society. If decisions taken in multiparty engagements (including coalitions) are not embraced as timeless constitutional values that are integral to democracy, then multipartyism will ultimately be dismissed as a defect in the system.

Approached differently, the ideal of multiparty democracy deserves more than the perfunctory attitude with which it has been greeted by some in South Africa. As democracies are increasingly characterised by irresolvable conflicts among groups, it is important to consider those attributes of multiparty democracy that need to remain permanent features of any functioning democracy, especially a stable one. A multiparty system should be seen not only as essential for the transition phase towards democracy, but also as a feature that will nurture democracy and prevent countries from sliding into impenetrable majoritarianism, where minority voices are not represented. A multiparty system has the potential to create an environment for consensus in policy formulation and implementation. The absence of an effective multiparty system in most democracies, including South Africa, has weakened both policy formulation and accountability.

Electoral competition, with realistic prospects of exchange of power between competing parties, has a positive effect on economic performance and the quality of democracy. But it also needs to offer options or policy alternatives to voters. The gains from competitive politics can be outweighed by the creation of fragmented political parties or an excessively tense political environment in which decision making becomes cumbersome, or nearly impossible. Intense electoral competition and political fragmentation tend to discourage many from pinning their hopes on coalition governments, particularly when such arrangements replace a one-party-dominant system.

Political fragmentation and coalitions

The emerging political culture, characterised by heightened political tensions and electoral competition, is putting strain on coalition politics and other formalised means of representation. Coalitions suggest that political parties can find each other and compromise on some of the issues that they advanced during their election campaigns. The key principle underscoring coalitions is that no single political party has been given an outright mandate to form a government. This also means that voters did not find any of the different manifestos presented by different political parties as sufficiently convincing on their own.

As South Africa approaches the 2024 general election, the country remains politically fragmented. The ANC has seen a noticeable electoral decline, while opposition parties have remained quite fragmented and divided on where they stand in relation to the still-dominant ANC. Although opposition parties are hoping to gain from the ongoing electoral fallout that the ANC is facing, they have not shown the necessary consolidation of support as an opposition camp. Given this dislocation among opposition parties, the prospects for a stable coalition agreement between these parties remain grim, to the detriment of voters.

The evidence emerging from municipalities thus far points to a lack of ability and willingness on the part of opposition parties to coalesce and sustain an alternative political agenda in South Africa. This then prompts the notion that coalition politics is synonymous with politics of chaos. Ironically, the ANC is already emphasising the need for voters to restore the party's majority to avoid a descent into chaotic coalitions, which has been necessitated by the very failures of the ANC to function under power-sharing arrangements that demand accountability. This flies in the face of voters' quest to spread their votes so as to dissolve a single dominant-party culture. If voters envision coalitions in the way that they vote, then it cannot be said that coalitions are a deviation from the democratic process. Coalitions rather serve to correct a defective system where political power is concentrated and tends to be abused.

It is the dominant-party system that has partially contributed to the political fragmentation and ideological schisms that have gripped the policy dialogue in South Africa, 30 years into democracy. This crisis cannot be resolved by advocating that the majority should naturally continue to identify with a single party for their challenges to be realistically addressed.

The real issue with coalitions: Fear of the unknown!

If experience counts for anything, South Africa has had a single dominant-party system since the end of apartheid, despite the constitutional provision that the country should embrace a multiparty democratic system. The domination of the ANC as a founding party of South Africa's democracy has cemented the idea that a single dominant-party system is appropriate for addressing the 'national question', including the transformation of society. Initially this was not widely challenged, as the ANC-led government enjoyed wider legitimacy. However, as evidence of flaws in this thinking began to emerge, the strong prospects of South Africa heading for coalition governments can no longer be ignored.

This is not simply about a shift towards a coalition system; it is also a correction aimed at addressing the concentration of political power in fewer hands, which ultimately affects accountability and the overall effectiveness of the system. Not all coalition governments will be effective or stable. However, the fundamental principle of power sharing overrides the short-term hiccups inevitably experienced in the early years of coalitions. Moreover, concerns about coalitions in South Africa are a reflection of misplaced expectations. Coalitions are expected to immediately address systemic crises that have beset South Africa for years, including those linked to mismanagement under the ANC-led government. The slow decision-making processes under coalition governments have been used as evidence to persuade voters to again put their trust in one party to govern. There is abundant evidence of the dominant-party system having failed South Africa. A reformed one-party-dominant system will not work either.

Conclusion

The Constitution of South Africa and the country's electoral law envision power-sharing arrangements in the country. Coalition arrangements are therefore an integral part of democratic consolidation in post-apartheid South Africa. The chief question is: what coalition arrangements will be optimal for South Africa? The answer does not lie in regulating coalitions in ways that would effectively curtail their dynamism. The chief characteristic of coalitions is that they are unpredictable and offer no guarantee either to smaller parties or their larger counterparts. While political parties participating in coalition arrangements may have proportionate influence (in line with the votes they obtained) over the direction of coalition governments, they are nevertheless vulnerable.

Even though the coalition arrangements in many municipalities have proven to be shambolic, coalitions provide an opportunity to embrace the constitutional principle of multiparty democracy. South Africa should be looking for better forms of coalitions and other necessary power-sharing arrangements and instruments, which improve the quality of legislation passed and overall policy effectiveness. With the adoption of the constituency system following the court ruling that allowed independent candidates to stand for elections in provincial and national legislatures, it is clear that the concentration of power in a political party is not envisioned in the Constitution.[9] This means that not only is there a place for coalition governments in South Africa, but they should also accommodate the smallest of political players. When big players dominate the scene, they tend to wrest political power from the electorate.

THREE

The economy, business and reform

Cas Coovadia

The (sorry) state of the nation

This contribution is being made at a juncture when people are debating whether South Africa has reached a tipping point. The basis of the debate is that South Africa is on the edge of a precipice and could either fall headfirst into turmoil or pull back into the relative safety of reform and wide-ranging transformation. This chapter explores why South Africa is at the edge of the precipice and what business is trying to do to arrest the country's perilous descent into darkness.

Business is playing an important role in giving the country space to address critical structural issues which, if implemented, could boost confidence and attract investment and put us onto an inclusive growth path. The quality and sustainability of economic transformation in South Africa will depend on how we manage that growth path. The following helps to illustrate why the country is at a precipice:

- Although we have recovered from Covid in the sense that we are back to pre-pandemic gross domestic product (GDP) figures, we were in a dismal situation pre-Covid; thus, getting back to a pre-Covid state is not progress. We must remember that GDP stood at 4.9 per cent in 2021, and it has fallen substantially since then.[1]
- In the second quarter of 2023, we had 74 000 fewer jobs than at the end of 2019 and our unemployment rate was a staggering 40.1 per cent.[2]

- In 2022, South Africa's poverty rate, based on the middle-income country poverty line, was 62.6 per cent.[3]
- The South African Revenue Service (SARS) estimates that the country loses approximately R100 billion annually due to illicit trade, which equates to approximately 1 per cent of GDP.[4]
- The World Bank ranks our key ports (Cape Town, Ngqura, Gqeberha and Durban) as four of the five worst-performing ports in the world for their operational (in)efficiency, which is a clear indication of the parlous state of our logistics and transport infrastructure.[5]
- The South African Reserve Bank (SARB) estimated that South Africa reached an all-time record of 14.8 days of loadshedding per month in the second quarter of 2022. Eskom recently said it had stabilised loadshedding at lower levels in the latter part of 2023, until it suddenly switched the country from stage 3 to stage 6 in one day!
- Transparency International's 2022 Corruption Perceptions Index ranked South Africa 72nd out of 180 countries (with 180 being the most corrupt) for the extent and impact of corruption in the country.[6]
- The major metropolitan municipalities in South Africa are in serious trouble. The State of City Finances Report 2022, published by the South African Cities Network, details the perilous state of finances in the country's major cities.[7] The causes thereof include high employee costs, substantial debt burdens and poor governance.
- South Africa has seen escalating social demands over the past two to three years, which are unsustainable from a fiscal standpoint.

The above are some of the economic factors contributing to the precarious situation in which South Africa finds itself. The business sector has been consistent in its position that these and other factors, like slow implementation of necessary structural reforms in the economy and poor service delivery by government, create a very difficult environment in which to operate.

The South African Chamber of Commerce and Industry (SACCI) Business Confidence Index (BCI) dropped from 106.6 in August 2023 to 108.2 in September 2023. Meanwhile, the Rand Merchant Bank (RMB)/Bureau for Economic Research (BER) Business Confidence Index (BCI) slipped by two points to 31 in the fourth quarter of 2023. These are indicative of low levels of confidence among businesses about the environment in which they operate, which in turn inhibits investment and limits growth.

There are also several social factors that must be considered in South Africa, as reported by Human Rights Watch in its World Report 2023:[8]

- People's right to a healthy environment is under threat as a result of poor implementation of policies and ongoing poverty, unemployment and inequality.
- Police conduct is having a negative impact on the rule of law.
- The ongoing violence against women and children is seriously eroding the rights of these vulnerable groups.
- Xenophobic tendencies are widespread.
- Climate change is taking its toll on urban and rural communities.

The above paints a bleak picture of the state that South Africa is in as well as some of the contributing factors. We must also factor in a weak state with little implementation capacity, expertise and (sometimes) political will as well as a very challenging geopolitical environment, making it difficult for the country to manage its respected non-aligned stance and the upcoming election. This will be the most significant since the first democratic election in 1994 and will be very complex, with a real possibility of coalition governments being formed at the national level and in some provinces. The fact that political parties are already in 'election mode' makes it difficult to adopt pragmatic, sustainable and long-term positions on critical legislation, most notably the contentious National Health Insurance (NHI) Bill.

Anticipating the future

In November 2023, the Indlulamithi South Africa Scenarios 2030 released scenarios for the country for 2035.[9] These give us a glimpse of the future and offer an interesting means to reflect on where the country could be in 2035 if tough decisions are not taken now. The 2035 scenarios come on the back of the scenarios for 2030 which, among other things, include a 'Gwara-Gwara' scenario. This refers to a floundering false dawn and a nation torn between immobility and restless energy in a demoralised land of disorder and decay. The situation in South Africa is such that the Gwara-Gwara scenario is already upon us in 2024!

The 2035 scenarios offer two broad possibilities. The Vulture Culture scenario depicts a nation characterised by a bloated government, authoritarian populism, low voter turnout, and the negative impact of the discovery of oil and gas reserves. The Weaver Work scenario depicts a nation in which cooperation, youth leadership, economic and social growth, and unity prevail. The Gwara-Gwara scenario has become a reality seven years before it was anticipated. Will we, in 12 years' time, find ourselves in the Vulture Culture scenario or the Weaver Work scenario? It all depends on the choices we make now.

On the edge of the precipice: Which way now?

South Africa is on the edge of the proverbial precipice. We could either hurtle towards the Vulture Culture scenario or earnestly strive to build the bright future depicted in the Weaver Work scenario.

Business in South Africa has long maintained that to overcome the myriad economic and social ills gripping the country, critical attention needs to be given to investment and growth. We are clear that there is no time for ideological debates and no time to prevaricate on the need to work together to create an environment for investment, on the back of which we can build sustainable and inclusive growth. Regrettably, we need to accept the fact that we are a small economy at the southern end of the globe and must chart our course within a global context that we can play in; yet we lack the ability to change the game. We are challenged by an exceedingly difficult and deteriorating geopolitical environment and a world moving towards multipolarity (which is in fact a good thing). However, we need to be strategic, pragmatic and intelligent about how we position ourselves in a multipolar world, which is ultimately to our benefit.

These are very difficult environments for businesses to operate in and add greatly to the cost of doing business. Policy and political uncertainty, poor implementation by government, high administrative costs, disintegrating metro governments, ongoing energy challenges, the inefficiencies and lack of competitiveness in the logistics and transport sectors, and increasing levels of crime and corruption are debilitating for sustainable business growth and new business formation. But identifying and implementing a limited number of critical interventions can stop the slide off the precipice and give us the space to address fundamental structural issues, with a view to bringing about sustainable change in key areas.

A couple of years ago, Business Unity South Africa (BUSA) addressed the conundrum of the role of business in these complex sets of circumstances. The conclusion at the time was that we essentially had three options:

- Indicate to President Ramaphosa that businesses would continue trying to run their operations to the best of their ability, despite the difficult environment, but would not work with government to address the crises we faced in the country. One reason for considering this option was the fear that business would become complicit in the lack of progress in the country if government was not committed to a real partnership. However, we also agreed that a decision by business to not work with government at all could have disastrous consequences for South Africa.
- Look at the President's priorities and offer to work with government in tackling these. But business was reluctant to work with government on an extensive list of priorities, as there was then the danger of not making progress in any of them.
- Identify critical areas with key interventions, which would move the needle on investment and growth and instil confidence in the country, and then ask the President if government would partner with business in tackling these. During its deliberations, business agreed that it would resource a limited number of interventions through a structured partnership with government.

BUSA met with the President in January 2022 to explore the third option and he agreed that business and government should form a partnership covering the following areas: energy, logistics and transport, water, other network industries, and law and order. BUSA decided to mobilise business in this effort on the Business for South

Africa (BSA) platform. However, in his State of the Nation Address (SONA) in February 2022, the President announced a process to agree a social compact at the National Economic Development and Labour Council (Nedlac) and did not refer to the proposed partnership with business. Business was thus unable to get any traction on the business–government partnership that year because it had been asked to engage on a social compact, which ultimately did not materialise.

BUSA met the President again in April 2023 and proposed a partnership on energy, logistics and transport, and crime and corruption. The President agreed to the establishment of a structured partnership between business and government to identify and achieve a limited number of critical interventions in each of these areas to stop the country's slide into oblivion. BUSA determined that the partnership, if successfully executed, had the potential to create 300 000 jobs and deliver a 3 per cent GDP growth rate by the end of 2024. It also agreed that the partnership would be confined to a limited number of focused interventions and must not replace increased efforts to address some of the fundamental structural problems in the economy.

A joint structure between the Presidency and business was formalised in June 2023, and BUSA mobilised influential CEOs to champion each of the workstreams, as follows:

- Energy: Nolitha Fakude (Anglo American) and Fleetwood Grobler (Sasol);
- Logistics and transportation: Mxolisi Mgojo (ex-Exxaro), Mpumi Zikalala (Kumba Iron Ore) and Andrew Kirby (Toyota);
- Crime and corruption: Neal Froneman (Sibanye) and Jannie Durand (Remgro).

BUSA also appointed executive heads for each of these streams to manage and coordinate the day-to-day work. Business and government representatives are currently collaborating in working groups under each of the streams. Figure 3.1 below illustrates the collaborative structure that was established.

Figure 3.1: Business–government collaborative structure

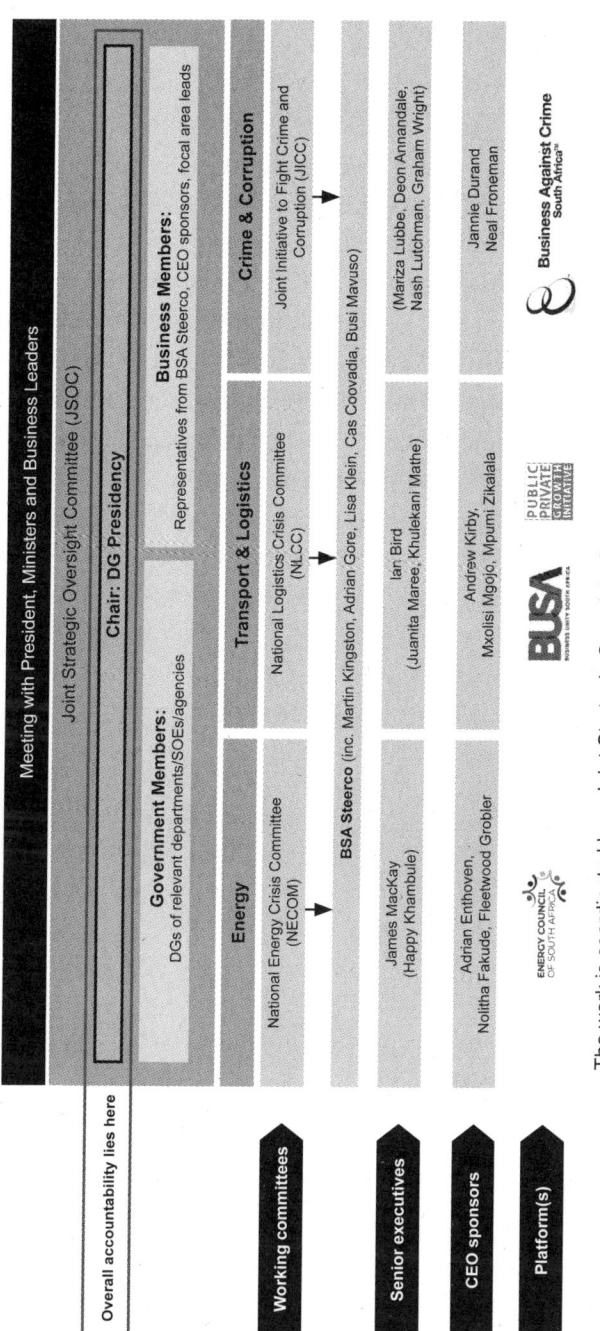

Source: BUSA

Consistent, though slow, progress has been made in each of these streams. Some of the critical milestones in this regard are as follows:

Energy

- The President announced the Energy Action Plan in mid-2022, a significant proportion of which business agreed with. In addition, he established the National Energy Crisis Committee (NECOM) in the Presidency to implement the plan.
- Business raised resources to secure appropriate expertise and allocated them to NECOM. The individuals in question have been working in NECOM since July 2023.
- Business seconded technical expertise to four power stations, leading to some stabilisation of loadshedding in mid-2023.
- The National Transmission Company of South Africa (NTCSA) has been licensed.
- Upwards of R4 billion in private-sector investment has been made in energy generation since the President lifted the ceiling on embedded energy.
- Business and government are working together in eight of the 10 workstreams under NECOM on issues such as strengthening and expanding the grid, wheeling and opening up more space for private-sector investment.

Logistics and transport

- A National Logistics Crisis Committee (NLCC) has been established in which business and government are collaborating.
- Business is working with government to clear the backlog at critical border posts like Lebombo and put in aerial surveillance at key posts to crack down on infrastructure theft.
- Business has agreed on a Logistics Roadmap, which is going through the Cabinet.
- The appointed business teams have worked well with the new Transnet board and the Minister of Public Enterprises in starting to address severe inefficiencies at Transnet and to open up space for private-sector operation of critical rail infrastructure.

THE ECONOMY, BUSINESS AND REFORM

Crime and corruption
- A Joint Initiative to Fight Crime and Corruption (JICC) has been established.
- The passage of the National Prosecuting Authority (NPA) Amendment Bill through Parliament is being awaited, which will enable business to capacitate the NPA.
- Business is piloting a project to modernise and improve the efficiency of the 10111 emergency line.
- Business is looking at developing a state-of-the-art forensic capability for the country.

Stepping stones to South Africa's future

Although this chapter has painted a picture of a country teetering on the edge of a cliff, South Africa remains a country with great opportunities. For example:
- We have a relatively large, diverse economy.
- We boast global businesses in health and life sciences, chemicals, consumer goods, automotives and related components, mining and resources, metals and agriculture, among others.
- We have one of the most advanced, stable and sophisticated financial sectors in the world.
- We have the potential to be one of the leading tourist destinations in the world, given our friendly people, high-quality resorts, diverse flora and fauna, beautiful beaches, historical landmarks and impressive landscapes.
- We play a critical role on the African continent which is also rich in potential.

Business believes that South Africa's unique blend of attractions, opportunities and enduring spirit can – and must – be positively exploited to prevent the country's descent into the void. It is entirely within our capabilities to forge an inclusive and transformative path into the future. We have a patriotic business sector that is committed to the country, which explains why business is prepared to partner with government to overcome some of the obstacles to investment and growth.

Of the three options that the business sector faced, the choice of a partnership with government is the only way to harness the country's considerable resources and ensure a collective effort in tackling some of the country's most intractable problems. In short, a surprisingly large number of people believe in South Africa and, under the right conditions, its ability to restore hope among the population and to find a new, more cohesive path.

May the upcoming elections mark the start of a new, more positive era for the country in which its long-hoped-for vision finally becomes the reality.

FOUR

Power struggles: Shedding light on South Africa's enduring energy challenges

Rod Crompton and Bruce Young

Introduction

The global energy system is currently experiencing two concurrent and interconnected transitions, and South Africa faces challenges in adapting to both. The first transition is related to increasing global concerns regarding the impact of human activities on the Earth's natural environment, particularly the over-utilisation of the planet's natural resources. This concern is often summarised in issues related to global warming and climate change. The second transition pertains to the technological tsunami occurring in the electricity sector, closely tied to the Fourth Industrial Revolution. While these are substantial topics, this chapter provides only a brief overview of each one and outlines the dilemmas that they create for South Africa.

Environmental concerns

Environmental concerns are predominantly centred on the energy sector, which is responsible for 68 per cent of greenhouse gas (GHG) emissions. In response to these concerns, the Paris Agreement of 2015 aimed to limit the global temperature increase to 1.5°C above pre-industrial levels and achieve net-zero carbon emissions by 2050.

By 2023, the likelihood of meeting these targets appeared to be slim, with much depending on the outcome of the 28th meeting of the United Nations Framework Convention on Climate Change Conference of the Parties (UNFCCC COP), which took place in late 2023. The success of this meeting hinged on the adoption of coordinated global policies and capital commitments necessary to attain these targets. If countries adhere to their current pledges, the world is projected to experience a temperature increase of 2.1–2.4°C above pre-industrial levels, in contrast to the 3–4°C increase under current policies.[1] Such a scenario could have major detrimental effects both on human populations and the natural environment.

Achieving a net-zero economy is a multifaceted and intricate endeavour, necessitating substantial transformation in people's lifestyles, work habits and resource consumption. The sheer magnitude of this quest may well be one of the most formidable challenges that humanity has ever faced. It will demand considerable sacrifices, concerted efforts, and investments from governments, businesses and individuals alike. According to a McKinsey study, the cost of this transition has been estimated at $US275 trillion, which is equivalent to 2.7 times the current global gross domestic product (GDP).[2] South Africa is poorly placed to meet the COP targets due to its heavy reliance on coal and oil, coupled with its highly energy-intensive economy.[3] Despite having only 0.75 per cent of the world's population, South Africa is responsible for 1.2 per cent of global GHG emissions.

The twin transitions are driving a gradual shift in the global economy from the Western and Northern regions to the Eastern and Southern regions, which offer more favourable renewable energy resources. This shift is exemplified by the establishment of the BRICS grouping (comprising Brazil, Russia, India, China and South Africa and, as of January 2024, Egypt, Ethiopia, Iran, Saudi Arabia and the United Arab Emirates (UAE)) and its aspiration to reduce the global economy's reliance on the United States (US) dollar, thus reflecting the evolving global economic landscape. South Africa faces a challenge in navigating its international relations as it seeks to balance traditional and emerging economic forces. Furthermore, there is a simultaneous transformation occurring in the global energy demand structure, with fossil fuels declining in significance and demand for renewable energy and electrification rising.[4]

Enthusiasm for these local and global transformations should be tempered by an understanding of the immense challenges associated with transitioning to a new global energy system. Fossil fuels remain the dominant source of primary energy supply in the world, and this holds true in South Africa as well. Despite a five-fold increase since 2015, solar power still accounts for less than 15 per cent of global energy capacity.[5] Meanwhile, global oil and gas supplies continue to expand, with non-OPEC (Organization of the Petroleum Exporting Countries) oil production growing by 10 per cent since 2015.[6] In South Africa, the value of petroleum-product sales significantly exceeds that of electricity retail sales,[7] underscoring the prevailing reliance on traditional energy sources. This highlights the major journey that renewable energy must undertake before it can fully substitute conventional energy carriers.

Technology tsunami

The technology tsunami in the energy sector is most evident in renewable electricity generation and storage technologies. These innovations have disrupted the traditional economies of scale associated with coal and nuclear-based power generation as well as the concentration of ownership within the power-generation sector. This disruption is also reshaping South Africa's minerals–energy complex[8] and challenging established interests in fossil fuels. Mainstream banks are progressively withdrawing from financing coal projects and, to a lesser degree, those related to oil and gas.

Interestingly, this shift away from economies of scale benefits consumers. For instance, solar-power generation now comes in a range of sizes, from small-scale installations to industrial-scale projects. Their capacity can be incrementally increased, and they are readily accessible online or at local hardware stores. This accessibility has proven to be advantageous for those looking to mitigate the impact of South Africa's intermittent rolling blackouts, termed loadshedding.

Eskom estimates that installed solar capacity doubled in just 12 months, reaching 4 800MW in September 2023,[9] up from 983MW in March 2022.[10] This growth in private investment in solar power, regardless of the government's plans, reflects a growing lack of confidence in the government's ability to resolve the electricity crisis in the short term. As solar energy becomes more widespread, negative electricity prices have been observed in some countries around midday. As the sun sets, alternative supply must be rapidly brought online. Similarly, on an overcast day, very little of the 4 800MW might be available, requiring a scramble for alternative supplies. System operators must adapt by implementing innovations like smart meters, smart grids and related technologies that are fundamentally transforming the electricity supply industry (ESI). Decentralisation, decarbonisation, democratisation and digitalisation have become the new watchwords for the electricity sector.

Emerging technologies are enabling consumers to transition to self-sufficiency, effectively turning them into 'prosumers' who can sell excess power to others. Such technological advances have rendered Eskom's traditional business model outdated, leading to a utility death spiral,[11] a phenomenon seen in vertically integrated utilities worldwide. The business model employed by South African municipalities is also no longer suitable, as they experience a loss of revenue from customers transitioning to off-grid or partially off-grid solutions. Amid these changes, the substantial capital investment burden in the electricity sector is being shifted from the state to the private sector.

These transformations are beginning to produce significant economic consequences and are triggering shifts in the political landscape. The once-dominant minerals–energy complex is engaged in a fierce struggle to maintain its supremacy. Yet some companies within this complex are seeking to enhance their 'green' image, to preserve export markets threatened by environmental taxes, or to explore opportunities in emerging energy carriers like hydrogen. Ironically, loadshedding is intensifying these developments.

Electricity

South Africa is currently facing a severe electricity crisis. The availability of electricity is a crucial, albeit insufficient, factor for modern industrial development. The country has grappled with loadshedding since 2008, and it has progressively worsened over the years. In 2022, President Ramaphosa acknowledged that the electricity crisis posed one of the most significant threats to economic and social progress in the country.[12] The government bears responsibility for addressing this issue, having assumed control of the procurement of generating capacity from Eskom in 2010.

There are many causes of loadshedding. These include government dithering in implementing market reforms, diminishing state capacity, delays in bringing additional capacity online, and the fallout from state capture and corruption, which largely centres on Eskom. Furthermore, a shortage of skilled personnel, overly optimistic construction assumptions, the ageing of Eskom's power stations and the growing trend of non-payment for electricity have all played a part. Notably, recurrent breakdowns in Eskom's coal-fired power stations, constituting 74 per cent of the nation's generating capacity, are a primary concern.[13] These problems persist unabated and are primarily rooted in government policies and their implementation, or lack thereof.

A convenient measure of Eskom's declining output is its energy availability factor (EAF) (Figure 4.1), which declined from about 80 per cent to 55 per cent in 2023.

Figure 4.1: Eskom's energy availability factor, 2021–2023

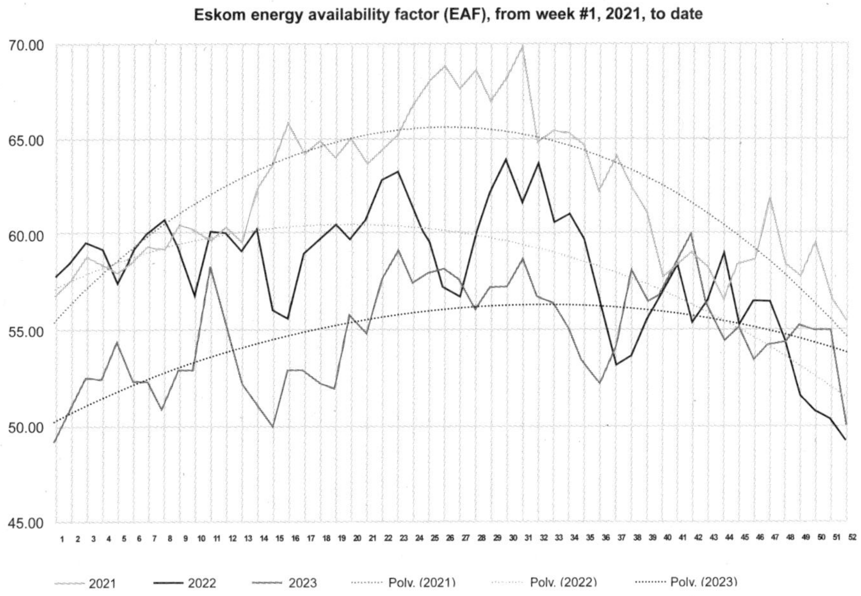

Source: EE Business Intelligence, Eskom data[14]

Energy issues in South Africa, as in many other countries, are inherently political. Von Holdt refers to the emergence of a pervasive informal political–economic system in South Africa, shaped by the intersection of patronage and factionalism, where patronage networks form political factions to gain influence within the state.[15] In the energy sector, this has manifested as the 'state capture' of entities such as Eskom and municipalities, alongside other state institutions.

This influence manifests in various ways, including criminal activities, a culture of non-payment for electricity, electricity theft, vandalism, and the theft of network infrastructure in both the petroleum and electricity sectors. In recent years, racketeering by coal and construction mafias has further threatened network industries, while law-enforcement agencies struggle to contain this growing problem.

Given that most of South Africa's energy is transmitted through various networks, energy planners are yet to devise effective solutions to address these internal threats. This in turn threatens the security of energy supply, a fundamental pillar of any energy system.

Electricity policy

The 1998 White Paper on Energy Policy established clear goals for South Africa's electricity sector, namely, to bring about market liberalisation and to address the challenges in municipal electricity distribution. However, neither of these goals has materialised. In 2003, the government initiated a process of reorganising the ESI by establishing the entity, Electricity Distribution Industry Holdings, and in 2012 it published the Independent System and Market Operator Bill. Unfortunately, both initiatives faltered and were abandoned. This was primarily due to a decline in support for such solutions within the ruling African National Congress (ANC), driven by a series of policy zigzags.[16]

It was not until 2019 that the Minister of Public Enterprises introduced a Roadmap for Eskom in a Reformed Electricity Supply Industry, which was a watered-down version of the 1998 White Paper. This marked a significant turning point in electricity reform. However, by this time, the pervasive influence of patronage networks and factionalism had seriously eroded many components of the state apparatus. Additionally, the impact of the ANC's cadre deployment policy, the Preferential Procurement Policy Framework Act, 2000 and state capture had left Eskom and numerous municipalities in dire straits.

In a quest to combat ongoing loadshedding, the Minister of Public Enterprises once again turned to market liberalisation and the unbundling of Eskom, stopping short of outright privatisation but opening the door to private-sector investment in the electricity sector. This shift appeared to set in motion a series of supportive policy measures aimed at addressing the challenges confronting the sector.

Market reform received a significant boost in 2022 when the President announced the removal of the 100MW licence-exemption cap for independent generators and introduced a proposal for a feed-in tariff for self-generating households and businesses.[17] The pursuit of market liberalisation was further advanced in the Minister of Finance's 2023 Budget Review, in which he reintroduced the possibility of private-sector investment in the transmission grid and announced investment incentives for industrial and residential customers looking to install solar panels.

This shift towards private investment as a solution to South Africa's crises is also apparent in the granting of Transnet port concessions to private operators and the Cabinet's approval of a National State Enterprises Bill in September 2023. This Bill aims to consolidate commercial state-owned companies (SOCs) under a single state asset management company, enabling private investment and creating the potential for stock exchange listings.[18]

Despite more policy zigzagging,[19] several supportive policies have emerged, including the Integrated Resource Plan (IRP), the Nationally Determined Contribution, the Just Transition Framework, the Just Energy Transition Investment Plan (JET-IP),[20] the Low Emissions Development Strategy, the National Infrastructure Plan 2030 and the Energy Action Plan. These initiatives were adopted following the President's pivotal speech in July 2022.

Amendments to the Electricity Regulation Act, 2006 are required to enable the functioning of the national transmission and market operator company, a crucial element in the ongoing process of market reform. This amendment faced significant delays but was eventually presented to Parliament in August 2023, partly due to renewed pressure from the National Energy Crisis Committee (NECOM).

Collectively, these policy developments bode well for ending loadshedding and establishing a stable ESI. However, the R1.5 trillion needed by 2027, as outlined in the Cabinet-approved JET-IP,[21] to expedite the energy transition and eliminate loadshedding, remains unsecured due to government delays and diminishing confidence. The outcome of the 2024 general election could determine whether South Africa continues along the path of market reform or, as certain factions within the ANC advocate, reverts to an ideological commitment to state ownership and 'ol' king coal'. Will the business and international community have sufficient confidence that there is policy certainty, which is sufficiently robust and longlasting to justify large investments in South Africa's energy infrastructure?

Such a policy direction has equity implications. Private investors expect a return on their investments, which implies higher costs for customers who pay. The substantial increase in electricity tariffs over the past decade has made it increasingly challenging for many to afford electricity. While the Free Basic Electricity subsidy offers some relief to the impoverished, it often does not reach its intended recipients, as municipalities sometimes allocate those funds for other purposes. Therefore, although there has been progress in the direction of market reform, it is likely to result in higher prices, even if only to enable Eskom to charge tariffs that reflect its actual costs. Meanwhile, there has been limited policy development concerning a safety net for the poor. Even if loadshedding is eliminated in the coming years, electricity prices may remain a political hot potato in the future.

Although a noticeable policy shift towards market reform has occurred, albeit somewhat reluctantly, the market views it as too little, too late. Customers, weary of awaiting a government-led solution to loadshedding, are now taking matters into their own hands. Market forces are assuming control, regardless of the government's stance. While this is a necessary step to eliminate loadshedding, these unmanaged transitions have social implications which the government will need to address in the future. This situation also raises the concern that future administrations may consider rolling back market reforms, similar to what transpired in Mexico.

Environmental concerns pose a significant challenge to power generation, especially as most of Eskom's coal-fired stations were built before increased awareness of emissions and public health impacts. The costly retrofitting required to bring these stations up to current environmental standards would not only be financially unviable but would also lead to reduced power output. Except for the recently built Medupi and Kusile coal power stations, the remaining coal fleet in South Africa is more than 40 years old and approaching the end of its operational life.

South Africa faces a crucial public-policy dilemma, simplistically characterised as a choice between addressing loadshedding or prioritising environmental and public health concerns. In 2022, Eskom initiated a Just Energy Transition to navigate this dilemma. However, it is too early to determine whether this approach will ultimately succeed.

Power generation

In the 20th century, fossil fuels played a pivotal role in elevating living standards, fostering significant population growth and facilitating the development of modern industrial societies. This was largely due to their high energy return on energy invested (EROEI). However, the repercussions of this growth, including climate change, have led to a global consensus on the need to phase out fossil fuels in favour of renewable energy sources.

Unfortunately, current renewable power-generation technologies are encountering obstacles in fully replacing fossil fuels. Their EROEI is notably lower,[22] necessitating a greater energy input to sustain current energy consumption levels. Presently, fossil fuels, with their higher EROEI, are utilised to manufacture renewable technologies with lower EROEI. Consequently, as the balance shifts and renewable energy's market share expands, renewable energy costs are likely to increase.

Renewable energy sources, such as solar and wind, have variable output. As a result, their effective deployment necessitates a complementary array of technologies, including storage options like pumped storage, batteries and synchronous condensers, and technologies that can rapidly ramp up supply, such as natural gas. Unfortunately, these additional costs are frequently omitted when estimating/quoting the costs of renewable energy, resulting in an overly optimistic perspective on these costs.

Eskom's coal-based power generation constitutes 86 per cent of South Africa's electricity supply,[23] while nuclear, hydroelectric and pumped storage make up smaller shares. Initiatives like the Renewable Energy Independent Power Producer Procurement Programme (REIPPPP) launched by the government in 2010, along with private investments, have begun to challenge Eskom's dominance in the market. However, decisions regarding the choice of generation technologies are determined by the Minister of Mineral Resources and Energy, through the various IRPs. These IRPs are intended to prioritise cost-effectiveness but also allow for technology choices based on 'strategic' considerations, which have been influenced by politicians. This is evident in a draft IRP 2023 published for comment in January 2024 (unfortunately without the dataset used to develop it), which has attracted widespread criticism. However, the relevance of IRPs has been somewhat diluted by the removal of the 100MW licence-exemption cap for independent generators.

The undesirably long intervals between IRPs (in rapidly changing circumstances) have been partially remedied as a result of legal action taken by a non-governmental organisation (NGO) in 2023 which compelled the President to belatedly enact a provision of the National Energy Act, 2008, obliging the Minister of Mineral Resources and Energy to publish an Integrated Energy Plan on an annual basis, commencing 1 April 2024.

With the mounting pressure to eliminate loadshedding, a contentious debate has arisen over the most suitable technologies, creating polarisation between advocates of coal and nuclear, on the one hand, and proponents of renewables, on the other. This dynamic reflects the highly contested political and economic landscape within the minerals–energy complex, which is playing out in plain view.

The influence of vested interests, combined with the emergence of social media and fake news, has made it more and more challenging for everyday South Africans to distinguish between facts and misinformation. This predicament is unfortunate, particularly at a time when factual information and evidence-based decision-making are most needed, as both are crucial for steering the ESI on a sensible path. The outcome of this situation remains uncertain, but three key imperatives are expected to shape South Africa's future trajectory.

First, coal is expected to remain in use for several decades. Eskom's newly established, large coal power stations have operational lifespans of 50 years. However, there may come a point, before the end of their operational life, when market conditions render them stranded assets. At this juncture, South Africa will face the decision to either close or subsidise these stations. Closure is likely to be met with fierce resistance from the coal lobby, particularly from the thousands of coal truckers. Second, the reduced barriers to entry and the lower cost of renewables, coupled with customers' imperative to ensure security of supply, enable consumers to vote with their feet. Third, international pressure, notably access to export markets, is being felt to an increasing extent and appears set to grow in importance.

Notwithstanding these imperatives, the immediate crisis is loadshedding. Since 2010, very credible generation-recovery strategies have been adopted – year after year, and Eskom CEO after Eskom CEO. What will be different this time around? There are several significant differences, stemming from renewed political will and desperation.

In addition to the market-oriented reforms mentioned earlier, financially stable municipalities have the option to source their power independently, outside of Eskom's purview. Solar power is experiencing rapid growth, now accounting for the highest share of renewable sources at 21.8 per cent in February 2023.[24] In just the second quarter of 2023, a remarkable R32 billion-worth of solar panels, batteries and inverters were imported, without burdening the national budget.[25] Furthermore, in late 2022, the President revealed that there was approximately 9000 MW of new private capacity in various stages of development.[26]

NECOM, comprising over a hundred high-ranking officials from various government departments and Eskom, collaborates closely with business and other stakeholders. This collaborative effort is overseen by the Presidency and signifies a fundamental change in government cooperation – one that advocates solutions, reforms and investments across governmental silos. A dedicated Minister of Electricity supports this initiative, introducing a fresh sense of urgency, concentration and accountability.

In 2023, Eskom received debt relief of R254 billion over a three-year period, with the condition that it refrain from further borrowing and making new investments in generation capacity for three to four years. This measure aims to address Eskom's unsustainable R423 billion debt[27] and place the organisation on a more sustainable financial footing. Also in 2023, the National Energy Regulator of South Africa (NERSA) approved a tariff increase for Eskom, which is a step towards achieving cost-reflective tariffs. Without such adjustments, Eskom would remain financially unsustainable and continue to pose the single largest risk to South Africa's economy. Eskom is also reforming its tariffs by introducing net billing schemes and offering to purchase surplus power.

Furthermore, Eskom is being unbundled into three subsidiaries: generation, transmission and distribution. The first step in this process is the establishment of a new National Transmission Company of South Africa (NTCSA), set to begin operations in April 2024, pending the passage of the Electricity Regulation Amendment Bill. These significant changes will usher in an electricity wholesale market. The government has also revealed plans to procure additional electricity capacity through subsequent bidding rounds. Bid Window 7 of the REIPPPP, launched in December 2023, represents the largest round to date, with a target of 5 000MW.

At long last, there is growing evidence of law-enforcement agencies performing their duties more effectively, although there is still a long way to go.[28] The military presence at Eskom's power stations, for example, serves as a symbolic deterrent against criminal activities and sabotage, while the forces of law and order are starting to make some modest progress in combating coal mafias and other criminal elements.

Despite these initiatives and efforts, the question on many people's lips is: when will loadshedding end? Much as the government hopes for it to end before the 2024 general elections, this is unlikely. The draft IRP 2023 envisages 2028. Over the past decade, Eskom's EAF has shown a consistent decline, as illustrated in Figure 4.1. Eskom's 52-week summer outlook for 2023/24 anticipates ongoing loadshedding at approximately stage 4 to stage 6. Unfortunately, Eskom's woes are not amenable to quick fixes. Yet, in among the intricacies, there are reasons for optimism.

Winkler's forecast suggests a substantial reduction in loadshedding in the latter part of 2024, with complete elimination anticipated four years after that.[29] Furthermore, as Eskom's market share diminishes, its impact on loadshedding should also decrease.

Key policy questions revolve around the prospects of the political will to reform either growing or waning, and whether the market will be permitted to make an optimal contribution to alleviate the problem of loadshedding.

Power transmission

South Africa's historical coal-centric electricity transmission network is primarily located in the north-eastern part of the country. However, the country's optimal wind and solar resources are situated in the south-western region, necessitating significant investment in the transmission grid for the transition to renewable technologies. The grid's capacity limitations in the south-western region became startlingly apparent during the sixth REIPPPP bidding round, where over 3 GW of renewable generation projects could not advance due to the absence of available connection capacity.[30]

In September 2023, the Minister of Electricity issued a warning about another impending electricity crisis.[31] He was referring to the need to build 14 000 kilometres of new transmission lines within the next eight to 10 years, which would require an unprecedented rate of construction. Alongside the construction challenges, there is also the financial hurdle of raising the required R235 billion, which is beyond the financial capacity of both Eskom and the state. Eskom is able to finance the R70 billion required between 2024 and 2028.[32] Nonetheless, it is evident that alternative financing mechanisms, likely involving private investment, must be found. The government will need to establish a supportive policy and regulatory framework to facilitate private-sector involvement in this substantial project.

The anticipated unbundling of Eskom's new NTCSA is expected to facilitate fundraising. However, the NTCSA will initially carry some of Eskom's existing debt, which will lower its credit quality. The NTCSA will initially assume multiple roles, including being the system owner and operator, the market operator and the central purchasing agency. These complex roles must be carried out amid the substantial challenges of loadshedding, a changing generation profile, new wheeling and curtailment arrangements, evolving market pricing, and the management of an extensive network expansion project.

The urgency of construction is being hindered by the necessity to secure rights of way through private properties, a notoriously slow process. Additionally, the NTCSA must adapt to evolving grid-access rules – that is, in 2023 it transitioned from a 'first-come, first-served' approach to a 'first-ready, first-served' approach. Achieving all these objectives concurrently is a formidable undertaking, particularly in a politically fractured society.

Power distribution

The electricity distribution crisis, primarily stemming from inadequate municipal maintenance of distribution grids, was initially recognised in the 1998 White Paper on Energy Policy. Attempts to address this issue through entities like Electricity Distribution Industry Holdings and regional electricity distributors proved unsuccessful, perpetuating the crisis. Annual reports from the Auditor-General have consistently highlighted the precarious state of municipal finances in South Africa, leading to several municipalities being placed under administration. In parallel, Eskom's escalating municipal debt reached R63 billion in 2023,[33] posing a significant threat to the ESI's survival. Despite efforts by both Eskom and the National Treasury to assist debt-ridden municipalities, success has been limited. Political solutions have also fallen short, with the legacy of non-payment from the apartheid era still prevalent today, notably in Soweto where 80 per cent of customers do not pay their bills.

Ironically, private investments in new renewable generation technologies are undermining municipal business models by reducing their electricity sales and consequently tax revenue from such sales. This phenomenon also hampers distribution-grid maintenance due to declining revenue and the migration of customers off the grid, resulting in reduced income. Tariff reform, such as increasing fixed charges, may offer some relief, but could disproportionately affect the poor. Implementing smart meters and smart grids presents a partial solution, although it will require investment and time.

The Achilles heel of the ESI is non-payment, together with the challenges posed to municipal business models. Failure to address these issues could lead to a growing divide within the ESI, with paying entities such as businesses and more affluent individuals having access to electricity, while those unable or unwilling to pay will have to depend on the state.

Transport

Land transportation in South Africa is primarily powered by petroleum products. On a global scale, oil demand is declining and is expected to continue doing so. This trend is attributed to the increasing efficiency of internal combustion engines (ICEs) and the expanding market presence of electric vehicles (EVs). In South Africa, the demand for petrol is declining, but the demand for diesel is on the rise, with the latter showing a compound annual growth rate of 2.68 per cent over the past 18 years – likely influenced by the demand for power generation.

Historically, South Africa has followed an import-substitution industrialisation policy, notably in the petroleum products manufacturing sector.[34] However, with the recent closure of three of the six refineries in the country, approximately 60 per cent of the refined fuel demand is now met through imports, rendering petroleum and fuels the most significant imports in terms of value.[35] This situation presents a compelling *prima facie* case for South Africa to transition to EVs, which could utilise local coal, wind and solar resources. Currently, government policy is biased against EVs in favour of ICE vehicles, despite calls from ICE manufacturers for an EV-supportive approach. After grappling with this issue for several years, the government has yet to extricate itself from its longstanding support programme for ICE vehicles.

With the decreasing global cost of EVs, South Africa faces a choice. It can either remain burdened with expensive ICE vehicles or it can adapt to global trends and simultaneously reduce its reliance on its most substantial import. Such a policy shift could significantly impact the country's GDP, thus underscoring the urgency of addressing the electricity crisis. A switch to EVs would also contribute to decarbonisation.

Buildings, heating and industry

Globally, there is an imminent need for decarbonisation, and South Africa is no exception in this regard. Carbon dioxide (CO_2) emissions are deeply ingrained in our activities and production processes. Notably, the heating and cooling of residential, commercial and industrial buildings are significant contributors to carbon emissions, introducing complex and costly challenges in the transition towards decarbonisation.

There is a growing consensus that heat pumps, powered by renewable electricity, offer the most efficient and cost-effective means of heating and cooling buildings in a decarbonised world.[36] Heat pumps can achieve up to 400 per cent efficiency, producing up to four times more heat energy than the electricity they consume.[37] Additionally, they can double as air conditioners for cooling during the summer. However, in Europe, replacing existing gas boilers with heat pumps is proving politically challenging, especially in Germany.[38] Although decarbonisation necessitates the eventual elimination of fossil fuels for heating buildings, the installation cost of heat pumps in domestic homes remains a significant financial burden, even in advanced economies. In the US, for example, installing a heat pump in one's home costs between R47 500 and R190 000, with the average homeowner spending R104 500.[39] Although labour costs may be different in South Africa, similar capital costs can be expected in the country.

Despite South Africa's milder climate compared to that of Europe, heating in winter and cooling in summer remain essential. Escalating electricity costs make traditional electric heaters increasingly unaffordable. Yet many South African households may struggle to afford the initial expense of heat-pump installations, prompting lower-income households to resort to higher-emission fuels, which could trigger political concerns. By contrast, larger commercial buildings are well-suited for heat-pump installations. Indeed, the heat-pump industry in South Africa is poised for significant growth, in line with the expansion of renewable electricity sources.

Industrial-process heat is necessary to create almost everything we use every day, such as food, textiles, cement, steel, composites, computer chips, plastics and glass. Industrial heat pumps can serve needs at temperatures of up to 150°C and are suitable for agriculture and the food industry. For higher-temperature process heat, options like direct renewable electricity usage, concentrated solar power, biomass combustion or green hydrogen are emerging possibilities. Exploring opportunities for collaboration with global heat-pump manufacturers and potential local production of heat pumps or components should be considered.

Natural gas

Natural gas is a contentious topic in South Africa, for several reasons. It currently accounts for a relatively small proportion of the country's primary energy supply. There is also a debate about whether to expand its use for gas-fired power generation, which could complement the increasing levels of renewable power generation. Environmentalists argue that while gas is better than coal, it still releases significant CO_2 emissions, suggesting that South Africa should consider transitioning directly to renewables instead of investing in gas.

Proponents of natural gas, however, highlight the substantial gas reserves recently discovered in northern Mozambique and southern Namibia, as well as TotalEnergies' oil and gas discoveries off the coast of Mossel Bay, which could potentially serve as an economic catalyst. Nevertheless, both Shell and Karpowership have faced legal challenges from environmentalists over their inadequate environmental impact assessments. Studies conducted by the National Business Initiative indicate that gas-to-power represents a crucial element in South Africa's future electricity mix. It is seen as a means of providing dispatchable electricity generation to complement the variable output from renewable sources.[40]

How South Africa strikes a balance between its carbon-reduction objectives, its economic-growth goals and its electricity-generation needs will be pivotal to future policy discussions. In the short term, Sasol has announced that its gas supplies from Mozambique are being depleted and that it will discontinue sales to certain industrial and commercial customers by 2026.[41] This poses a significant challenge to these customers as viable alternatives are currently unavailable and there is a lack of infrastructure to support gas imports. Shifting back to options like liquefied petroleum gas (LPG), coal or fuel oil would necessitate additional investments, particularly in the light of impending carbon taxes, and potentially result in increased emissions. LPG seems to be the more probable choice for many, although it is expected to lead to price increases.

Green hydrogen

A consensus has emerged, evident at COP26[42] in 2021 and in the oil and gas industry,[43] about the potentially pivotal role that green hydrogen could play in the transition to renewable energy. Green hydrogen is generated through water electrolysis, using renewable electricity. It does not result in direct CO_2 emissions and is not a novel concept. The current surge of interest globally in green hydrogen marks the third wave, with previous waves occurring in the 1970s and early 2000s.[44] Whether this current wave of enthusiasm will lead to the widespread adoption envisaged by its proponents, remains unclear.

Nevertheless, there is substantial agreement that several multi-GW green hydrogen facilities will be established over the next decade,[45] including those dedicated to the export of green hydrogen from the southern hemisphere to the northern hemisphere. Construction has commenced on a US$5 billion 4 GW project in Saudi Arabia to produce 1.2 million tonnes annually of green ammonia[46] made from green hydrogen, with production set to start in 2026.[47] Two of the referenced projects are located on the west coast of southern Africa, while the third is situated in northern Australia. These regions were chosen due to their arid, sparsely populated environments, making them ideal for solar and wind electricity-generation projects, free from the regulatory and space constraints typically found in densely populated First World countries.

However, industry and political consensus and forecasts are not always reliable predictors of developments in the energy sector. For instance, in 1974, General Electric listened to the prevailing industry consensus and projected that by 2000, approximately 90 per cent of the US's electricity would be sourced from fast-breeder nuclear reactors.[48] However, this anticipated expansion of nuclear power did not materialise due to safety, cost and technology-related concerns, resulting in the construction of only two fast-breeder reactors to date.

Green hydrogen is envisaged for many end-use applications, but there are competing green-technology options, particularly the direct use of electricity, for several of these applications.[49] Therefore, it is not a given that green hydrogen will be used for all the applications for which it is currently being considered.

The International Renewable Energy Agency (IRENA) estimates a wide range of green hydrogen production costs, ranging from US$2.7 to US$6 per kilogram.[50] Another IRENA study examined the optimal means of transporting green hydrogen, suggesting that transporting it over long distances (>7 000 kilometres) would add an additional US$2.5 to US$4.2 per kilogram to the factory gate price.[51]

Optimists anticipate a delivered green hydrogen price range of US$5 to US$8 per kilogram for the initial wave of green hydrogen projects up to 2030. This translates into an equivalent oil price range of US$247 to US$395 per barrel. With oil hovering in the price range of US$80 to US$100 per barrel, green hydrogen is considerably more expensive. As a result, regulatory and government interventions will be necessary to incentivise the construction of the first generation of plants. It is doubtful that South Africa can afford to subsidise green hydrogen.

Conclusion

South Africa finds itself in a very tough position insofar as energy is concerned. On the one hand, the electricity crisis is prompting the start of an unmanaged energy transition led by market forces, with a weakened state trying to introduce some market reforms. South Africa is caught in the maelstrom of the Fourth Industrial Revolution and an electricity technology tsunami, coupled with international pressure to decarbonise its economy (one of the most carbon-intensive economies in the world), despite the country's powerful and vociferous coal lobby. To compound matters, South Africa is gripped by high levels of unemployment and industrial decline while fractured politics is riven by the intersection of patronage and factionalism. In such a context, it is reasonable to expect political turmoil and policy zigzags to continue.

Nevertheless, there are prospects for a better future. Market reforms are starting to get under way and more space is being created for the private sector in the ESI. Moreover, new technologies with lower barriers to entry are democratising an electricity system that, historically, was heavily centralised.

Key to governing this tempestuous collection of pressures will be an astute state capable of riding the waves while simultaneously providing policy direction. This is unlikely to occur without significant pressure being exerted on government by private enterprise, civil society, and the local and international financial communities.

FIVE

Do geopolitics and trade clash? South Africa's foreign and trade policy options

Anthoni van Nieuwkerk

Introduction

Globally, South Africa is regarded as a small, open economy, accounting for 0.6 per cent of global gross domestic product (GDP). With a GDP of R4.6 trillion in 2022, South Africa's economy is nevertheless the biggest in Africa. It is also the most industrialised, technologically advanced and diversified economy on the continent.[1] Despite several socioeconomic challenges, including poverty and unemployment, and infrastructure failures, especially in electricity supply, South Africa is an upper-middle-income country, one of a few such countries in Africa. It is also a leading member of the Southern African Development Community (SADC).[2] South Africa's trade with the rest of the world is outlined in Table 5.1.

The natural resource extraction industry remains one of the largest industries in the country, contributing R200 billion to GDP annually. Since the end of apartheid, the South African economy has diversified, particularly towards services. For example, in 2019, the financial services industry contributed R74.5 billion to GDP, while in 2021, South Africa-based financial institutions managed more than R26 trillion in assets. In October 2021, the total market capitalisation of the Johannesburg Stock Exchange stood at R24 trillion. Furthermore, the country's advanced financial infrastructure and efficiency present opportunities for international investors.[3]

Table 5.1: South Africa's trade with the rest of the world, 2022 (R billions)

	Exports	Imports	Trade balance
Total	2 013.4	1 817.9	+195.6
Agriculture	118.4	39.0	+79.5
Manufacturing	909.4	1 679.5	-770.1
Commodities	942.9	63.1	+879.8

Source: Department of Trade, Industry and Competition (DTIC)[4]

Like Brazil in Latin America, South Africa can be viewed as a 'Southern middle power' (or emerging economy) in an African context. Middle powers have some capacity to pursue internationalisms that promote collective responses to global challenges, to coordinate coalitions of like-minded actors, and to sustain the operation of existing multilateral institutions.[5] However, Southern middle powers also exercise ambivalent internationalism – in other words, they choose whom to engage with and when. As argued below, South Africa strives to strike a balance between exercising leadership of the Global South through anti-imperialist rhetoric and maintaining beneficial trade and investment relationships with Western economies.[6]

South Africa's foreign policy and strategy: An ambivalent middle power?

Since the first democratic election in 1994, the South African government's international relations and foreign policy and strategy have been shaped by the ruling African National Congress (ANC). The ANC's worldview is powerfully shaped by its intellectual history. During the struggle for liberation from minority rule in South Africa, the ANC managed to develop bilateral and multilateral ties with non-state actors and states across the globe. Since it officially attained 'ruling party' status in 1994, the ANC has not abandoned its ideological worldviews and international character.[7] Indeed, the ANC has set out to strengthen its historical ties with former liberation organisations or individuals, both in Africa and in other parts of the world.

The ANC professes to embrace progressive internationalism, an approach to global relations that is anchored in the pursuit of global solidarity, social justice, joint development and human security. Progressive internationalism envisages a just, equitable, non-racial, non-patriarchal, diverse, democratic and equal world system. To fundamentally transform the global balance of forces – evidenced in a radical restructuring of global governance and a progressive global movement – advocacy is required. These principles, the ANC argues, have informed its stance as a liberation movement since its formation in 1912, which has been affirmed at successive conferences. However, its internal discussion documents highlight a range of challenges, failures and shortcomings – especially the failure to mobilise 'progressive forces' on the continent, the inability to work together and speak as one, capacity constraints at its headquarters, and policy drift.[8]

The approach of the Department of International Relations and Cooperation (DIRCO) as a key foreign policy implementor is aligned with that of the ruling ANC but is arguably more nuanced. 'Party-to-party' relations are different from the formal, rules-bound world of diplomacy where 'state-to-state' relations dominate. For DIRCO, South Africa is required to engage strategically in 'an uncertain international environment' and, moreover, to 'use its strong bilateral footprint and respected multilateral presence' to continue to advance the interests and values of South Africa, Africa and the Global South.[9]

South Africa's multilateral engagements are therefore premised on the need to advance its national interest and safeguard its national position, advance the development priorities of developing countries and promote an equitable, rules-based multilateral system. According to DIRCO, the Economic Reconstruction and Recovery Plan (ERRP) remains the standard programme to rebuild the economy. The ERRP is not without its critics, though, who attest to policy failure in the face of increasing poverty, inequality and unemployment.[10]

DIRCO often refers to the national interest. It is therefore worth pointing out the key characteristics of the government's recently adopted national interest framework document.[11] The framework document characterises South Africa's national interest as the protection and promotion of its national sovereignty and constitutional order; the well-being, safety and prosperity of its citizens; and a better Africa and world. It also notes that the promotion of South Africa's national interest globally must serve to deliver on the national goal of reviving and growing the economy to levels set in the National Development Plan (NDP).

Because South Africa needs faster and more sustainable economic growth, higher investment, increased employment and productivity-linked growth, the document recommends the following:

- Attract sustainable and responsible investment which supports industrial development and higher levels of localisation.
- Combat illicit financial flows, including money laundering, tax evasion, illicit trade, trade mispricing and under-invoicing.
- Leverage the African Continental Free Trade Area (AfCFTA), which promises to support structural transformation in Africa through greater market integration, more trade and investment, and improved value-added production and productivity-linked growth.
- Elevate the importance of technology transfer to the country, while also attracting critical skills.
- Enable citizens to acquire skills that are critical for growing the economy and building a robust society.
- Create the necessary conditions for accelerated growth in the green and blue economies.

Clearly, economic diplomacy is a priority for the national interest and foreign policy doctrines. However, South Africa's trade performance has been disappointing. Reasons include the structure of the country's export basket (dominated by commodity products), the country's dependence on a limited number of large but mature export markets, and the high cost and deteriorating competitiveness of the general business environment.[12] South Africa seems to be maintaining a cautious approach to trade agreements and prefers localisation.

Against this background, one can ask: are the current foreign, trade and national interest strategies relevant and sufficient to save South Africa from the volatile, uncertain, complex and ambiguous (VUCA) world it faces?

The current state of affairs

Similar to the collapse of the Soviet Union and the end of the Cold War in the late 1980s and early 1990s, and the rise of the 'unipolar moment' in the United States (US) in the 1990s, which came to an end with the attack on its symbols of power in 2001 ('9/11'), the world is once again in the throes of fundamental change. What are the contours of the changing world order within which South Africa needs to find its place?

The world we live in

Humanity hardly had time to grasp the impact of the global Covid-19 pandemic when underlying, post-Cold War tensions between Russia and members of the North Atlantic Treaty Organization (NATO) surfaced. The US stepped up efforts to isolate Russia by supporting the integration of peripheral parts of the former Soviet Union into European and Atlantic institutions. Not for the first time, Russia pushed back against what it perceived to be an encroachment on its sphere of influence. Following a series of crisis events, Russia launched a full-spectrum attack on Ukraine on 24 February 2022. On that day, the world changed. Writing soon after the invasion got under way, well-known liberal US commentator Anne Applebaum said: 'History has accelerated; the impossible has become possible. Shifts that no one imagined weeks ago are unfolding with incredible speed.'[13]

On 7 October 2023, the world again recoiled in horror as Hamas, a militant Palestinian group, unleashed violence against Israelis living in the vicinity of the Gaza Strip. Not to be outdone, the Israeli government, supported by the US and European governments, responded by conducting a relentless bombing campaign against the Palestinian population in Gaza and the West Bank. At the time of writing, many thousands had died, and a regional conflagration was not out of the question.

Conflagrations of this nature – which are increasingly dangerous and cruel – have severe consequences for the world. The strategic calculations informing the leaders of the Global North and Global South are under scrutiny by experts and the public alike: do they desire peace, or should they use violence to reshape global affairs?

What are these unimaginable shifts?

The Western, liberal, rules-based world order – designed to make the world a safe haven for democracy and capitalism – is on the back foot, with its failures having led to a deepening division and conflict between and within the Global North and Global South. Multilateral diplomacy appears to be unable to ensure international peace and security, to manage financial stability or to act meaningfully on climate change. The Ukraine and Gaza crises have weakened the United Nations (UN) and reduced its role to that of a provider of humanitarian aid, instead of a leader of global efforts to maintain peace. It is unclear whether the system can be reformed.[14]

The activities of the world's mega arms manufacturers and dealers (particularly the five permanent members of the UN Security Council) keep the world in a perpetual state of conflict, which is further complicated by organised crime and the trafficking of arms and ammunition. It is unlikely that this exploitative and corrupt stranglehold can be broken. Conflict is escalating, mutating and spreading. The big powers might revert to weapons of mass destruction in their attempts to neutralise or annihilate one another. These failures appear to be a temporary setback for the 'rules-based liberal world order'. But if the leaders of the Global North proceed with a unilateral restoration or recalibrated order without accommodating the interests of the Global South, the world will experience a Cold War 2.0 or, if violence goes unchecked, the Third World War.

Faced with the rise of these contending Northern and Southern power blocs, how should the South African government protect and advance the country's national interests? Is membership (or associateship) of one or the other unavoidable? Or can it craft a hybrid strategy to benefit from both? Importantly, what are the options for engaging all possible trade and investment partners? The ensuing sections examine the relevant options and offer pointers regarding the construction of a hybrid economic diplomacy approach.

The Global North

The Global North refers to the 38 members of the Organisation for Economic Co-operation and Development (OECD). Full members come from North America, Europe and Australasia, as well as Chile in South America and Japan and Korea in Asia.¹⁵ No African country belongs to the OECD, except South Africa as a 'partner'. The OECD gathers and interprets data for policymaking and standard setting on global themes. These agenda-setting activities by the OECD, which impact the rest of the world, are meant to advance the interests of its members.

A smaller, more focused group of OECD member countries work together under the banner of the Group of Seven (G7). The G7 is an informal political forum consisting of Canada, France, Germany, Italy, Japan, the US, the United Kingdom (UK), and the European Union (EU) as an associate. G7 members are the major advanced economies and account for over half the world's net wealth (at over R3.7 trillion), 30–43 per cent of global gross domestic product (GDP) and 10 per cent of the world's population (770 million people). Its members maintain close political, economic, diplomatic and military ties on matters relating to global affairs. However, its relevance is in question in an increasingly multipolar world, represented by alternative institutions such as the Group of 20 (G20).¹⁶

The Global South

The Global South refers to the members of the Group of 77 (G77). The G77, established in 1964 by 77 developing countries, is the largest intergovernmental organisation in the UN, providing the means for the countries of the South to articulate and promote their collective economic interests, to enhance their joint negotiating capacity on all major international economic issues within the UN system and to promote South–South cooperation for the purpose of development.¹⁷ Although the membership of the G-77 has grown to 134 countries, the original name has been retained due to its historical significance.

A smaller, more focused group of G77 member countries work together under the BRICS banner. BRICS is an acronym for Brazil, Russia, India, China and South Africa. The group was initially called BRIC (without South Africa) by Goldman Sachs economist Jim O'Neill in 2001. He believed that by 2050 the four BRIC emerging economies would come to dominate the global economy. South Africa was added to the list in 2010. BRICS is an important yet informal grouping that brings together the major emerging economies in the world. It accounts for 41 per cent of the world's population, 24 per cent of global GDP and over 16 per cent of global trade (based on 2019 World Bank data).[18] BRICS countries deliberate on important issues under the three pillars of political and security, economic and financial, and cultural exchanges.

In 2023, BRICS announced it would expand its membership ranks by admitting another five countries in early 2024: Egypt, Ethiopia, Iran, Saudi Arabia and the United Arab Emirates (UAE). As noted in a recent report by the Economist Intelligence Unit, expanding the bloc from five to 10 members will create a group of impressive economic size in terms of their share of global population, GDP and merchandise exports. Crucially, too, the addition of Iran, Saudi Arabia and the UAE will elevate BRICS's share of global oil production from about 20 per cent to 43 per cent in 2024.

As Saher Liaqat recently argued, BRICS's assertive stance and its pursuit of greater representation and influence in global affairs signify a significant challenge to the US-led international order.[19] While not aiming to replace the West, BRICS seeks to reform and reshape the existing international system to be more inclusive and equitable. This shift reflects changing global power dynamics. BRICS and potentially other nations seeking to join the bloc are collectively working towards an alternative model of global governance which challenges the traditional Western dominance.

The trade and investment relationship between South Africa and the G7

Within the OECD, South Africa's trade relations with the EU and US stand out. South Africa and the EU are preferential trading partners. Since its entry into force in 2016, the Southern African Development Community (SADC)–EU Economic Partnership Agreement (EPA) has been the foundation of a trade and investment relationship, characterised by regular exchanges between the partners.

The EU, with its 27 member states, is not only South Africa's biggest trading partner but also its dominant source of foreign direct investment (FDI). EU-generated investment has created more than 300 000 jobs in South Africa and has significant potential in areas such as green technologies, manufacturing, energy, digital/

automation and services. Roughly 50 per cent of South Africa's exports to the EU consist of manufactured goods, which contribute directly to beneficiation and employment in the country, and thus to inclusive growth. South Africa's main exports to the EU are fuels and mining products (27 per cent), machinery and transport equipment (18 per cent) and other semi-manufactured goods (16 per cent). EU exports to South Africa are primarily machinery and transport equipment (50 per cent), chemicals (15 per cent) and other semi-manufactured machinery (10 per cent).[20] South Africa's trade with the EU is outlined in Table 5.2.

Table 5.2: South Africa's trade with the European Union, 2022 (R billions)

	Exports	**Imports**	**Trade balance**
Total	436.2	398.3	+38.0
Agriculture	31.5	3.8	+27.8
Manufacturing	211.3	375.5	-164.2
Commodities	173.4	3.7	+169.7

Source: Department of Trade, Industry and Competition (DTIC)[21]

In 2022, bilateral trade between South Africa and the US was estimated at R467 billion, while the US's goods and services trade deficit with South Africa was R129 billion.[22] The two countries signed a formal bilateral trade and investment framework agreement in 1999, which was amended in 2012. The thriving economic links between the countries are attributable in large part to the African Growth and Opportunity Act (AGOA), under which South Africa is eligible for preferential treatment for its exports to the US as well as special textile and apparel benefits. Industrial supplies and materials are the largest component of trade flows in both directions. South Africa is also a net beneficiary of strong investment ties between the two countries.

In 2022, the value of US FDI (stock) in South Africa amounted to R138 billion. US direct investment in South Africa is mainly directed at manufacturing, finance and insurance, and mining.

US multinationals operating in South Africa employed an estimated 134 600 people in 2022.

The trade and investment relationship between South Africa and BRICS

South Africa's trade with the BRICS bloc increased by an average of 10 per cent every year over the period 2017–2021.[23] South Africa's total trade with BRICS countries reached R830 billion in 2022, an increase of more than 70 per cent from R487 billion in 2017. In 2020, the member countries adopted the Strategy for BRICS Economic Partnership to increase access to one another's markets, promote mutual trade and investment, and create a business-friendly environment for investors in all BRICS member countries. In 2015, BRICS launched the New Development Bank to mainly finance and support infrastructure and sustainable development projects. To date, the New Development Bank has provided funding for 12 projects in South Africa valued at over R100 billion.

President Ramaphosa has listed the following as key benefits of South Africa's membership of BRICS: increased tourism; enhanced energy security; access to funding from the New Development Bank for energy, transport and water; and (with an expanded membership) enhanced prospects of economic partnerships in oil and energy, information and communication technology (ICT), agriculture, textile, logistics, air transportation, tourism and medicine. President Ramaphosa is of the view that membership of BRICS has made a valuable contribution to the implementation of the government's ERRP.

Within BRICS, China is a key strategic partner, given its established political and economic relations with South Africa. South African exports to China totalled R218 billion in 2022.[24] According to South Africa's Minister of Trade, Industry and Competition, the value of two-way trade (recorded in 2023) between China and South Africa now exceeds R900 billion, while South Africa's exports to China exceed R500 billion.[25] In the Minister's view, this is a reflection of the success of the first phase of the country's relationship with China, which was deepened after the establishment of political relations in 1994. The second phase of the relationship with China has been geared towards achieving greater equity in terms of Chinese and South African companies' investment in the respective economies. Today, the value of Chinese investment in South Africa stands at close to R200 billion, according to the Minister.

Analysts, however, caution that there are risks associated with China being South Africa's major BRICS trading partner – particularly as China's investment activity in the country is mainly of the portfolio (as opposed to the direct) investment type, where Chinese companies 'exploit' South African resources and neglect to contribute to skills transfer, job creation, and so on.[26]

Potential for a hybrid economic diplomatic strategy

South Africa and its economy stand to benefit from a political strategy designed to maintain trade and investment relations with both the Global North and the Global South. In fact, South Africa's recalibrated foreign policy, designed to deal with today's increasingly turbulent world, should build on the successes of an earlier trade and industry-designed 'butterfly' trade strategy.[27] It uses the analogy of the four wings of a butterfly, representing South Africa's outreach to North and South America on the one side, and Europe and Asia on the other. South Africa's strategic relationships with the US and Brazil should anchor the two wings on the left, and its strategic relationship with the EU and China should anchor the wings on the right. This strategy, though, needs to be embellished with another key outreach imperative – trade with Africa. As demonstrated in Table 5.3, South Africa's exports to the rest of Africa were valued at over R494 billion in 2022, slightly eclipsing total trade with the EU, which stood at R436 billion in 2022.

Table 5.3: South Africa's trade with the rest of Africa, 2022 (R billions)

	Exports	**Imports**	**Trade balance**
Total	494.5	160.3	+334.2
Agriculture	20.4	13.7	+6.8
Manufacturing	389.5	119.1	+270.4
Commodities	73.2	22.3	+50.9

Source: Department of Trade, Industry and Competition (DTIC)[28]

The reality, however, is that much of this Africa trade is concentrated in the Southern African Customs Union (SACU) and a few neighbouring markets. Six of South Africa's top seven African export destinations in 2019 were its immediate neighbours and, together, these six countries made up close to 70 per cent of South Africa's total exports to Africa.[29] A more ambitious and far-reaching strategy would be to anchor trade with the rest of Africa via the nascent African Continental Free Trade Area (AfCFTA) Agreement. The AfCFTA aims to provide broader and deeper economic integration across the continent as well as attract investment, boost trade, provide better jobs, reduce poverty and increase shared prosperity in Africa. If fully implemented and supported by South Africa's North and South trading partners, it could raise incomes by 9 per cent by 2035 and lift 50 million people out of extreme poverty.[30] However, it is also necessary to recognise the obstacles to realising these ambitious goals; some analysts ask whether Africa is ready and prepared to commit to a free trade regime.[31]

There are other challenges associated with strategy formulation and implementation, and in this case, the assessment contained in the government's recent 25-Year Review, rings true.[32] It argues that for the country to see the benefits of economic diplomacy, it needs three key ingredients. The first ingredient is that economic diplomacy must be embedded in a clearly articulated national interest. As discussed above, DIRCO has released a national interest framework document; however, it requires refinement.[33]

The second ingredient is that the state's economic diplomacy capabilities must be further strengthened and deepened. DIRCO's training academy requires a revival and professionalisation to produce savvy African diplomats with the skill set to engage and negotiate with external players on the country's behalf.

The third ingredient is that economic diplomacy must flow from closer collaboration between government and the business sector so that there is true synergy between them, both at home and abroad. South Africa's hosting of the 15th BRICS Summit in 2023, which included a BRICS Business Council meeting (chaired by the vibrant South African chapter), set a high standard of engagement, and is worth emulating.

On reflection, a fourth ingredient emerges: an appropriate trade policy. An updated and comprehensive trade policy is needed for the following reasons: to guide South Africa's approach to trade support and negotiations, both across the continent and internationally; to develop consistent positions on newer trade issues, such as e-commerce; to consider the impact of changed international conditions, such as climate change and the emergence of global value chains; and to promote serious trade facilitation reforms at and beyond the country's borders.[34]

The country's National Development Plan, adopted by the government and the ANC in 2012, has by all objective measures failed, due in no small measure to unfavourable external conditions but also weak state capacity.[35] Given this reality, the formulation of a comprehensive trade policy, aligned to a realistic economic recovery plan and supported by fresh foreign and security policies, will be an urgent task for the post-2024 elections administration.

SIX

Is Africa open for business?

Daniel Mminele

Introduction

The 2024 national election in South Africa will mark 30 years since the advent of democracy, causing many to reflect on the hopes and aspirations that accompanied the watershed election in 1994. As South Africa was charting its new domestic path, the country was also being welcomed back into the community of nations and readmitted to various continental and global bodies, while enjoying a significant amount of goodwill from those who hoped to see the country succeed.

With various African countries having played a significant role in the liberation struggle, both through displays of solidarity and the provision of material support to liberation groups, and with many South Africans living in exile, the continent and the world were waiting to see what contribution the new South Africa, under its new dispensation, would make to the ongoing development of the continent. This chapter examines what has been achieved, but more importantly, what potentially lies ahead for South Africa's economic relationship with the rest of the African continent, with an emphasis on Sub-Saharan Africa.

Beset by war, corruption, bad governance and poor macro-economic policies, Africa was labelled 'the hopeless continent' by *The Economist* in 2000. A decade later, on the back of a commodities boom, expanding manufacturing and services sectors, and many

African countries improving their governance and adopting sound macroeconomic and market-friendly policies, the label had changed to a more inspiring 'Africa rising'.

While the global financial crisis caused turmoil in both advanced economies and emerging markets, the direct effects on Africa were relatively muted, given the limited integration of African financial markets into international capital markets. However, a number of post-crisis spillover effects did register, leading to a pause in the 'Africa rising' narrative. This came in the wake of a deceleration in Africa's growth trajectory and rising expectations that global central banks would start normalising ultra-loose monetary policy, which would lead to capital outflows from many emerging markets, including those on the African continent.

In the more recent period characterised by post-pandemic recovery and transitions to low(er)-carbon, more climate-resilient and environmentally sustainable economies, the narrative has changed to 'the new scramble for Africa', referring to increasing competition for diplomatic influence, strategic and commercial ties, and natural resources critical for the energy transition. Many countries on the continent have undergone democratic transitions, have achieved higher levels of political stability, and have generally been focusing on policy reforms aimed at creating a conducive climate for both domestic and international investment. Some commentators are optimistically calling the 21st century 'Africa's golden century', on the strengths of the progress made to date in the areas of governance, infrastructure and technology, thereby paving the way for investment and growth, underpinned by innovation and a more business-friendly economic environment.

Africa's potential

The continent is generally seen to hold immense potential for investment and growth, given its infrastructure development needs, its abundant natural resources, and a young and growing population, which represents a significant consumer market for the future. The World Bank projects that over the next three decades, Sub-Saharan Africa will experience the fastest increase in the working population of all regions, with a projected net increase of 740 million people by

2050.¹ The World Economic Forum, in turn, projects that by 2030 young Africans are expected to constitute 42 per cent of the global youth.²

Another reason to be optimistic about Africa's future is the speed with which the continent has adopted mobile technology, which is helping to drive the integration of people across the continent into the mainstream financial services arena. There is some scepticism about Africa's ability to 'leapfrog' into the digital age because the African workforce lacks the skills to capitalise on the opportunities presented by data analytics, machine learning and other manifestations of artificial intelligence (AI). However, the World Economic Forum contends that huge strides made in mobile and digital banking on the continent have already helped millions of Africans to access finance in areas not covered by traditional banking services.³

Africa's well-documented 'mobile revolution' has made the continent the world's mobile banking leader, with the highest number of services, account holders and transactions. A well-functioning and modern financial and banking system acts as a catalyst to unlock business opportunities and is critical for a country's growth and development.

South Africa in the broader African context

South Africa's economic ties with the rest of the African continent have been broadly influenced by the country's political relationship with the continent. When South Africa faced international isolation and sanctions in the wake of widespread condemnation of the apartheid system, its economic ties with other African countries weakened. However, in the post-apartheid era, these ties have been significantly expanded. South Africa is currently the third-largest economy (behind Nigeria and Egypt) on the continent by gross domestic product (GDP) and is the most sophisticated, technologically advanced, diversified and industrialised economy in Africa.

South Africa's economic ties with the rest of the continent prior to the advent of democracy were limited, both because of the economic and diplomatic sanctions it faced and because South Africa was pursuing inward-looking policies aimed at self-sufficiency to avoid becoming overly reliant on external trade and investment. However,

South Africa developed close economic ties with some countries on the sub-continent that were economically dependent on it and formed part of the Southern African Customs Union (SACU).

As reiterated in successive State of the Nation Addresses and Budget Speeches, growing ties with African countries and advancing regional integration have been one of the cornerstones of South Africa's economic policy in the post-apartheid era. This has also been demonstrated by the preferential treatment granted to African countries in the areas of exchange controls and external investment allowances, where typically higher limits have been permitted. Meanwhile, economic strategies have been driven through membership of key continental bodies, such as the African Union (AU), the Southern African Development Community (SADC) and SACU. According to tralac,[4] South Africa's trade with the rest of the continent is mainly concentrated in the SADC region where it leverages its strong domestic position in sectors such as financial services, telecommunications, mining, retail and construction, with South African companies already having a significant presence in many other countries on the continent.

The increasingly important role that Africa is anticipated to play in shaping the global political and economic agendas going forward was demonstrated in the G20's elevation of the African Union (AU) recently from 'invited international organisation' to full member and in the International Monetary Fund's (IMF) recent decision to grant a third seat on its executive board to Sub-Saharan Africa. These important developments provide a clear signal to South Africa that the country needs to strengthen its position and stature and participate more actively in continental and global fora.

Even if not directly mandated as such, South Africa is generally regarded by the international community as a representative of the continent in fora where other African countries are not represented, such as BRICS. BRICS comprises the original members (Brazil, Russia, India, China and South Africa) and the new members as of 1 January 2024 (Egypt, Ethiopia, Iran, Saudi Arabia and the United Arab Emirates (UAE)). In adopting a 'continental voice', South Africa needs to ensure that the interests of Africa as a whole are heard and considered.

How South Africa can leverage its know-how and resources in and for Africa

One of the most important avenues through which South Africa can leverage its business know-how and resources in Africa is the African Continental Free Trade Area (AfCFTA), an ambitious integration project aimed at expanding trade and investment on the continent, especially through regional value chains. The AfCFTA, which came into effect on 1 January 2021, is the largest free trade area in the world in terms of participating countries, connecting 1.4 billion people in 55 countries, with a combined GDP of about US$3.4 trillion. By 2030, these figures will rise to 1.7 billion people and a combined GDP of US$6.7 trillion.[5] The ultimate vision is to create a single African market.

In 2022, Calvin Phume, Director of Africa Bilateral Economic Trade in the Department of Trade, Industry and Competition (DTIC), summed up the immense potential of the AfCFTA for the continent and South Africa as follows:[6]

> We are poised to witness a surge in trade activities, fuelling economic growth and fostering cross-border collaboration. With the AfCFTA now in full swing, South Africa stands at the forefront of a momentous trade revolution that will shape the future of the continent, encouraging innovation and promoting the development of value chains, thereby spurring industrialisation and job creation across sectors.

The World Economic Forum and the AfCFTA released a report in January 2023.[7] Among the highlights were that the automotive, agricultural and agro-processing, pharmaceuticals, transport and logistics industries in Africa are poised for growth. Africa's automotive industry, for example, is projected to grow by 40 per cent by 2027, adding about R735 billion to Africa's economy. Contributing factors to this growth are increasing urbanisation and a growing middle class. Meanwhile, the rapid growth of the pharmaceutical industry will be influenced by factors such as a growing commercial environment and a rise in genericisation, according to the United Nations Industrial Development Organization (UNIDO), which is quoted in the report.

It is common to hear people referring to the AfCFTA as a gamechanger, both for South Africa and the continent as a whole. However, key to the effectiveness of the AfCFTA is the removal of obstacles that hamper intra-Africa trade, such as tariff barriers, complex border and customs procedures, and onerous or non-harmonised rules and regulations that make it difficult to move goods and services (and people) from one country to the next in a cost-efficient manner. The steps involved in dismantling these obstacles and the relevant timeframes form the foundation of the free trade agreement underpinning the AfCFTA.

At present, Africa accounts for only 2 per cent of global trade, and, according to the United Nations Economic Commission for Africa (UNECA), only 17 per cent of trade is intra-African trade. This is significantly less than in other economic blocs, such as the European Union (EU) and the Association of Southeast Asian Nations (ASEAN) blocs where the proportion is 50–60 per cent or higher.

A significant development in today's post-pandemic period, which will support the AfCFTA and intra-African trade, is the greater emphasis being placed on regional value chains, which also help to shield economies and regions from external shocks – as demonstrated, for example, in the severe disruptions to global supply chains induced by the Covid pandemic.

To capitalise on the opportunity to unlock trade through the AfCFTA, it is important for African countries – and South Africa in particular – to move from talk to more action, from potential to lived reality. While good progress has been made, the negotiations pertaining to the various phases of the AfCFTA are still under way. A faster pace is required here, with countries needing to more readily accept that trade-offs are necessary between national and continental objectives.

From a sectoral perspective, South Africa is Africa's leading investor in renewable energy (both public- and private-sector projects). The commendable progress that South Africa has made in the areas of policy development, project preparation, investment planning and innovative funding could be of benefit to other African countries in their transition efforts. Successful energy transitions must take into account countries' specific circumstances, while also leveraging expert knowledge to arrive at optimal solutions. In this regard, South Africa has gained valuable experience from its Just Energy Transition Partnership, a decarbonisation programme backed by key members of the G7 and European Union (EU), and from working with various international partners that provide finance at scale to support energy transitions. Significant potential can be unlocked by further extending the scope of energy transitions in South Africa and other African countries from their current focus on mitigation to adaptation and resilience.

The energy sector offers substantial business opportunities, which South Africa is well placed to tap. The McKinsey Global Institute, in a report titled 'Reimagining Growth in Africa', revealed:

> ... eight manufacturing opportunities could together generate up to US$2 billion a year in revenue and create 700 000 new jobs by 2030. These business opportunities include assembly of off-grid and micro-grid solar systems and electric two-wheelers, as well as potential and nascent next-generation opportunities such as electric vehicle charging stations and production of cross-laminated timber.[8]

The report adds that Africa could become a major source of materials needed to support the world's transition to a low-carbon economy, with Africa holding 93 per cent of the world's platinum reserves, nearly half the cobalt and manganese reserves, a third of the aluminium reserves, and 11 per cent of the copper and lithium reserves.

Another area in which African countries require high levels of investment is infrastructure (rail, road, ports and telecommunications), which will be an important driver of the continent's development in the years ahead and a catalyst for stronger connectivity and regional integration. According to World Bank estimates, Sub-Saharan Africa needs to invest around 7 per cent of GDP in infrastructure annually until 2030 to meet its Sustainable Development Goals; yet investments are currently running at half that rate.[9] The scale of these investments will require already-strained public finances to be topped up with significant amounts of private finance. South Africa could leverage its well-developed and sophisticated financial markets to provide innovative solutions to support sustainable infrastructure financing on the continent.

Tourism is another industry in which South Africa, given its experience and resources, can make profitable inroads on the continent. Tourism has been making a post-pandemic recovery and seems poised to play an increasingly important role in economic growth and job creation, which were interrupted by Covid-19. The IMF has identified tourism as an important contributor to Africa's economic recovery and growth,[10] a view echoed by the UN World Tourism Organization, which forecasts a return to 95 per cent of pre-pandemic tourist numbers by the end of 2023, with steady growth into the future.[11]

Data from Statista indicate that the contribution of travel and tourism to Africa's GDP in 2022 was anticipated to be 5.9 per cent, compared to 7.2 per cent in the EU and 7.6 per cent in the Asia-Pacific region.[12] Moreover, tourism features in the African Union's Agenda 2063 roadmap as an important dimension of sustainable economic development on the continent. With the exception of well-known Indian Ocean island resorts and popular wildlife destinations in certain parts of the continent, the potential of tourism still needs to be more aggressively tapped if it is to make a more substantial contribution to Africa's GDP.

A reality check: Facing up to Africa's polycrises

Africa clearly presents many important medium- and long-term trade and investment opportunities for South Africa which, if tapped, could help to drive domestic growth and make a dent in the systemic challenges of unemployment, inequality and poverty. However, South Africa needs to successfully navigate a range of polycrises (or severe challenges) that are potential stumbling blocks to the country's more active engagement with the continent. Some of these apply to all African countries; others are South Africa-specific.

A common Africa-wide crisis is the lingering macroeconomic effects of the Covid pandemic, which are particularly evident in countries' growth and inflation dynamics, cost-of-living trends and sovereign debt levels. Another crisis is the accelerating pace of climate change and the pressure that countries are under to transition to low(er)-carbon and more climate-resilient economic structures and activities. Such transitions need to be safe, inclusive and just, with the latter provision aimed at ensuring that there is equitable sharing of opportunities, risks, challenges and responsibilities among and within countries.

In addition, African countries are currently caught in the crossfire in the battle between various global superpowers (such as the United States, China, Russia, Iran and others), which has resulted in increasing geopolitical fragmentation. How African countries choose to position themselves geopolitically will be key to the preservation of their long-term interests and credibility in the eyes of the world.

Domestically, the most pressing crisis is South Africa's persistently low growth rate, which in turn has helped to fuel the country's record-high unemployment levels, declining productivity and widespread poverty. It is also contributing to the growing inequality phenomenon. Getting growth moving again is essential if the country is to have a fighting chance of tackling its many pressing socioeconomic ills. Among the most significant goals are unlocking the country's energy potential (and ensuring energy security while migrating to more sustainable energy sources), tackling the country's transport and logistics infrastructure backlog and inefficiencies, taking decisive action against perpetrators of crime and corruption, and entrenching a culture of integrity and accountability in the public and private sectors.

It is almost a cliché to say that South Africa needs bold and visionary leadership. Yet this is exactly what is required – individuals who are willing to accept power legitimately and responsibly and to use it to drive change, underpinned by a common purpose among stakeholders, aligned goals, a collaborative spirit, courage and urgency.

Critical success factors for leveraging Africa's potential

If South African policymakers and businesses are to leverage the country's strong economic position on the continent, as well as its combined policy, technical and business know-how and resources, several critical success factors need to be in place:

- Policy certainty: South Africa needs transparent and consistent government policies, with reasonably predictable outcomes, to enable businesses to expand into or increase their market share and influence in Africa.

- Commitment to regional integration: South Africa needs to use its 'continental voice' to promote the value of effective regional integration and the removal of diplomatic, financial and physical obstacles that have given rise to the continent's fragmented trade and investment environment. Regional integration should not be focused simply on seeking strength in numbers or pitting winners against losers. It should be about balancing national (which are often short-term) and regional (which are often longer-term) interests.
- Harmonisation of policies, regulations and standards: Notwithstanding the benefits of having ready access to a regional market, it is challenging operating in multiple jurisdictions with different policies, regulations and standards. These can add to the cost of doing business and deter investment. Greater harmonisation of policies, regulations and standards (including financial reporting requirements) across borders will make it easier for African businesses to pursue opportunities elsewhere on the continent. This will generate more income for Africa, which will *remain* in Africa to fuel ongoing growth and development.
- Sound governance and accountability frameworks: The South African government needs to create the necessary policy and regulatory environment to support the establishment of sound governance and accountability frameworks. Businesses, in turn, need to be even-handed and consistent when applying governance and accountability frameworks across all the African markets in which they operate.
- Effective public–private partnerships: The scale of the investment, technologies, expertise and capacity needed to fast-track Africa's growth and development in new and more traditional sectors, and to ensure that the AfCFTA delivers on its promises, calls for strong and committed collaboration between the public and private sectors. Lumkile Mondi asserts that efforts by South Africa's business community to expand into other African countries have been influenced (for better or for worse) by the evolving nature of state–business relations in South Africa since the transition to democracy.[13] Notwithstanding the government's constrained resources, such resources can still be

strategically deployed to crowd in domestic and international private finance for projects with high potential.
- Strong business and community ties: South African businesses with continental or regional aspirations or existing inroads need to foster informed partnerships with local businesses and communities in other African countries, with a view to leveraging their superior knowledge of conditions 'on the ground' and ensuring that their business interests are aligned with the worldviews and needs at the local level. Businesses that have made successful forays into Africa usually have a great deal of experience of what can go wrong (and how costly it can be) if different countries' market dynamics and cultural nuances are not properly understood.
- Local and international skills and experience: Africa has a skills shortage (both management and technical skills), and South Africa is no exception in this regard. Business success will come to those who continuously invest in human resources, with an appropriate blend of expatriates and locals, supported with the right tools and technologies to ensure their efficiency and effectiveness.

Taking stock

Is Africa open for business? The answer to this question has to be an emphatic 'YES'. This chapter has shown that, despite its many challenges, Africa has considerable potential in a range of sectors (notably mining, telecommunications, financial services, energy and tourism), which makes it an attractive region from a trade and investment standpoint. It also has a very large market, which – being youthful – is automatically wired for expansion. Moreover, it has taken steps towards forging stronger links between countries across the continent through the AfCFTA and other regional integration initiatives.

Many people tend to focus on what Africa *lacks*, such as a strong track record in policy implementation and good governance, harmonised policies and regulations, adequate infrastructure, and the know-how and skills required to run effective governments and profitable businesses in the 21st century. Yet it is these very weaknesses or gaps that constitute *opportunities* for countries like South Africa, which is endowed with considerable talent, resources and experience and already enjoys a strong presence in many African countries through its established trade and investment ties. In addition, South Africa's familiarity with the problems experienced by many other countries on the continent is valuable – whether it is engaged in high-level diplomatic discussions or championing the cause of micro businesses.

Another compelling reason for South Africa putting effort into extending its reach across Africa is that it *must*. In global terms, South Africa still has a relatively small market with a small export basket that has a heavy concentration of commodities. Global competition is becoming increasingly fierce, and trade is heavily influenced by global and regional value chains. A more united African continent, reinforced by regional value chains in key sectors, will put South Africa and its African trade and investment partners in a stronger position when they compete for business opportunities in global markets, while also opening up important economic pathways on the continent itself, to the benefit of countries, businesses and communities.

The 2024 election in South Africa has been called a watershed election because so much is at stake, so much could change, and there will be no turning back. A restless electorate, a long list of intractable problems and a whole continent on its doorstep could be the perfect brew to get South Africa going (and growing) again.

SEVEN

South Africa's financial future: Keeping the debt trap at bay

Isaah Mhlanga

Introduction

The International Monetary Fund's (IMF) October 2023 World Economic Outlook projected that South Africa's debt ratio would reach 85 per cent of gross domestic product (GDP) by 2028. This is the third-highest debt ratio among 14 major peer emerging economies, with Brazil in the lead (105 per cent of GDP), followed by China (96 per cent of GDP).[1] Social spending continues to rise unabated without matching permanent revenues.

South Africa's 2023 fiscal policy stance combined with its historical record of overspending will inevitably lead to a fiscal crisis, as the rapid growth in public debt will result in increased debt-service costs, which will crowd out public and private investment in growth-boosting infrastructure. Without a change in fiscal stance and growth-enhancing measures, a debt spiral is likely. This will put the country into an unsustainable low-growth and high-debt equilibrium, further eroding spending on social services, with the potential for igniting social instability far greater and wider than the July 2021 episode.

This prospect must be avoided at all costs because a return to higher business and consumer confidence, higher investment, faster economic growth and job creation, and a more stable society is not guaranteed once society loses confidence in the ability of the state to manage the economy in a manner that brings them improved living standards.

Debt dynamics: From the global financial crisis to the great Covid crisis

The global response to the global financial crisis (GFC) included central banks reducing policy interest rates to the zero lower-bound level and instituting bond-buying programmes that kept interest rates close to zero, particularly in advanced economies. In South Africa, this coincided with the preparation for the 2010 Soccer World Cup, which required investment in infrastructure. In 2008, South Africa had a debt-to-GDP ratio of 24 per cent, ahead of Bulgaria's 15 per cent and Saudi Arabia's 12 per cent (see Figure 7.1). The South African government borrowed an additional 7 per cent of GDP, which took its debt ratio to 31.2 per cent of GDP by the end of 2010. China also borrowed an additional 7 per cent of GDP, while Hungary borrowed an additional 9 per cent of GDP. By contrast, Bulgaria, Indonesia, Mexico and Saudi Arabia all reduced their debt ratios. Across the major peer emerging economies, debt ratios increased by an average of only 2 per cent of GDP – three and a half times less than the increase in South Africa's debt ratio.[2]

From 2010 to 2019, the lure of decade-long low interest rates driven by the quantitative easing programmes of major global central banks – particularly the United States (US) Federal Reserve (Fed), the European Central Bank (ECB), the Bank of Japan (BoJ) and the Bank of England (BoE) – encouraged many countries to borrow, with reduced concerns about the cost of debt. The search for higher-yielding emerging-economy debt by global investors, given the negative-yielding advanced-economy debt, made it easy for emerging economies to access funding. Even countries whose spending choices did not build the necessary capacity for their economies to grow and generate tax revenues on a sustained basis continued to borrow cheaply from international capital markets. South Africa fell into this cohort of countries, which increased their debt levels but had little to show for it in terms of growth.

South Africa added another 25 per cent of GDP to its debt ratio, which stood at 56 per cent of GDP by the end of 2019. China and Brazil added comparable debt of 26 per cent and 25 per cent of GDP, respectively. Colombia added the fourth-highest debt of 16 per cent of GDP over the same period. Excluding these four countries, the rest of the peer countries added an average of 2 per cent of GDP to their debt ratios, which is 14 times less than the increase in South Africa's debt ratio.[3]

Figure 7.1: Debt-to-GDP ratio in selected major emerging economies, 2008–2028

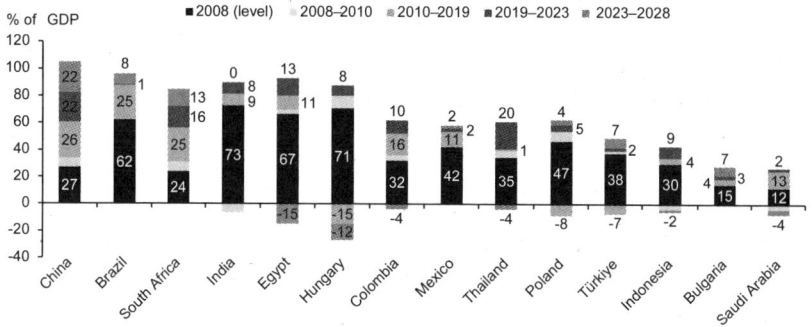

Source: Author's calculations[4]

When the Covid-19 virus pandemic struck in 2020, nearly 30 per cent of countries that had fiscal rules (relating to spending, deficits or debt limits) breached and suspended them due to the need to decisively respond to the health crisis caused by the virus and the income crisis caused by the lockdowns.[5] South Africa was in the same situation, dropping its expenditure ceiling anchor during the pandemic. This increased its debt ratio by 16 per cent of GDP between 2020 and 2023, the third highest among peer emerging economies, after China and Thailand increased their debt ratios by 22 per cent and 20 per cent of GDP respectively. Excluding these two countries, the average increase in the debt ratio among peer emerging economies was 6 per cent of GDP, nearly three times less than the increase in South Africa's debt ratio.[6]

An examination of the 15-year period between the GFC and the end of Covid-19 provides a clear indication that, relative to peer emerging economies, South Africa's increased debt was driven not only by global shocks beyond the control of policymakers. Imprudent fiscal policy choices were made, which shaped the country's debt trajectory. South Africa added 48 per cent of GDP to its debt ratio, with only China adding more (55 per cent of GDP) to its debt ratio. Next in the sequence were Colombia, which added 30 per cent of GDP, followed by Brazil, Egypt and Thailand, which each added 26 per cent of GDP. Excluding China and South Africa, the remaining peer emerging economies added an average of 13 per cent of GDP to their debt ratios between 2008 to 2023, nearly four times less than the increase in South Africa's debt ratio.[7]

Debt dynamics in future: South Africa's continued unsustainable path

Looking ahead to 2028, the IMF data show that the only country among the major emerging economies whose debt ratio will increase faster than South Africa's is China which is expected to add 22 per cent of GDP, taking its debt ratio to 105 per cent. South Africa is projected to add 13 per cent of GDP, taking its debt ratio to 85 per cent. Excluding China and South Africa, peer emerging economies are expected to reduce their debt ratios by an average of 1 per cent of GDP between 2023 and 2028. Columbia, Hungary, Indonesia, Saudi Arabia, Egypt and Thailand are all expected to reduce their debt ratios by an average of 7 per cent of GDP. India's debt ratio will remain unchanged at 84 per cent of GDP. Brazil, Türkiye and Bulgaria will add about half of what South Africa is projected to add to its debt ratio. Across peer emerging economies, China and Brazil are the only countries whose debt ratios are projected to be higher than South Africa's by 2028, at 105 per cent and 95 per cent of GDP, respectively.[8]

South Africa's debt management has been poor in that it has resulted in an unsustainable debt trajectory (Figure 7.2). Economic shocks such as the 2008 GFC and the 2020 Covid-19 pandemic were common across countries, but South Africa's fiscal policy response and policy choices have clearly put the country on the wrong (unsustainable) path. Given the lack of dynamism in the South African economy relative to China, Brazil and India – countries that closely mirror South Africa from a debt-dynamics perspective – a combination of policy choices is needed, which will ensure fiscal sustainability. If drastic adjustments are not made to the current fiscal stance and path, a fiscal crisis over the next decade is a real possibility, with dire economic and sociopolitical consequences.

Figure 7.2: Debt-to-GDP ratio in select emerging economies, 2000–2028

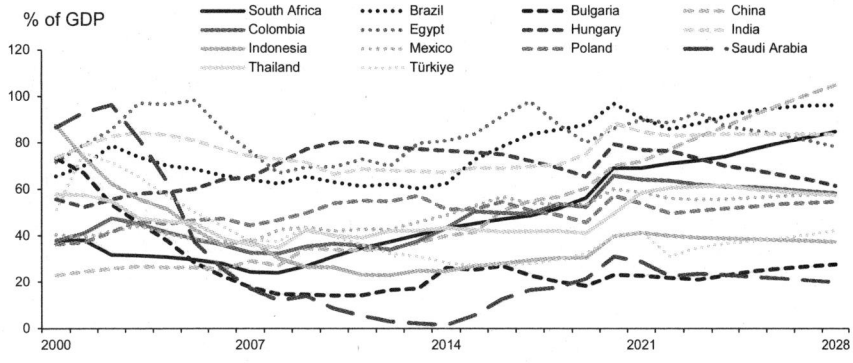

Source: Author's calculations[9]

Unsound fiscal policy choices in recent decades

There are several fiscal policy choices that South Africa has made over the past two decades that have disproportionately contributed to the country's rising debt levels. They offer important lessons about the impact of fiscal policy choices on economic growth and debt sustainability. The four policy choices that stand out are:

1. Unconditional bailouts of state-owned enterprises (SOEs)

The continuous unconditional bailouts of SOEs over the past two decades, necessitated by the government's failure to free economic sectors from inefficient and improperly run SOE monopolies, has been one of the main drivers of an unsustainable fiscus. The Gauteng Division (Pretoria) of the High Court, in a recent ruling involving the Democratic Alliance (DA), United Democratic Movement (UDM) and South African Local Government Association (SALGA), demonstrates the extent of SOEs' influence over fiscal outcomes. The High Court ruling had this to say:

> ... the non-realisation of the Government's intention in the late 1990s to open the energy sector to competition with private actors and to timeously implement the Independent Power Producer procurement programme, the delays in the decisions and implementation to build Medupi and Kusile power stations, the decisions to run power stations beyond their capabilities without maintenance, the failure to ensure or approve sufficient revenue for its services and the failure to take adequate steps to protect Eskom from criminal activity, corruption and state capture, individually and collectively, and the resultant energy crisis manifested by loadshedding and continued failure to remedy the crisis, constituted and still constitute breaches by the respondent organs of state to protect and promote the rights contained in the Bill of Rights.

These failures resulted into Eskom receiving R182 billion in bailouts in fiscal years 2015/16–2022/23, which followed R83 billion in bailouts in 2008–2014.[10] What the High Court said about government's decisions regarding Eskom and the energy sector can also be applied to SOEs in transport and logistics (Transnet, SA Express, South African Airways (SAA), South African National Roads Agency Limited (SANRAL), Airports Company South Africa (ACSA), South African Post Office (SAPO)), telecommunications (South African Broadcasting Corporation (SABC)) and defence (Denel). Together with Eskom, these SOEs received R331.2 billion in state bailouts in the period 2014–2023,[11] which could have been avoided had the state opened these sectors to private competition, run the SOEs efficiently, and prevented mismanagement and corruption.

2. Fee-free higher education[12]

Government implemented its fee-free higher education policy in 2018, contrary to the recommendation of the Heher Commission on the Feasibility of Fee-Free Higher Education and Training.[13] Mlambo et al. concluded that the rushed implementation of free higher education would have a negative impact on growth and service delivery in the country, given the need to divert resources towards education with a fiscus that was already heavily constrained.[14]

3. Social relief of distress grant

With the Covid-19 pandemic, the government implemented the social relief of distress (SRD) grant as a temporary measure to reduce poverty among those who had lost their jobs. The SRD grant has been extended for the fourth time – the latest extension due to end in March 2025.[15] In the period 2020/2021–2023/2024, R124 billion has been spent on the SRD grant. An additional (approximately) R33.6 billion will be spent in 2024/2025, which will take the cumulative spending on the SRD grant since its introduction to R157.3 billion by 2024/2025.[16] As things stand, what was initiated as a temporary relief measure has been crystallised in the budget without an accompanying permanent revenue source.

4. Growth in public-sector wages

This has outstripped inflation and private-sector wage growth over much of the past decade. One of the reasons for this is that there is a misalignment in the timing between the government's and the public-sector unions' wage agreement, on the one hand, and the budget, on the other hand. This results in lower budget increases than were eventually agreed at the bargaining council. For example, the 2023 budget provided for a 1.5 per cent increase, but the wage agreement eventually had a settlement figure of 7.5 per cent.

What is clear from these four contributing factors is that South Africa's unsustainable debt trajectory is not just a fiscal management issue; its genesis can be traced to the broader public sector, including SOEs over which the National Treasury has limited immediate control, thus making it difficult to ensure fiscal sustainability. The fiscus reflects how legislation, regulation, law enforcement, project planning and implementation across the different levels of government and SOEs, politics and policy decisions all interact to produce an unstable equilibrium of low economic growth and tax-revenue collection, and continually rising and unfunded spending needs. The consequences of an unsound fiscal policy are explored below.

Consequences of an unsound fiscal policy: The case of South Africa

Former US Treasury Secretary, Robert Rubin, detailed six

consequences of an unsound fiscal policy in the case of the US.[17] These consequences are generally applicable across both advanced economies and emerging economies, including South Africa.

Decline in business confidence

When businesses are unsure about their future debt trajectory and therefore the appropriate tax policy to adopt, they tend to make very short-term decisions which, by nature, are not supportive of long-term investments. When an unsustainable debt path is obvious, as is currently the case in South Africa, business confidence declines or remains low, resulting in low levels of private-sector investment, low economic growth and limited job creation. South Africa's business confidence, as measured by the Rand Merchant Bank (RMB)/Bureau for Economic Research (BER) Business Confidence Index, has been low for a very long time, reflecting (among other things) policy uncertainty in general but also an unsustainable debt trajectory more recently.

Crowding out of public and private investment

When government spending rises faster than tax revenue collection, government debt rises, which ultimately increases debt-service costs. Given the stickiness of current spending, especially social spending, public investment is usually the first to be displaced by higher debt-service costs. The continued rise in public debt requires domestic savings to be directed towards funding the government deficit, which then crowds out private investment, stifles economic growth and further restricts the ability to generate tax revenues.

Increased financial stability risks

Domestic banks are one of the lenders of money to the government. Given their role in the economy, they are required to invest in government bonds that qualify as highly liquid capital to meet the capital adequacy requirements of the South African Reserve Bank (SARB). When banks are overexposed to government debt, it weakens their ability to respond to economic shocks, which in turn increases financial stability risks for the economy.

Reduced resilience to economic shocks

An overindebted government usually has few or no fiscal buffers, which reduces the resilience of the economy to deal with future economic shocks. South Africa has plenty of experience of being hit by economic shocks without having fiscal buffers in place and then having to resort to borrowing to deal with the shocks. When the Covid-19 pandemic struck, the government was already running large fiscal deficits of 6.5 per cent of GDP, which meant that the only way to finance the response to the pandemic was to increase borrowings.[18]

Higher costs of funding for the whole economy

When debt is unsustainable, credit rating agencies reduce the credit rating of the government, which also reduces the credit rating of SOEs, banks and corporates. This is because in most cases no individual company can have a better credit rating than the government due to the latter's ability to increases taxes and service its debt, which private companies are unable to do. A reduced credit rating results in investors requiring higher compensation to lend to both the government and corporates, which also filters through to the rest of the economy, making it more expensive to fund investments.

Sudden stop in access to international capital markets

When foreign investors assess a country's credit risk to be rising, with the likelihood of a default also rising, they demand higher compensation to take on that credit risk. This is reflected in increasing government bond yields and/or the shortening of the duration over which investors are willing to bear the risk. When the debt trajectory is unsustainable, credit rating agencies reduce a country's debt ratings, which will also be reflected in higher bond yields. This increases the cost of borrowing for the government, banks, corporates and ultimately households.

The deterioration in credit quality can be gradual or rapid. Market access can continue for a long time until it suddenly stops, often without warning. Mexico experienced sudden stops in access to international funding in 1982 and in 1994–1995; Korea and Indonesia experienced sudden stops during the 1997 Asian crisis; and

Argentina's sudden stop occurred in 2001.[19] Regaining market access can require significant structural adjustments in economic policy, including debt restructuring, which can take a long time. The longer it takes for government to regain market access, the more costly it is for the economy.

Keeping the debt trap at bay: A two-pronged approach

When the debt-to-GDP ratio continues to rise, even at lower debt levels, the debt is unsustainable. This happens when the interest cost of financing debt is higher than the economic growth rate, which is also reflected in a more rapid increase in debt relative to economic growth.

Putting the debt ratio back onto a sustainable path requires the narrowing of the fiscal deficit. This can be achieved by reducing the real growth of public spending or increasing tax revenues by increasing the pace of economic growth, or both. In South Africa's case, government will need to run primary (non-interest) fiscal surpluses for a couple of years while implementing growth-boosting reforms in network industries, including energy, logistics, water, and safety and security. A combination of the following will help to put the debt ratio onto a sustainable path:

- Cut government spending by between 5 per cent and 10 per cent, which will be difficult given the political constraints.
- Raise revenues through an increase in value-added tax (VAT) (by 1–2 per cent) to fund unfunded SRD grants so that the grants are neutral to the budget.
- Create a set of fiscal policy anchors through legislated fiscal rules, which could include adherence to the current expenditure ceiling framework, a medium-term target for the debt-to-GDP ratio and fiscal deficit, and rules pertaining to the use of unexpected tax revenues for debt reduction instead of current spending.
- Reform the relationship between national government and local government and SOEs such that the National Treasury can intervene quickly where there are bad spending practices.
- Align government wage bargaining with the budget process so that the budget is based on agreed wage rates.

Concluding remarks

Various policies can be employed to wind down the country's critical debt ratio to a more sustainable level and in the process fend off a worst-case fiscal scenario for South Africa. However, keeping the debt trap at bay means that the risks to the fiscal outlook discussed in this chapter must be urgently addressed and several tough choices and decisions must be expeditiously made.

EIGHT

Banking on credibility: The central bank and monetary policy after 2024

Hilary Joffe

Introduction

South Africa's institutional strengths are often cited by rating agencies and lenders as a reason why the country remains attractive to investors, despite its low economic growth and high public debt. The South African Reserve Bank (SARB or the Bank) is chief among those institutions. But it faces a period in which its independence and credibility could be tested, in a shifting and uncertain landscape, both at home and abroad.

South Africa's 2024 general election has the potential to usher in a coalition government with a more populist slant. This could increase pressure to add employment and growth objectives to the SARB's core mandate of price stability. South Africa's public debt level is already unsustainable and may get even worse, especially if the general election delivers an unstable or populist coalition. That could put pressure on the SARB to use its balance sheet to help shore up the government's fiscal position, despite the risk this poses to the rand and inflation as well as the challenges it could create for financial stability.[1]

The external backdrop is daunting. Central banks globally are grappling with a new and unpredictable set of economic and geopolitical realities. These could mean that inflation and interest rates in advanced economies will not return to the ultra-low levels of the decade following the 2008–2009 global financial crisis any time soon. This 'higher-for-longer' scenario for interest rates has far-reaching implications for emerging markets, including South Africa. Tight global financial conditions will weigh on capital flows and currencies, making it harder and more costly to borrow on international markets and more difficult to calibrate monetary and fiscal policy.

All of this is occurring at a delicate time for the SARB. The governor and all three of his deputy governors are due to be replaced – or reappointed – by the President before November 2024. South Africa's Constitution protects the independence of the central bank and enshrines its price-stability mandate, while the country's financial legislation tasks it with safeguarding financial stability. However, the implementation of those safeguards in practice requires independent-minded and astute executive leadership at the SARB.

Four key tests (or questions) will therefore shape South Africa's central bank and monetary policy after 2024. The first is: who will lead the Bank? The second is: what political pressures might be brought to bear on its mandate and independence? The third is: how will it respond to the fallout from global inflation and interest rate dynamics? The final question is: what risks will South Africa's fiscal predicament pose for the Bank's ability to maintain price and financial stability, and how will it manage these?

The question of succession

South Africa's democratic Constitution mandates the Bank 'to protect the value of the currency in the interests of balanced and sustainable economic growth in the Republic' and safeguard its independence.[2] New financial sector legislation in 2017 added a second mandate – to protect financial stability. South Africa followed international best practice in 2000 by adopting inflation targeting as the anchor for monetary policy, clarifying the goal of the Bank's core price-stability mandate and bringing transparency and predictability to its task of containing inflation. The government sets the target, but the Bank has full operational independence in how it implements it.

These institutional safeguards are an important bulwark against political interference. However, its executive leadership matters a great deal to the Bank's independence in practice, and to the integrity and effectiveness with which it implements its mandates to support economic growth in the way the Constitution intends. This applies not just to monetary policy but also to the Bank's other responsibilities, each of which is crucial to South Africa's economic fortunes. The Bank is responsible for the prudential regulation of the banking and financial system as well as for South Africa's payments system and the management of the country's gold and foreign exchange reserves. And it is the banker to the government, with a central role in the bond and money markets.

The Bank's strength as an institution in the democratic era has been supported by an exceptionally talented and stable executive leadership team, comprising the governor and three deputy governors, which combines political experience with extensive economic and financial expertise and is highly regarded by market players and economists as well as by international peers.

Yet the entire senior executive leadership is in flux, with all four senior posts up for appointment or renewal during 2024. Governor Lesetja Kganyago's second five-year term of office ends in November 2024. The terms of office of two of the deputy governors, Rashad Cassim and Nomfundo (Fundi) Tshazibana, end in August 2024. All three individuals may be open to serving further terms of office should the President choose to reappoint them, as he is entitled to do. There is no limit on the number of repeat terms, which can be shorter than five years.

Deputy Governor Kuben Naidoo's second five-year term of office was due to end in March 2025, but it emerged in October 2023 that he had tendered his resignation early, to spread his wings after 29 years in the public service.[3] By February 2024, President Cyril Ramaphosa had yet to announce the appointment of a successor. The clustering of the governor's and deputy governors' terms of office introduces an unusual level of uncertainty at the Bank, especially in the context of the uncertainty surrounding the outcome of South Africa's 2024 general election. The governorships are essentially political appointments over which the President has complete power. The President is required to consult with the Minister of Finance and the board of the SARB, but he appoints 'after' rather than 'in' consultation – a significant distinction which means that he is not obliged to take their advice.

The Bank's legislation requires the governor to be 'a person of tested banking experience', a provision that has been interpreted to mean that some central banking experience is required. But there are no specific requirements for deputy governors, which means that there are limited institutional safeguards to ensure that strong candidates with the necessary expertise are appointed. Crucially, the President has the power to hire, but he does not have the power to fire. This helps to safeguard the Bank's independence, buffering it from a Türkiye-type scenario in which that country's president fires governors if he does not like their interest rate decisions, causing inflation to spiral and the currency to crash.

In the absence of clear criteria for appointments, the most powerful sanction against bad choices by the Bank is the power of the market. The rand exchange rate and government bond yields could be expected to respond swiftly and aggressively to any appointments at the SARB that would undermine its credibility and integrity – just as they did when former President Jacob Zuma appointed an unknown finance minister and put the Treasury's credibility at risk in December 2015. President Ramaphosa understands markets and might be inclined to make sound appointments – but it is hard to predict what post-election political trade-offs might have to be made.

The market tends to focus on what the appointments at the Bank will mean for monetary policy and interest rates. In an important sense, the quality of the leadership may matter even more in other areas of the Bank's work, such as banking regulation and financial markets, where the goals are not as clearly defined as they are in monetary policy and the Bank's activities are not subject to public scrutiny in the same way. Unlike good monetary policy, good banking and financial market regulation is largely behind the scenes; the public generally gets to hear of it only when it goes wrong.

Clearly, personalities do matter when it comes to interest rate decisions, which are made by a Monetary Policy Committee (MPC) of up to eight individuals appointed by the governor, which includes the three deputies.[4] The outcome of any given MPC meeting may depend on the balance between so-called hawks and doves – between those more focused on price stability and those more focused on economic growth. However, there is only limited value in categorising governors and deputy governors according to their perceived preferences and trying to predict the interest rate trajectory accordingly. Those preferences are not hard wired; if they were, there would be no point in the Bank's three-day MPC meetings.

And while the balance within the Committee can influence interest rates at the margins, pushing them 25 or 50 basis points higher or lower at any given meeting or over the cycle, in the end the Committee must deliver on its price-stability mandate. It must meet the inflation target set by government or explain its failure to do so. It has a single, blunt instrument that it can use – interest rates. However – and this is crucial – it also has the power to influence inflation expectations through its communications as well as the signals it sends with its interest rate decisions.

The past two decades of inflation targeting have shown how much inflation expectations matter to inflation outcomes. Businesses calibrate their prices, and trade unions their wage demands, in line with where they see inflation going in future, and that, in turn, influences the outcome. Where the central bank is credible and everyone believes it will get inflation back within target, even if prices spike, interest rates may not have to rise all that much to curb inflation when it ticks upwards. When the central bank lacks credibility, such as when it is seen to be vulnerable to interference by politicians who dislike high interest rates, inflation is more likely to spiral and sharper interest rate hikes will be needed to get prices under control, with significant damage to economic growth.[5]

The credibility of the governor and the deputies therefore matters as much for inflation outcomes as any hawkish or dovish leanings. The individuals in question must demonstrate their commitment to their mandate through the actions that they take and must be able and willing to communicate it clearly to those price and wage setters and to the market. Their credibility may well be tested after 2024 in the face of tough global financial conditions as well as a tough domestic environment with deteriorating public finances. As discussed in due course, it may also be tested by challenges to the Bank's very mandate.

Nationalisation? Inflation?

Contestation inside and outside the African National Congress (ANC) alliance over the Bank's ownership and its price-stability mandate could grow after 2024, especially if the election results in an ANC-led coalition that includes the Economic Freedom Fighters (EFF).

The Bank is one of only eight central banks globally that still has private shareholders. It is state controlled, in that the President appoints the majority on the board and the board cannot influence monetary policy. Yet calls to 'nationalise' the Bank have been a rallying cry for populist political factions over the past decade – either because politicians genuinely believe that removing the private shareholding could shift the Bank's priorities or simply because it represents a convenient attack on a fiercely independent institution. The EFF's 2013 founding manifesto called for the Bank to be nationalised,[6] and party leader Julius Malema unsuccessfully tabled a motion in Parliament to effect this in 2017. The ANC's 2017 national conference resolved to nationalise the Bank, as did its 2022 conference.

However, nationalisation may be a cover for the real political debate – which is about inflation targeting. Calls to add employment and/or economic growth targets to the price-stability mandate have grown as South Africa's economic growth performance has lagged, its unemployment rate has climbed, and its politics have become more contested and more populist, inside and outside the ANC. Politicians have also sought to load functional public institutions – such as the courts, competition authorities and central bank – with socioeconomic objectives that a dysfunctional state has failed to achieve.

The ANC itself is clearly divided within. The party's 2019 election manifesto committed it to a 'flexible monetary policy regime', which takes employment creation and growth into account 'without sacrificing price stability'. But ANC leaders speaking after the party's 2022 national conference said the party was looking to expand the mandate to meet the needs of the economy and to address high unemployment levels and low economic growth.[7] President Ramaphosa subsequently told Parliament in November 2023 that there was no intention to change the Bank's mandate – the price-stability mandate already supported economic growth, and a more accommodative monetary policy stance would not address South Africa's structural growth problem.[8]

Reflecting the economy's structural constraints, the Bank's estimated potential or trend growth – the rate of growth that the economy can sustain without fuelling inflation – is just 0.1 per cent for 2023, rising to 1 per cent in 2024 as the electricity supply improves. This indicates that the economy risks inflation, and so interest rate hikes may be justified, even when growth is very weak, thus making the task of monetary policymakers tougher and more likely to be politically contested.

Nor can monetary policy, which is designed to manage cyclical fluctuations, do much about South Africa's electricity or logistics or skills constraints, other than to urge government to implement structural reforms to lift growth and so make monetary policy more effective. Kganyago has said that if the government wanted to give the Bank a formal jobs target, it would have to give it the tools to deliver on such a target, such as the power and independence to intervene in labour-market regulation.

Challenges to inflation targeting may lose heat once interest rates start to decline, but they are unlikely to disappear. Arguably, though, they will prove to be less of a threat to the Bank's independence and core mandate than the pressure the Bank is under to use its balance sheet to shore up the public finances, as will be discussed below.

South Africa is not alone in this. The new era of high inflation and high interest rates in advanced economies has made inflation targets controversial. High public-debt levels and debt costs have roused concerns that governments will exert political pressure on central banks to help limit borrowing costs by keeping interest rates lower than necessary to combat inflation.

Former Bank of Israel and Federal Reserve (Fed) governor, Jacob Frenkel, and his colleagues argued recently that 'central banks cannot solve all that ails our economies. They should not be expected to solve problems that other actors can better address ...' Their price-stability, financial-stability and macroeconomic-stability goals are hard enough to achieve, say Frenkel and his colleagues, who advocate a humble approach to central banking. 'We should dial back public expectations that central banks can or should do more than this.'[9]

It is also worth taking heed of the clear reminder they issued on the link between mandate and central bank independence: 'To achieve their core goals, central banks require independence from political interference. With independence comes a heavy burden of responsibility, and this is a key reason why central bankers must accept the deliberately narrow mandate that the humble approach implies.' They added: 'Crucially, once inflation is allowed to take hold, if independence and credibility are lacking, people's inflationary expectations for the future are adversely affected and the results can be deeply harmful.'

Facing up to 'high-for-longer' global rates

Going into 2024, monetary policy appears to be at a turning point in South Africa – as it is globally – with lower inflation fuelling expectations that the central bank now has the space to consider when it might start reducing interest rates.

Like many other emerging markets, South Africa was more alert to the dangers of inflation, when prices climbed in 2021, than advanced-economy central banks were, and it started raising interest rates earlier. The MPC implemented its first interest rate increase in November 2021 and paused its hiking cycle only after the May 2023 meeting, when the policy repurchase (repo) rate had reached 8.25 per cent – up from the four-decade low of 3.50 per cent to which the Bank had cut interest rates in the depths of the Covid crisis in May 2020. Following its May meeting, the MPC's view was that the interest rate in real terms was now 'in restrictive territory' – in other words, at a level where it restricts the economy to squeeze inflation back to target rather than to accommodate economic growth.

In contrast to the United States (US) and Europe, where headline inflation reached double-digit highs in the wake of Russia's invasion of Ukraine in 2022, South Africa's headline inflation rate rose quite gradually, peaking at 7.8 per cent in July 2022 before subsiding as fuel and food prices started to decline. Though inflation eased to below 6 per cent from June 2023, the MPC has repeatedly made it clear that it is targeting the 4.5 per cent mid-point of the inflation target range, not the 6 per cent top limit, and that it will start to reduce interest rates only once inflation is headed sustainably towards that mid-point. By the end of 2023, the Bank's forecasts showed inflation declining to 4.5 per cent in the second half of 2024 and stabilising at that level on average in 2025 and 2026. In addition, the Bank's own quarterly projection model, which it uses as a decision-making guide, showed interest rate cuts through 2024 and 2025.

In theory, then, the space should be there for monetary policy to be loosened quite considerably from 2024 onwards. This is especially so, given that while economic growth is expected to gain pace as the electricity supply improves, the Bank is forecasting that growth will remain very weak at 1 per cent, rising to just 1.6 per cent by 2026. In practice, though, loosening prematurely and too aggressively could put the currency and the Bank's credibility at risk in a volatile external environment that is very different from that which prevailed after the 2008–2009 global financial crisis and more challenging for emerging markets in general and South Africa in particular.

Going into 2023, the leading advanced-economy central banks were tightening monetary policy aggressively, and economic recessions were expected to be the way to bring inflation under control. Going into 2024, the Fed, in particular, appeared to have engineered a 'soft landing', with inflation declining amid strong economic growth and employment and Fed chairman, Jerome Powell, starting to signal interest rate cuts. However, interest rates in the US and Europe are expected to remain high until there is clear evidence that inflation is returning sustainably to their 2 per cent target. Even when it does, it is unlikely that interest rates will again fall to the near-zero levels that prevailed in the decade following the global financial crisis.

Several factors could drive the natural or neutral (or 'steady-state') interest rate to a permanently higher level than before the Covid crisis, including high global public-debt levels and the need to spend more on ageing populations and climate change mitigation. Furthermore, Gita Gopinath, Deputy Managing Director of the International Monetary Fund (IMF), suggests that central banks could react more aggressively to supply shocks than they did before the pandemic and 'shy away from over-easy policies when inflation is only modestly below target and labour markets are close to full employment'.[10]

In the 'low-for-long' years, global investors sought higher yields and had plenty of appetite for riskier assets, including emerging-market currencies and bonds. A 'higher-for-longer' environment means global financial conditions are tougher. And as Gopinath has emphasised, financing conditions for emerging markets will remain challenging. It has become more costly and more difficult for emerging-market governments to borrow on international markets since the US started its aggressive tightening cycle. Capital flows into emerging-market equity and bond markets have decreased sharply.

This is an environment in which emerging markets that depend on foreign inflows will feel the pain in their currencies. It is also an environment in which investors become more discriminating in their choice of emerging markets, avoiding those regarded as particularly high risk. South Africa ticked both boxes in 2023. The rand was among the worst-performing emerging-market currencies, hitting an all-time low against the dollar in May as loadshedding and low economic growth, together with South Africa's perceived support for Russia, succeeded in driving away international investors. This is in a context in which South Africa's dependence on foreign capital is increasing because its fiscal deficit is expanding and the current (trade) account in its balance of payments has swung from surplus into deficit, with the latter expected to widen as commodity exports diminish while imports rise.

The growing twin deficits will themselves keep the risk premium that investors attach to South Africa elevated after 2024,[11] even if one assumes progress in mitigating some of the idiosyncratic risks, such as foreign policy or loadshedding. The higher risk premium means that they will demand higher returns, raising South Africa's cost of borrowing. The Bank estimates that average policy interest rates in G3 economies will remain high at 4.3 per cent in 2024, against 1.1 per cent in 2022.

'These tighter global financial conditions will raise the risk profile of economies needing foreign capital' is a frequent refrain from the MPC.[12] This will influence monetary policy through at least two channels from 2024. One channel is the rand exchange rate, which affects inflation. The central bank targets inflation, not the exchange rate. However, the exchange rate is a key input in the inflation forecast. The rand's volatility and depreciation were constant concerns for the MPC in 2023. They will remain so, given South Africa's need for foreign capital and the currency's sensitivity to idiosyncratic risks. The outcome of the 2024 general election is clearly one of those potential risks. Also, the Bank's own monetary stance has a material impact on the value of the rand. Unofficially, it will carefully steer interest rates to ensure it does not get too far behind the Fed, because that would widen the yield gap between South Africa and the US, weighing on capital inflows or even prompting outflows which, in turn, would further weaken the rand. The other channel is South Africa's neutral or natural real rate of interest. This is the real, inflation-adjusted rate that neither stimulates nor contracts the economy. When the MPC says interest rates are 'restrictive', it means that they are above that neutral rate – and the question then is: how restrictive do interest rates need to be to get inflation back to a given target?

The Bank adds its estimate of South Africa's country-risk premium to the global real neutral rate to arrive at South Africa's real neutral rate, which it currently estimates at 2.5 per cent for 2023, rising to 2.8 per cent by 2026. A higher neutral rate implies that tighter monetary policy will be required to reduce inflation to the target. The increase in the global neutral rate therefore implies a 'higher-for-longer' scenario for South Africa. An increase in the country-risk premium after 2024 makes this even more likely, and the state of the public finances is key to that risk premium. If fiscal policy is too loose, as it seems highly likely to be after 2024 (given political pressures), monetary policy will have to be tighter than it would otherwise have been to offset it. As discussed below, the fiscal outlook is a growing concern for monetary policy and financial stability.

Yet a more immediate concern for monetary policy is that inflation expectations remain intractable, hovering around the top of the target range. And though South Africa has done relatively well in limiting the recent rise in inflation, in significant part because of the Bank's credibility, in absolute terms the inflation rate remains high by global and emerging-market standards. Kganyago has long been keen to reduce the target itself, ideally towards a point target of 3 per cent (rather than a range), to bring it closer to that of South Africa's major trading partners and to make the country more competitive. That would help to manage inflation expectations, and ultimately inflation, at sustainably lower levels – as the Bank succeeded in doing after 2017 when it effectively re-set the target at 4.5 per cent.[13]

Assuming some degree of continuity in the leadership, the aspiration for a lower target could mean that the Bank will implement only moderate rate cuts after 2024, in an effort to massage inflation expectations downwards towards sustainably lower levels so that a lower target can be eased in gradually and at little cost to the economy. It is hard to see how there would be any political appetite for a lower formal inflation target. But the aspiration may shape the Bank's approach, underpinning its credibility in a context in which this may be more important than ever to investor perceptions of South Africa.

The weight of the public-debt burden

Fiscal policy has stepped firmly onto the radar screens of monetary policymakers as global public-debt levels have climbed and borrowing costs have risen, thus complicating central bankers' efforts to combat inflation and introducing new risks to financial stability. In South Africa's case, the government's unsustainable level of public debt and the sharply rising yields that investors are demanding to buy longer-term debt are key factors keeping interest rates elevated. Over a three- to five-year time horizon, investors will intensify their demands for domestic banks and fund managers to absorb more debt and will put pressure on the Bank to deploy its own balance sheet to assist a government that is more likely to be profligate than prudent.

MPC statements during 2023 urged government to achieve a prudent public-debt level that would 'strengthen monetary policy effectiveness and its transmission to the broader economy'.[14] The Bank has become increasingly concerned about the yield curve for sovereign bonds, which is one of the steepest in emerging markets. This reflects investors' pessimism over the longer-term outlook for the public debt – despite lower inflation and the Bank's inflation-fighting credibility, which should have lowered medium- to long-term inflation expectations and yields, and despite government's commitment to stabilising the debt. In 2023 alone, South Africa's debt level rose by about 11 percentage points, while medium- to longer-term bond yields have on average risen from 8 per cent to 11 per cent over the past decade.[15]

The November 2023 Medium-Term Budget pencilled in a path that relies on steep spending cuts to get the debt to stabilise by 2026, albeit at more than 77 per cent of GDP. However, the spending cuts appear implausible, with the government under pressure to raise, not reduce, social spending. In the absence of far higher rates of economic growth, South Africa's public debt and debt costs will probably keep rising, as the IMF and most private-sector economists expect.

The outcome of the 2024 election will influence the pace and depth of the unfolding fiscal crisis. However, South Africa is unlikely to suddenly fall off a fiscal cliff, defaulting on its debts and running to the IMF to be rescued. Far more likely is a slow-burn route to what economists call 'financial repression', which could prove more painful for the economy than an IMF bailout and could pose significant risks to financial stability.

South Africa has deep pools of local capital and well-developed domestic markets. Government has kept the lid on dollar-denominated foreign borrowing. It did rely on large quantities of foreign money to ramp up the public debt after the global financial crisis, but much of that went into rand-denominated bonds on the domestic market. As foreigners have fled, local banks and fund managers have picked up their bonds. They now own three-quarters of government bonds, up from a low of below 60 per cent in the 'Ramaphoria' period of early 2018. This means that the fortunes of the domestic financial sector are ever more closely tied to government's fiscal fortunes, increasing the risk that a sovereign bond crisis would rapidly become a banking or broader financial-sector crisis. The Bank has, since 2020, been flagging this 'sovereign financial-sector nexus' as a risk to South Africa's financial stability.[16]

Tight global financial conditions and limited foreign-investor appetite for South Africa's risk assets can only make it more difficult and costly for government to meet its borrowing requirement, which is running at about R2 billion a day, with the quantum of government debt set to rise to R6 trillion over the medium term. Domestic capital markets are deep but not bottomless, and domestic investors may already be reaching prudential limits.[17] That is the scenario in which government can be expected to resort to financial repression which, in the words of economist Carmen Reinhart, is 'when governments implement policies to channel to themselves funds that in a deregulated market environment would go elsewhere'.[18] Almost by definition, it means an inefficient allocation of capital, usually at below-market rates, and it is bad for savings, investment and economic growth.

Arguably, South Africa is already there in some form, given the extent to which banks, pension funds and unit trusts have already run up their sovereign-bond holdings at the expense of making loans for more productive investments. After 2024, however, there could be political pressure to force more financial repression through regulation. The ANC has already suggested a return to apartheid-era prescribed assets, which required pension funds and insurers to invest a proportion of their assets in public-sector bonds and the Public Investment Commissioners (now the Public Investment Corporation (PIC)) to invest the bulk of its funds in bonds. The PIC could be an early target for a post-election government seeking to go this route.

Banks are already required to hold significant amounts of government paper to meet reserve and liquid-asset requirements. But this is designed to ensure prudent management of their balance sheets, not to help the government sell more bonds into a saturated market. Any attempt to do this would likely face resistance from the private financial sector. An independent central bank with a mandate to protect financial stability should in theory push back. Whether the Bank would do this after 2024 would depend on its leadership.

The likelihood of a pushback might be greater if government were to put pressure on the Bank to use its own balance sheet to intervene in the bond market, either to reduce interest rates or to buy bonds in the secondary market. The Bank did that during the early Covid-19 financial crisis, buying government paper to stabilise the market, which had frozen up. But that is quite different from intervening to help the government out with a fiscal crisis. It comes with costs if it is to be done without fuelling inflation, and these may have to be borne by the central bank. It comes with the risk of 'moral hazard', in the sense that government may have little incentive to manage its public finances prudently if it can effectively monetise the public debt by getting the central bank to buy it. And to the extent that it might risk the Bank's independence and credibility in the eyes of investors, it could further increase government's borrowing costs and worsen the fiscal crisis.

South Africa would not be alone. Central banks in some advanced and emerging markets have been persuaded to intervene in bond markets to assist their governments. In South Africa during the Covid pandemic, a former senior Treasury official controversially called for the Bank to intervene in the market in an effort to flatten the yield curve and reduce borrowing costs for the duration of the crisis.[19]

Late 2023 saw the start of a debate on whether government should ask the Bank to realise the significant paper profits on South Africa's gold and foreign exchange reserves to reduce government's borrowing requirement. Calls to do this, from the left-wing Institute for Economic Justice as well as some in the market,[20] relate to the so-called Gold and Foreign Exchange Contingency Reserve Account (GFECRA), which houses the unrealised profits on the reserves. Rand depreciation and gold price appreciation increased those profits to about R500 billion by the end of 2023. The reserves themselves sit on the Bank's balance sheet, but South Africa's central banking legislation is unusual in that it requires that when the reserves are marked to market, the profits or losses are for the Treasury's account.

Realising the profits would mean that the Bank would either have to sell down the foreign exchange reserves themselves or monetise the profits by simply crediting the amounts to the Treasury, probably at the tax-and-loan accounts that the Treasury holds at commercial banks. The latter is the most plausible route, but it would come at a significant cost, because to prevent it being inflationary the Bank would have to 'sterilise' the transfers, issuing bonds or bills on which it would have to pay interest. This raises the key question: who would bear that cost? If, in theory, the Bank were to realise the full R500 billion to hand over to the Treasury, the annual interest cost – at about R40 billion – would exceed the Bank's R27 billion in capital. This would effectively bankrupt the institution for the sake of a cash sum equivalent to less than the government's borrowing requirement for a single year.

A case could, however, be made to draw down the GFECRA to a limited extent and to put protocols in place for how and when profits might be realised, and whether the Treasury would bear the associated costs.[21] The Bank and the Treasury undertook a review of the options towards the end of 2023, with assistance from the IMF. The quality and integrity of the Bank's leadership, as well as that of the Treasury, will be key to whether strategies that risk being seen by the market as a raid on the foreign reserves can be pursued without running up inflation and running down institutional credibility after 2024.

Yet none of the fiscal pressure is inevitable. Higher rates of economic growth would quickly solve much of the problematic fiscal arithmetic and remove the need for financial repression or for incursions into the Bank's balance sheet. Faster structural economic reforms by government hold the key to the realisation of that hope.

Looking ahead

Central bankers everywhere face tricky times after 2024, as the interest rate cycle turns. It is also a tricky time in global politics, with countries housing more than 50 per cent of the world's population due to go to the polls in 2024,[22] South Africa among them. The outcome of South Africa's election – the first in the democratic era in which the ANC is at risk of losing its majority – could materially affect the environment for monetary policy. It could amplify calls for the Bank's mandate to be expanded to include employment, growth or other targets beyond its core price-stability mandates. It raises questions about continuity at the Bank, at a delicate moment in which all four of its governors are scheduled to be renewed or replaced in a single year, in an appointment process that is ultimately at the discretion of the President.

South Africa's monetary policymakers will be tested by the impact on the currency and the country risk premium of a 'high-for-longer' interest rate scenario which will make for difficult global financial conditions. They will be tested at home by rising public-debt levels that will weigh on monetary policy, increase risks to financial stability, and increase pressure on the Bank to use its balance sheet in some form to monetise the public debt.

In this context, the Bank will have to retain a clear focus on its core inflation-targeting mandate and its responsibility to ensure financial stability, while also communicating clearly, effectively and widely. It will need to continue spelling out the limits of what a central bank can do and the risks involved in mandating it to do more.

Yet it must also be cognisant of the profound growth and employment challenges facing South Africa and partner with government to ensure that structural reforms to address these are fast-tracked. A post-election government must, in turn, remain fully aware of the important role that the central bank can and must play in providing a bedrock of macroeconomic stability, as well as the costly sanctions that markets can impose if the credibility of South Africa's key economic institutions is undermined.

NINE

Broadening farm ownership for successful transformation in South African agriculture

Johann Kirsten and Wandile Sihlobo

Introduction

One of the dominant questions surrounding South Africa's agricultural policy since the dawn of democracy has been how to accelerate land reform to ensure the inclusion of black farmers in the agricultural sector. Failed attempts to bring this about prompted some political parties in December 2017 to call for the expropriation of land without compensation through an amendment to section 25 of the Constitution of the Republic of South Africa, 1996. This motion was tabled in the National Assembly, but it failed. On the margins, some began to ask, 'Is farm ownership a requirement for success in the South African context?' Of course, this is a broad question, and the answer would depend on each individual farmer's financial status. Yet, working from the premise that farming is a long-term endeavour requiring intensive capital investment, farm ownership is crucial.

For this fundamental reason, South Africa is still discussing (and wrestling with) the issue of land ownership, which will be explored in this chapter – not from a historical perspective but in terms of the options available to accelerate land reform from now on. But first it is important to highlight the progress made so far in the area of land reform.

Progress with land reform

There is a general perception that the land reform programme has failed to deliver a recognisable shift in ownership patterns. However, the real situation is more nuanced. This is because land reform covers different components, including redistribution, restitution, financial compensation, private acquisition and state acquisition. Some have shown more progress than others. Hence, it is important to examine what has happened to the state acquisition of farmland which, for the most part, is then leased to entrepreneurs wanting to become farmers. The factors that stand in the way of success are discussed below. These factors have been drawn from reports and from farmers themselves and are also based on the experience of the authors (of this chapter) as agricultural economists in the South African farming sector.

The National Development Plan (NDP), adopted in 2012, had a target of redistributing (or restoring) 30 per cent (or 23.7 million hectares) of all freehold agricultural land to black South Africans by 2030. In 1994, when South Africa held its first democratic election, the 77.58 million hectares of farmland in the country with registered title deeds were mainly owned by white farmers. Since then, by the authors' calculations, the total area with land rights that has been transferred away from white ownership – either to the state or black beneficiaries, or where financial compensation has been made for land claims – is 19.16 million hectares. This is equivalent to 24.7 per cent of all freehold agricultural land (Figure 9.1). Although the number may look heartening, given that it is close to the 30 per cent target set out in the NDP, the area of concern is that the state is now a major owner of agricultural land (more than 2.5 million hectares).[1] This is a problem, for various reasons.

The Agricultural Land Holding Account Trading Entity is responsible for the acquisition of land and other property (movable and immovable) under the Proactive Land Acquisition Strategy (PLAS), which was implemented in 2006. Through this scheme the land is held by the state for use by lessees of the land reform programme.

By June 2023, the state had acquired 2.5 million hectares of productive farmland through the programme. Most of the roughly 2 500 beneficiaries have a 30-year lease agreement with the state, although there are several farms where no agreement has been signed. The arrangement involves the leasing of land. But there is no mention of the transfer or sale of land to beneficiaries. The acquisition strategy was a noble attempt at land reform. It had some clear objectives: acquire land with high agricultural potential; integrate black farmers into the commercial agricultural sector; improve the beneficiary-selection process; improve land-use planning; and ensure optimal productive land use.

Figure 9.1: Land reform progress in South Africa, 1994–August 2023 (hectares)

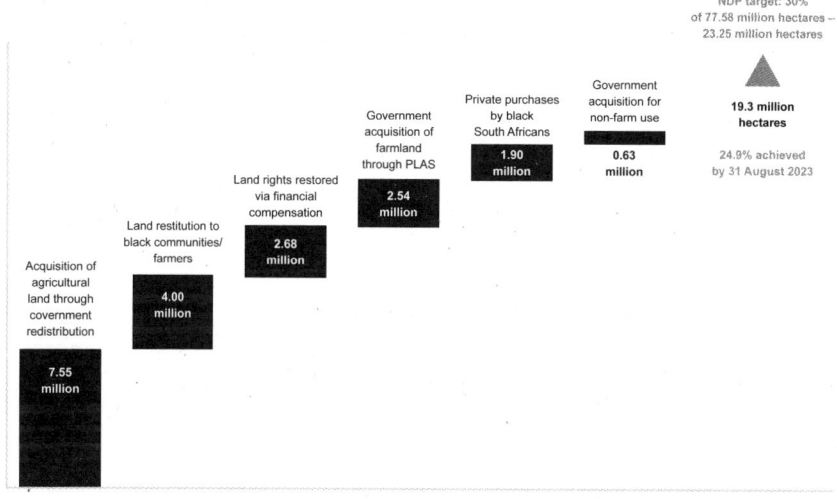

Source: BER (2023)[2]

Virtually none of the land acquired through the PLAS programme has been transferred to individuals (although, at the end of 2023, there was a sudden drive by the Minister of Agriculture, Land Reform and Rural Development to transfer land to those beneficiaries who were up to date with their lease payments and had no arrears on their municipal accounts). Most land is leased to beneficiaries and in some cases the farms are illegally occupied. More than half the current beneficiaries on the leased land have not shown any significant agricultural production. This implies that valuable agricultural resources are not being utilised and are lying fallow. The factors behind this failure are set out in a recently published article.³ The article was based on findings that were first collated in a research report compiled by the Agricultural Research Council for the (then) Department of Rural Development and Land Reform (DRDLR) and released in 2019. However, its findings were never publicised.

The disappointing outcomes of the PLAS programme can be attributed to a number of factors. First, land tenure is insecure. This makes it difficult – or impossible – to invest in the land or secure loans for improvements and growth. Beneficiaries must rely on government grants to do business, and the grants are often not enough. Moreover, the process is often slow. Second, there is the problem of bureaucratic red tape. For example, there is clear evidence of excessive layers of approval being required, with repetitive documentation. This causes significant delays. Third, there is a lack of access to finance. Farmers have limited credit history, collateral or access to formal financial institutions because of the nature of their lease arrangement. Fourth, the process of leasing state land and engaging bureaucrats to conduct the beneficiary-selection process and manage farm-related decisions is simply setting beneficiaries up to fail.

Actions that need to be taken to accelerate land reform

The South African government has bought land on behalf of beneficiaries at market value. But it lacks the capacity and resources to manage the land assets and generate any return in the form of rents, improve the capital asset base or even perform general maintenance of the physical assets that may be on the land. A solution would be for the government to transfer the asset to an institution with a vested interest and the capacity to provide both oversight and finance. One such institution might be the Land Reform and Agricultural Development Agency announced by the President in his State of the Nation Address (SONA) in February 2021. This mechanism is discussed in detail below.

However, it is first worth highlighting that the 'low-hanging fruit' are the 2.5 million hectares that the state has already acquired and should now allocate to eligible beneficiaries. This could be done in an orderly way by offering the land to beneficiaries for purchase, provided they meet specific criteria, at half the purchase price. Beneficiaries would pay the purchase price (minus rent) to the state over time and register a mortgage with the Land Bank at the prime rate minus 6 per cent. This would have the additional benefit of recapitalising the Land Bank without any pressure on the fiscus and ensuring that the new farmers would have sufficient 'skin in the game'.

Creation of the Land Reform and Agricultural Development Agency

The NDP (Chapter 6) and the report by the Presidential Advisory Panel on Land Reform and Agriculture[4] offer a clear guide on how the redistribution of agricultural land can be accelerated. In essence, they locate the responsibility for redistributive land reform with local (district- or municipal-level) land committees. These committees would design context-specific, locally based solutions centred on the dominant farming enterprises, while also considering community and social dynamics in the location in question. In this way, the task of land acquisition and redistribution would be taken out of the government sphere.

To leverage land and funds for land redistribution through local land and agricultural development projects, there is a need for a national coordinating agency. This could be satisfied through the creation of the Land Reform and Agricultural Development Agency – a one-stop shop to ensure that all elements of successful land reform are in place. The concept of a 'land reform agency' was announced by President Ramaphosa in his SONA in 2021 and echoed again in 2022. The Agency should ideally have five broad tasks:

- enabling policy and bureaucratic processes to facilitate land donations;
- creating and managing recognition mechanisms given to farmers donating land and/or providing financial and other support to beneficiary farmers;
- establishing and managing a land reform fund;
- recording and monitoring progress on land transactions;
- prescribing the rules of local land committees.

The Agency could be established by the Minister of Agriculture, Land Reform and Rural Development in terms of Clause 26 (2) of the Land

Bank Act, 2002. The Agency would not require any additional fiscal outlays but would activate contributions from the private sector and would therefore only record land transactions and accept land for redistribution. This could be regarded as a land observatory, where the true extent of the redistribution of land would be assessed on the basis of improved statistics on land transferred and the productive status of the land.

Most importantly, the Agency would monitor progress with land reform and, in the process, advise on partnerships between farmers and beneficiaries. The process of monitoring would also enable the Agency to report to the government on the quality and sustainability of the various initiatives developed and implemented at the local level. At the district level, farmers, communities, agribusinesses and other private-sector role players would craft solutions within a framework of clearly identified incentives and recognition mechanisms managed by the Agency.

With all the enablers and recognition mechanisms in place, confidence in the land reform process would be fostered. This would encourage the voluntary release of land (by mines, churches, municipalities, state-owned enterprises (SOEs), government departments or absentee landlords) directly to beneficiary households, communities or to the Agency. The Agency would keep a proper record of all these land parcels and provide a certificate of recognition to the donor. The certificate would entitle the holder to certain benefits, such as points on the broad-based black economic empowerment (B-BBEE) scorecard, which might entitle the beneficiary to procurement preferences or a range of preferential financial arrangements.

Development of the Land Reform and Agricultural Development Fund

Coupled with the establishment of the Agency, it is proposed that a Land Reform and Agricultural Development Fund be set up. The Fund would be created specifically for land beneficiaries and land donors, providing financial assistance to beneficiaries and encouraging large farmers to be partners in the redistribution process. The sources of capital for the Fund should include:
- donations by companies and private individuals (for which they

would receive B-BBEE recognition);
- international donors and development finance institutions, such as the Development Bank of Southern Africa (DBSA), with donor funds ideally constituting the major share of the Fund;
- joint-venture financing models, particularly those implemented by agribusinesses, large commercial farmers, property developers and commercial banks, among others;
- transfers from the Department of Agriculture, Land Reform and Rural Development (DALRRD), which are earmarked for land reform grants and farmer support programmes as well as other funds from the annual budget for land reform and food security over the Medium-Term Expenditure Framework (MTEF) period 2021/22 to 2024/25. Conservative estimates suggest that around R5–9 billion could be available for this purpose.

These sources of funding should enable the Agency to provide finance to beneficiaries and commercial farmers donating land at affordable interest rates and with beneficial terms, such as deferred repayments or deferred interest payments. Donors, the National Treasury and members of the Agency should be trustees of the Fund. In this way, many more people could afford to develop allocated land for farming purposes and access bridging finance and seasonal finance at an affordable rate of about 2.5 per cent, given that the cost of capital would be only about 1.1 per cent or lower.

Throughout this process, opportunities would be created for other investors to contribute to the goals of restoring social justice, equitable land ownership, decent housing and fair economic opportunities. This would include a call for voluntary financial donations from the financial services industry, as well as the mining and manufacturing and other non-agricultural sectors. This would apply in particular to businesses that do not own any landed property.

Implementation of a land-redistribution strategy for underutilised and unproductive land

In addition to the initial endowment of state-owned land by various departments and SOEs, the state has, over the past decade, acquired a total of 2.46 million hectares of productive farmland through the

PLAS for redistribution to beneficiaries. Owing to bureaucratic red tape, patronage and various other problems, few (if any) of these farms have been redistributed to land reform beneficiaries. These farms are only rented out to specific farmers under short-term contracts and as a result, many of the farms are unproductive or producing sub-optimally. The inability to access finance due to the insecurity of tenure is one of the primary reasons for this.

One option is to transfer the state's land holding to the Land Bank as a mechanism to capitalise the bank. The latter would take responsibility for selecting bona fide farmers as beneficiaries and transferring the title deeds to them. The bank could then provide start-up capital, under close supervision, to these farmers with the land serving as collateral. Such an arrangement is essentially a no-brainer and would help to fill the gap in the market for empowered farmers. The establishment of the Fund, together with the land, would help the Land Bank to carry out its developmental mandate.

Anecdotal evidence suggests that if the above recommendations are implemented, there would be a dramatic expansion of production (especially by black farmers) in three agricultural sub-sectors of grains, beef and poultry. For this to occur, three critical steps need to be taken:

- Land ownership (title deeds) should be transferred to qualifying beneficiaries who are selected according to the approved beneficiary-selection policy. Strict selection based on merit and a skills and means test should be applied.
- Production finance (via the Land Reform and Agricultural Development Fund and the Land Bank at beneficial rates) should be secured through the title deeds. Comprehensive Agricultural Support Programme (CASP) funding (which would need to be redesigned) could be sought for improvements to immovable assets and farm infrastructure.
- Links should be established with commercial value chains, agribusinesses and government procurement schemes.

Amendments to the beneficiary-selection process

The importance of a transparent beneficiary-selection process cannot be stressed enough. Following the suggestion by the Presidential Advisory Panel to formulate a policy on who should be prioritised for land allocation and how these beneficiaries should be selected, the DALRRD developed the Draft National Policy on Beneficiary Selection and Land Allocation. This policy was made available for public comment in 2020 but has not progressed further. It is recommended that this process be expedited and the policy signed into law, taking the following into consideration:

- The draft policy suggests that an independent selection panel should be established for land allocation at both the provincial and national level. The policy indicates that the panel would be a non-statutory, multi-disciplinary group consisting of representatives of relevant stakeholders. It is recommended that this panel also include private-sector individuals to increase transparency and send a signal to the public that private–public cooperation is taking place.
- The draft policy suggests that all applicants should be subject to a skills audit to determine their training needs and the programmes that they would need to undergo before they could take ownership of the land. It is recommended that a skills audit be conducted among new applicants as well as existing beneficiaries to ensure that all beneficiaries have the training, skills and experience needed to manage a farming operation. These would include agricultural degrees and/or other qualifications, learnerships, internships, apprenticeships and practical experience. While certain categories of applicant, such as women and people with disabilities, are prioritised in the land-redistribution process, it is important that they, too, have the correct skills and experience. If they do not, they should be given the opportunity to develop the needed expertise.
- The draft policy indicates that monitoring and evaluation should take place through the Chief Directorate: Monitoring and Evaluation. Evaluations would be based on development indicators for land reform initiatives using different scales and would take place during the first three years of the farming lease. It is suggested that evaluations take place annually and that extension officers be included as evaluation agents. In addition, a database containing the details of each land recipient should be created for monitoring purposes and to prevent the allocation of land to unqualified individuals or those with political connections.

Supporting beneficiaries

In essence, the land reform support programme must not be hamstrung by bureaucratic red tape and endless committee meetings. These time wasters are among the reasons why the current CASP has failed to reach as many farmers as possible. The following principles should apply:

- Avoid project-based and piecemeal approaches to farmer support.
- No public tenders for farm input purchases or on-farm investments must be issued. This would ensure that time is not wasted and opportunities for patronage are minimised.
- Only on-farm infrastructure should be supported. This would include boreholes, animal-handling facilities, poultry houses, fencing, orchards and barns.
- Fixed improvements to land, such as conservation works, fences, contouring, soil improvement programmes and investment for 'regenerative agriculture', should also qualify.
- For financing, a universal flat rate per specific item should be introduced for refund claims by farmers. The rate should be no more than 80 per cent of the market rate/value of the item.
- Farmers should be able to appoint any service provider, following initial budget approval and initial inspection by government officials. Payment should be processed following implementation inspection and the furnishing of full documentation as well as proof of payment to the service provider.
- Production and operating expenses such as wages, fuel, seeds and fertiliser should be funded with production finance from co-ops, agribusinesses or commercial banks.
- Machinery and farming implements should be financed through term loans from dealers, banks or agribusinesses.

New farmers find it hard to survive in the initial years before a revenue stream has been established. It would therefore be sensible to support the family with a personal maintenance allowance of R3 500 per month for the first 24 months. A programme like this would play an essential role in ensuring a successful outcome for South Africa's land reform programme and the building of a new 'crop' of commercially oriented black farmers.

Ensuring a robust and stable agricultural sector

In summary, farm ownership is important yet challenging. South Africa provides many examples of the challenges associated with making the agricultural sector more inclusive and dynamic, but it is encouraging that the question of ownership (through land reform) has been central to policy debates in recent years.

In an increasingly turbulent world and in the face of persistent socioeconomic challenges on the home front, South Africa desperately needs a robust and stable agricultural sector. The policy interventions discussed in this chapter, notably the establishment of the Land Reform and Agricultural Development Agency and the Land Reform and Agricultural Development Fund, represent opportunities to do things differently in the area of land reform and to achieve better and more sustainable results.

Land reform will remain a key focus area for policymakers for many years to come, but it will only gain traction if land ownership is prioritised, with support provided by both public- and private-sector entities. The implementation of key policy interventions in this crucial arena would be an important tipping point for South Africa.

TEN

Can we conquer corruption in South Africa?

Jan van Romburgh

Introduction

The findings from the Zondo Commission of Inquiry provide an authoritative yet devastating picture of the scale and depth of state capture and corruption in South Africa. But before we can answer the question posed in the title of this chapter, we need to accept the fact that people's worldviews and perceptions of right and wrong differ – sometimes quite dramatically.

The moral conceptualisation of, among other things, facilitation payments, gifts and items of gratitude right through to the manoeuvring of undisclosed interests and payments to influence decision makers, and the consequent flow of economic value, differs from person to person. Likewise, a narrow-minded view that limits economic crime to corruption only conceals the range of mechanisms used by perpetrators to gain an unfair economic advantage over the victims of dubious economic practices and crimes. Corruption is certainly one of the most virulent strains of economic crime, but there are others. However, the term has come to be used almost in a generic sense in South Africa to describe a host of activities spanning a lengthy continuum, from small-scale financial irregularities to widespread state capture.

Without going into further academic debate about the precise definition, parameters and consequences of economic crime, this chapter presents a number of arguments on what can be done about it and various attempts that are currently under way to identify and curtail economic crime – including corruption. These observations are based on the accumulated experience of the author (a forensic accountant) who has held various strategic management positions throughout his professional career, conducted many forensic investigations, developed a curriculum for forensic accounting and taught the subject at the undergraduate and postgraduate levels, and lectured on strategic management to Master of Business Administration (MBA) students.

The arguments presented in the chapter fall into two categories: the 'world of pre-crime' and the 'world of post-crime'.

World of pre-crime

Although they have become clichés, the following two expressions remain powerful and relevant:

'Prevention is better than cure.' 'He who fails to plan, plans to fail.'

It is better to prevent a problem than to attempt to cure it, which is likely to be a much more difficult task. In addition, a lack of foresight and planning could snowball into an insurmountable (and usually unexpected) hurdle later. Both truisms can be applied to the fight against economic crime in South Africa. To this end, the following steps are recommended:

Formulate a clear and transparent economic crime-prevention strategy

All entities – both in the private and public sectors – should have a deliberate strategy for preventing and curbing economic crime, which is sufficiently detailed as to cover all the bases (who, what, where, when and how). The top management would be responsible for clearly and transparently setting out what the strategy would entail, underpinned by the organisation's position on ethics, governance and sustainability.

It is important that the strategy leaves no doubt as to which transactions, contracts and business activities are permissible or otherwise. Even though certain types of conduct are accepted under a country's law or traditional customs, an organisation may follow a different path, for its own reasons. Moreover, while there have been many philosophical attempts at defining and communicating the importance of 'good ethics' and 'strong governance', such definitions are often vague and detached from the day-to-day reality. In the absence of a practical, easy-to-follow code, people can be vulnerable to the illicit temptations of the commercial world.

Employ the right people (who will not succumb to temptation)

Probably the best preventative measure that an organisation can take in the fight against economic crime is to recruit and employ the right people. Once the wrong person becomes part of an organisation, it is often a long, expensive and cumbersome process to part ways with that person in the event of transgressions. While a normal recruitment and selection process involves the assessment of documentation relating to qualifications and a limited interview process (usually one interview) followed by a telephone call or two to the candidate's nominated referee(s), it often happens that very little vetting and verification of candidates takes place. Gaps in employment history go unexplained and possible wrongdoings at previous places of employment go undetected.

Although it may be argued that the vetting process is more rigorous in the case of senior (and therefore 'more important') appointments, economic crimes can be committed at any level of an organisation – from very junior (clerks) to very senior (executives). It is therefore essential to invest in the proper verification of prospective employees by acquiring evidence of their performance at tertiary institutions or places of previous affiliation, vetting their professed qualifications, interviewing their previous employers, investigating their general business interests and testing their ethical behaviour, such as through case study-based simulations.

Because people (and their circumstances) change, they should not be exposed to unnecessary temptation, although the cost thereof should not offset the benefit. A simple, yet golden, rule is: 'Segregate the books and the asset.' In other words, all reasonable steps should be taken to avoid a situation in which the person responsible for accounting in respect of a specific asset also has the opportunity to misuse that asset. For example, if person X has control over the bank account, then person Y should be the one recording and explaining the transactions processed through the account. That way, person X and person Y would have to collude with each other to cause harm, which would be more difficult to do than if one person caused the harm – assuming they had the power to do so.

Ensure transparency through lifestyle audits and other disclosures

The need for transparency aligns with the obligation to protect stakeholders and to uphold the public interest. In the accounting field, for example, entities with a certain public-interest score must undergo compulsory external audits. One such type is a lifestyle audit whose overarching principle is that wealth accumulation needs to be explained and, importantly, acted upon where necessary. This need not be a complicated process. Salaried employees, and public officials in particular, should have a starting balance sheet, with full disclosure of all assets and business interests – including those of 'connected' persons (with the notion of 'connected' itself being the subject of debate).

The results of the initial disclosure should be a consideration in the selection process. The starting balance sheet should then be compared to subsequent balance sheets during and (definitely) at the end of the term of employment. Unexplained wealth should be highlighted and probed. It seems to have become the norm that when so-called 'conflicts of interest' are declared, nothing further needs to be done. But this is where organisations are getting it wrong. The declared business interests should be subject to approval, and how these are to be managed should be clearly articulated – including, for example, the provision that no contracts may be entered into with such identified entities or 'connected persons'.

Leverage the power of artificial intelligence and other technologies to reduce risk

Leveraging the power of artificial intelligence (AI) and big data analytics should be non-negotiable goals for competitively minded organisations that are intent on reducing the risk of corruption and malfeasance. There are several excellent interfaces used for the identification of 'red flags' in both public- and private-sector operations. For example, if the National Treasury has the ability to perform online monitoring of transactions performed by state-owned enterprises (SOEs), the early detection of 'red flags' would be extremely valuable. Preventative mechanisms are often overlooked because of the difficulty (or inability) to justify the associated costs. However, the timeous identification of 'red flags' could ensure swift, mitigating action, which could be a significant cost saver in the end.

Understand the roles (and scope) of internal and external auditors

South Africa has experienced much turbulence in recent years. To add insult to injury, all sorts of economic crimes and corporate failures have been exposed. The country has strong cohorts of internal and external auditors whose job may be perceived as exposing corruption and malfeasance in public- and private-sector organisations before they escalate. This then prompts the question: where were the auditors when these governance lapses and economic crimes were occurring?

Part of the problem is an expectation gap. In other words, there is a lack of alignment between what auditors are supposed to do and what the public expects of them. Related to this is an over-reliance on so-called 'clean audits'. A clean audit is in essence the unqualified expression of an opinion on the fair (or otherwise) presentation of a set of financial statements. It does not certify the absence of fraud and/or corruption.

There is therefore a misplaced reliance on correctly presented financial statements (for which many organisations pay considerable sums of money), while the underlying bank accounts and the assets of the state or corporate entities are being plundered. It may be argued that the higher fees paid to external auditors to produce 'better-quality' financial statements may be better spent by actively searching for 'red flags' and their underlying causes, or by expanding the internal audit and risk-assessment capacity to timeously identify risks and take appropriate action.

World of post-crime

Much can be said about the ability (or inability) to act when transgressions occur. 'Negative reinforcement' theory suggests that perpetrators will continue to abuse the system if there are no consequences for their actions. Simply allowing them to resign from their position and take up new (and often successive rounds of) employment elsewhere in a so-called revolving door pattern, without being properly investigated and successfully prosecuted, creates a fearless and reckless transgressor who has the potential to unleash much harm on public- or private-sector organisations.

What can be done to enhance economic-crime detection practices and prosecution in an organisational context? A number of recommendations appear below.

Formulate and activate a clear response plan

Organisations and their appointed officers should know exactly, from a procedural standpoint, what to do if and when a crime is suspected. The modus operandi should be clearly spelt out in a response plan, which should include the steps involved in obtaining evidence, dealing with the suspect(s) and obtaining professional assistance where necessary. Importantly, the plan should be acted upon with speed and resolve, and not left on paper – where so many plans sadly tend to languish.

Establish public–private partnerships to boost investigative capacity

As became the norm in South Africa, the private sector was allowed or 'empowered' to take over various roles traditionally played by the government. However, while skills shifted to the private sector, the legislative powers remained with government. This applies in particular to investigative work and crime prevention. Clearly, public–private partnerships are required to make meaningful progress in these areas.

Public-sector organisations should therefore vigorously seek the skills and resources available in the private sector to anticipate and curtail economic crimes in the workplace and to administer justice where required. Of course, this should not simply become a money-making racket for private consultants. Private forensic work needs to be performed in collaboration with the South African Police Service (SAPS) and other public-sector law-enforcement agencies and role players. To enhance the effectiveness of public–private partnerships in the crime-detection and crime-prevention arenas, legislative or regulatory amendments may be required.

Optimise information sharing through public–private partnerships

Information sharing is a noble principle, but it is complex in practice. It is common cause that the vital information needed to conduct thorough investigations and prosecute economic crimes is spread across various clusters of role players, including banks, registrar(s) of companies, credit agencies, crypto exchanges, cell phone companies, and many others that store and manage data.

There is an inherent conflict in the sharing of information because personal data is increasingly being protected under various laws. A careful and legitimate balance therefore needs to be struck between safeguarding personal and private information and making it accessible to investigators. This conundrum goes to the heart of public–private partnerships in the investigative space, with differing contractual arrangements adding to the dilemma. To get around some of the private–public contractual complexities, loose associations such as 'task teams' or 'fusion centres' are sometimes created, although such arrangements have yielded few success stories.

If the concept of public–private partnerships is out of the question in certain scenarios, then at least the process of information sharing should be streamlined between state institutions with investigative powers, such as the SAPS, the Special Investigating Unit (SIU), the National Prosecuting Authority (NPA), the South African Revenue Service (SARS), the Auditor-General (AG) and the Companies and Intellectual Property Commission (CIPC), to name a few.

Conduct specific, focused audits

An important question should be posed: why have forensic investigations (especially by the private sector) become so prevalent over the past 15 years? Apart from the government's deteriorating capacity to investigate and prosecute economic crimes as well as a general decline in the morality of society, organisations have become increasingly aware of the importance of being proactive and responding to 'red flags' and other internal alerts, rather than relying entirely on the traditional external audit outcomes. If the quality of these investigations/audits is good, it will complement and assist the work of the relevant law-enforcement agencies and provide greater clarity to other stakeholders.

Prioritise training

The need for ongoing training (for all role players) in the investigative and crime-prevention fields cannot be stressed enough – particularly as fraudsters are learning new evasion techniques and tricks at an alarming rate. As technological advances and adoption accelerate, training needs to focus in particular on digital applications where economic crimes are often skilfully concealed from the non-tech savvy.

Empower the Auditor-General for greater effectiveness

In the public sector, the AG is normally the first in line to do an assessment of an entity's finances and has the opportunity (by law) and the necessary access to information to uncover (within the constraints of its mandate) economic crimes. However, if the AG's effectiveness is being compromised by resource scarcity, then this elephant in the room needs to be confronted. It is better to deploy the available resources to the AG's office to enhance their ability to do sufficiently intensive performance audits, which could expose unwarranted and irregular expenditure, than to spend excessive amounts of time attending to complicated disclosure requirements linked to fairly meaningless financial statements, where the goal is to curb economic crime.

Perhaps it is time for people to turn their attention once more to the basics of accounting, such as recording transactions when the cash flows, and limiting the use of subjective judgements and theoretical interpretations, as dictated by the relevant accounting standards. Moreover, the necessary resources need to be channelled in the right directions to ensure efficient and honest procurement and service delivery.

Can we conquer corruption in South Africa?

Can we conquer corruption (in the broadest sense of the word)? Yes, if all the relevant stakeholders (and especially the public and private sectors) collaborate in a proactive manner and their collective endeavours are infused with strong leadership and unwavering commitment. Already, much has been done, in the form of the Zondo Commission and other exposés, to highlight the extent of economic crimes in South Africa, which have had and continue to have such devastating consequences for business and society. Yet there can be no let-up in the pace at which economic crime, in all its permutations, is tackled – especially as criminals are becoming more and more creative, thanks to technological advances and lackadaisical prevention and detection efforts.

With many things in life, it is a good idea to start small in the fight against corruption and other forms of economic crime – introducing effective, yet manageable, systems and nipping trouble in the bud before it has the opportunity to escalate and become practically unstoppable. Having the necessary systems and procedures in place is therefore crucial, with 'prevention is better than cure' being an important mantra for all organisations. Of course, detection and prevention aside, *why* people are lured into economic crime is a fundamental consideration too, which lends itself to extensive debate for another day!

ELEVEN

Local government in South Africa after the 2024 election: Will the desirable or the probable outcome prevail?

Erwin Schwella

Setting the scene

Governance in the public sector in South Africa has long been tainted by corruption. President Ramaphosa and the ruling African National Congress (ANC) have confirmed this. In a letter to ANC members in 2020, the President wrote:

> Today, the ANC and its leaders stand accused of corruption. The ANC may not stand alone in the dock, but it does stand as accused number one. This is the stark reality that we must now confront. We must have the political courage and the honesty to acknowledge that ANC leaders, public representatives and members have on numerous occasions been implicated in such forms of corruption.[1]

Expanding on this destructive picture that he painted, the President said that the capture of state institutions had been facilitated by politicians and officials at the highest level. In this regard, the Zondo Commission revealed disturbing levels of grand corruption, where individuals were deliberately deployed to institutions to manipulate procurement and other processes with a view to siphoning off massive amounts of money for an elite network of mostly ANC politicians, public servants and businesspeople. It is well known that the impact of state capture has been devastating – a disaster, in fact.

Billions of rands intended for improved public transport, better infrastructure for the poor, reliable and affordable electricity, the empowerment of emerging black farmers and the broader development of South Africa were stolen to line the pockets of well-connected individuals. Many public institutions have been left deeply dysfunctional, with some virtually destroyed. Huge damage has been inflicted on the economy and the capacity of the state. Many claim that Cyril Ramaphosa's expressed good intentions to deal with bad governance have done little to spur government into action, despite the recommendations of the Zondo Commission of Inquiry into Allegations of State Capture. Current evidence suggests that the significant underperformance in recent years is continuing unabated. Indeed, extraordinarily little has changed.

In 2023, Chief Justice Raymond Zondo announced that, one year after the release of the Commission's report, extremely limited progress had been made (if any at all) in implementing the recommendations of the Commission.[2] Despite feeling proud of the role that he played in the state capture inquiry, Zondo expressed the fear that citizens remained vulnerable to the impact of corruption and other forms of malfeasance. In his view, the inadequate oversight role that Parliament played for many years has not improved. Therefore, if another group of people were to attempt state capture, they would undoubtedly succeed, as Parliament would once again fail to stop them. After all, it all boils down to the quality of governance. Was the Zondo Commission – with its painstaking analysis and well-considered recommendations – all in vain?

There is mounting substantive and substantiated evidence that governance in the public sector in South Africa has been and continues to be in a state of crisis. This is particularly apparent at the local government level. The disastrous impact of governance failures (from ethical breaches to profound service-delivery shortcomings) is evident in scores of municipalities across the country.

South Africa once again appears to be at the proverbial cross-roads, faced with the opportunity to start afresh but evidently still chained to its bad old ways. As Charles Dickens famously said in *A Tale of Two Cities*:

It was the best of times, it was the worst of times ... it was the spring of hope, it was the winter of despair, we had everything before us, we had nothing before us, we were all going direct to Heaven, we were all going direct the other way ...[3]

Sadly, current trends indicate that most South African municipalities are 'going the other way', eschewing the benefits that would flow from committed and ethical local government. Roads are in disrepair, buildings are neglected, housing and public transport are inadequate, healthcare standards are falling, utilities (like power and water) are erratic, crime is increasing, the landscape is scarred with unsightly litter, and the mood is grim.

According to Rotberg,[4] when governments perform effectively and display strong leadership, they (along with the population in general) can confidently claim their place in the global community. Among the hallmarks of effective governments are high-quality public education and healthcare, an economic model geared for sustainable growth, efficient public institutions, an orderly society, respect for the rule of law, and safe living and working environments. Other clear signs are that the arteries of commerce are not clogged with unnecessary red tape, the population enjoys myriad personal freedoms as well as a sense of belonging and commitment to their communities, and the natural environment is nurtured for the benefit of current and future generations. Government leaders are more interested in being remembered for improving the lives of many than the fortunes of a few.

Two possible future scenarios for local government in South Africa

Meier indicated that, when contemplating the future, different scenarios present themselves.[5] Some are positive and encouraging and others are quite bleak. Moreover, while some scenarios may be desirable and possible, they are not necessarily probable, given the prevailing circumstances.

The broad contextualisation provided above leads one to two possible future scenarios for local government (municipalities) in South Africa: a high-road or 'dedicated desires' scenario and a low-road or 'destructive disasters' scenario. The former is the ideal scenario for local government in South Africa, but the latter is the more probable. These two scenarios are discussed below.

Dedicated desires scenario – pie in the sky?

The 'dedicated desires' scenario draws on the provisions of the Constitution of the Republic of South Africa, 1996,[6] and the legislative, policy and service-delivery guidelines that underpinned the creation of various democratic institutions post 1994. Broadly, this scenario paints a picture of good governance and professional service delivery in all spheres of activity, including at the local government level.

For example, according to the Constitution, municipalities are mandated to provide efficient and sustainable services and to remain accountable to the communities under their administration; to ensure a safe and healthy environment; to promote social and economic development within their jurisdictions; and to cooperate with provincial and national government. The Municipal Systems Act, 2000 regulates the process of assigning powers and functions to local government.[7] Such functions include establishing a framework for planning, standard setting, and performance management and monitoring; carrying out efficient credit control and debt collection; investing in infrastructure and related services; and making provision for community participation.

Clearly, local government is critical to the proper functioning and general well-being of communities. However, large numbers of municipalities throughout South Africa have not lived up to the vision espoused in the 'dedicated desires' scenario. Their democratic transition has been far from smooth, with severe operational, managerial and financial shortcomings having become the rule rather than the exception, and poor service delivery the unfortunate outcome. Many municipalities are bereft of effective leadership; instead, they are convenient vehicles for cadre deployment and politically motivated largesse, which benefit a cabal of the well-connected at the expense of the greater population spread across cities, towns and rural communities.

The National Development Plan (NDP), launched in 2012, gave considerable attention to the responsibilities and functions of local government. To a large extent, the focus on local government was a reaction to some of the observed deficiencies (evident from the NDP diagnostics) in the ways municipalities were being run in South Africa.[8] The NDP advocated the strengthening of municipalities so that they could better serve as vehicles of effective service delivery and inclusive development.

Among the NDP's key recommendations were: building capacity among municipal officials; prioritising the development and maintenance of infrastructure; rooting out corruption and enhancing financial management (greater transparency and accountability, less wasteful expenditure, and better revenue collection and debt management); addressing the consequences of poor spatial planning; enhancing service delivery in the areas of education, housing, healthcare and other social services; supporting local economic development (including job creation) initiatives; ensuring sustainable environmental practices; and promoting active citizen engagement and participation.

Evidence, however, shows that very few, if any, of these recommendations were acted upon, with the result that the quality of local government has in most cases not improved. In fact, it has worsened. Even the importance attached to '*ubuntu*' in African culture has not been able to reverse the steady deterioration in the ethical character and performance of municipalities. Bolden described *ubuntu* as an alternative to individualistic and utilitarian philosophies.[9] Broadly, it refers to 'humanness', meaning that a person is a person only through other people. It therefore begs the question: is *ubuntu* frequently spoken about but seldom practised?

Destructive disasters scenario – the more probable outcome?

The 'dedicated desires' scenario – so vividly described in the NDP and other plans, policies and blueprints for the country – has been eclipsed by a host of problems that more closely mirror the 'destructive disasters' scenario.

No disaster of governance can come close to the unmitigated governance disaster perpetuated by apartheid, largely because of the sheer magnitude of the neglect shown towards marginalised non-white communities. However, with the start of the post-apartheid era, there was a genuine desire to turn the page on the past and embrace healthy transformation, evidenced in community engagement, efficient service delivery, clear accountability and observance of the rule of law. The 'dedicated desires' scenario quickly began to take shape, fuelled by widespread optimism and the reformulation of many local government regulations and procedures.

During the Mandela and first Mbeki administrations, there were signs that the 'dedicated desires' scenario was gaining traction. Progress was being made in fulfilling the promises outlined in the new, post-1994 legislation, policies and service delivery guidelines. However, things started to slip during the second Mbeki administration, with confidence in government taking a knock in the wake of the HIV/AIDS (denial) debacle and the Zimbabwe diplomatic relations disaster.

And then came the Zuma administration. At the annual meeting of the World Economic Forum (WEF) in 2019, President Ramaphosa (Zuma's successor) referred to the nine lost years under the Zuma presidency, a period in which the country lost its way and succumbed to widespread governance failures and corruption. Although Ramaphosa, upon his election as president, was seen to be the embodiment of hope, with an ability to restore the fading 'dedicated desires' scenario, his commitment and capabilities have been increasingly called into question, as corruption has remained rampant and performance at all levels of government has been on a downward spiral.

An African National Congress (ANC) stalwart and previous government minister, Mathews Phosa, recently asserted that the reality in Africa is that 'colonisation was replaced by "theft at state level" [with] politicians cooking up deals benefiting them selling state assets to Chinese and other foreign companies'. Referring to 'most' African countries, he continued: 'We steal like hell from taxpayers ... South Africa is throttled by corruption. There are always unaccountable billions of rands at municipal level. We are not accountable. We've got a bunch of thieves ruling us.'[10]

Mathews was not coy when he described the crumbling road infrastructure, the electricity woes, the decaying schools, the floods of sewage spilling onto the roads, the unfilled potholes – all pointing to the fact that the country's leaders have no plan. Nelson Mandela was his hero, and he believed that there was no corruption under Mbeki. But after Mbeki, the rot set in, and it was allowed to fester and grow. A major contributing factor, according to Phosa, is that Ramaphosa is indecisive. Chief Justice Zondo declared that a year after Ramaphosa had received the Zondo Commission report, no real action had been taken. Phosa emphasised that a country cannot be run by commissions and committees. Ramaphosa must take decisions, and his priority should be to destroy the rot.

Tracking the decline in local government in South Africa since 1994

The decline in local government in South Africa should be seen within the context of deteriorating governance and professional service delivery. The evidence can be found in reports from various observers of municipalities, including official constitutional oversight structures in South Africa. A selection of these is covered below.

Auditor-General South Africa

The Auditor-General South Africa (AGSA) is a constitutional Chapter 9 oversight institution. It produces annual audit reports on all government departments and public entities, including municipalities. Municipalities are subject to local governance and service delivery requirements under the Municipal Finance Management Act, 2003. AGSA states that the aim of its municipal audits is the following:

> We focus on auditing areas that matter to achieve the country's sustainable development goals and objectives. These focus areas use a majority of our public funds and have the greatest impact on the lives of our people. They therefore require stringent oversight to ensure that our people feel the benefit of these services and those funds are used in a way that creates the best value for money for the people of our country.[11]

Since 1994, the results of the municipal audits have been on a consistent downward trajectory. The AGSA report on local government audit outcomes (2016–17) lamented the decline in the performance of municipalities since 2011–12 and their repeated failure to heed the advice and recommendations of the AGSA.[12] In the 2011–12 audit year, there were already clear signs of weakness in internal controls, and things got steadily worse after that.

The most recent AGSA report on local government audit outcomes (2021–22) confirms this decline:

> Our previous general report showed that the local government audit outcomes were in a poor state when the previous administration took over in 2016–17 and did not improve over its term. The administration was characterised by accountability and service delivery failures, poor governance, weak institutional capacity, and instability. The behaviour and conduct of leaders and officials led to a local government culture that was largely devoid of performance, accountability, transparency, and integrity.[13]

The report cited poor planning and reporting on basic services, failing infrastructure, deteriorating financial health, ineffective financial reporting practices, procurement and payment transgressions, and inefficient use of information technology systems. Disclaimed audit opinions were all too frequent. Of particular concern was the absence of consequences for wrongdoing, which meant that there was little incentive to improve. There were some exceptions, with the municipalities in question working diligently to serve their communities and deliver a strong overall performance. However, these cases are quite rare, and the number of star performers is dwindling as times go by.

At most municipalities, irregular expenditure has increased – sometimes dramatically. Relatively few municipalities produce quality financial statements that receive clean audits, and only a small percentage of municipalities are deemed to be fully compliant with key pieces of legislation.

Not surprisingly, President Ramaphosa recently weighed in on the governance crisis at the local government level, stating:

> Government needs to urgently address service delivery issues at local government level that can mostly be ascribed to a lack of requisite skills and competencies, governance failures and lack of accountability and inadequate consequence management. It is vital that we enhance the mobilisation of resources to be provided

by national and provincial Government to support and strengthen the capacity of municipalities in the exercise of their powers and performance of their functions in accordance with section 154 of the Constitution. Our Constitution acknowledges that local government is everybody's business.[14]

And, as usual, given the 'shock' that President Ramaphosa feels at the parlous state of the country's municipalities, he is likely to engage in prolonged consultations and assemble a war room or a commission of inquiry to thoroughly investigate the consistent failures at the local level.

Organisation Undoing Tax Abuse

The Organisation Undoing Tax Abuse (OUTA) is a civil society organisation whose mission is to fight tax abuse and other financial crime in South Africa. In a recent blog, it stated:

> Every year we see service delivery getting worse, our roads getting more potholes, our water quality deteriorating or being interrupted, and electricity coming and going. Yet municipal charges increase, and politicians get clever in adding additional tariffs to generate more money, whilst municipalities are externalising costs to residents who are forced to start looking after themselves. We see more people buying bottled water, fixing potholes, or cleaning the curbs. As civil society, we now need to draw a line in the sand.[15]

Corruption Watch

In 2021, Corruption Watch reported on the failures of local government to deal with corruption, stating that more than 5 000 whistle-blowers had approached the organisation since 2012 with personal accounts of corruption at the local government level.[16] These accounts provide a chilling snapshot of how some municipalities have been captured to serve private interests, how municipal managers abuse their power and position, and how procurement and employment processes are continuously subverted – all of which result in vulnerable communities being denied access to basic services, which is a human right.

Edelman Trust Barometer

Trust in government is strongly correlated with perceptions of legitimacy and legality of public institutions. At present, South Africans' trust in government is at a low ebb. The 2023 Edelman Trust Barometer South Africa report shows that South Africa has the largest percentage-point difference (40 points) between trust in business and trust in government among all the countries surveyed, with 62 per cent trusting business and 22 per cent trusting government.[17]

Human Sciences Research Council

The Human Sciences Research Council (HSRC) tracks trust in government over a longer period, using the annual South African Social Attitudes Survey. Surveys conducted over the years revealed that from 2003–2021, there was a consistent decrease in trust in all three spheres of government (national, provincial and local). Of particular concern is that the dismally low level of trust in national government is still higher than trust in provincial and local government.

Joleen Steyn and Ben Rogers, the researchers involved in the HSRC surveys, report that the mood among South Africans has definitely soured.[18] Some of the signs of this are declining levels of satisfaction with democracy and life in general, a growing sense of despondency and heightened fears about the future. The despondency about democracy is particularly worrying and does not auger well for the future of democracy in South Africa. Previous studies on attitudes in South Africa revealed that while South Africans were becoming increasingly dissatisfied with democracy, their satisfaction with life in general remained intact. More recent results, however, show a significant decline in satisfaction with life due to increased despondency about the perceived failings of democracy, deteriorating political efficacy and mediocre public service delivery. There is a growing sense of hopelessness, which could potentially trigger political instability in the future.

Steyn and Rogers emphasise that these disturbing trends witnessed in South Africa in recent years have been strongly influenced by people's perceptions of the quality of government, the trustworthiness of institutions and the value of democracy. Those who have more positive attitudes are also more positively disposed towards government and its ability to deliver services to a reasonable standard, including water and electricity supply, sanitation, tackling of crime and corruption, job creation and the administration of social grants. Those who believe that the standard of service delivery has deteriorated have a more negative outlook. Similarly, those who trust the national and local government, Parliament, the Electoral Commission of South Africa (IEC), political parties and politicians display more optimism than those who are more sceptical about these entities.

Figure 11.1 illustrates the link between survey respondents' satisfaction with democracy and their anticipated satisfaction with life over the next five years, tracked over the period 2014–2021.

Figure 11.1: Link between satisfaction with democracy and anticipated satisfaction with life over the next five years

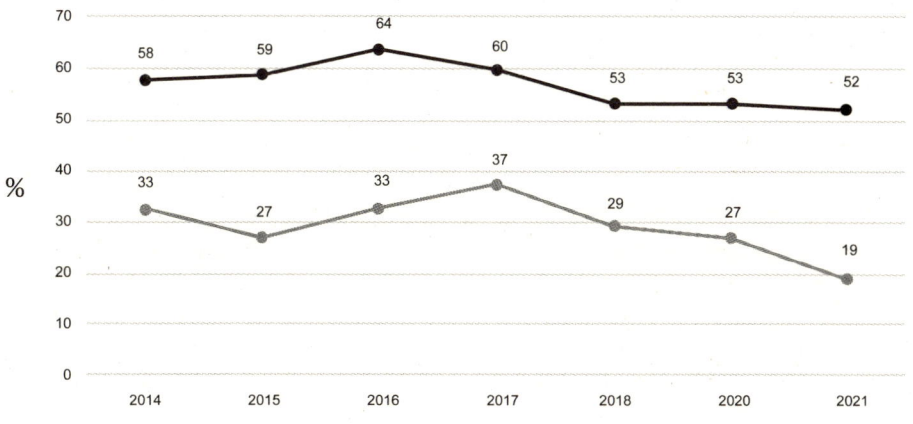

% saying life will improve for those satisfied with democracy

Source: HSRC, South African Social Attitudes Survey (SASAS), 2014–2021

On average, the difference between the two groups was 28 per cent in 2014, rising to 33 per cent in 2021.

Evidence suggests that South Africans are becoming increasingly concerned about poor governance and service delivery, particularly within municipalities, which in turn influences their impressions of democracy. Expectations of, and trust in, government are at record-low levels and are continuing to decline. As 'democracy despondency' increases, so too does a sense of hopelessness among many South Africa.

Understanding the decline in local government in South Africa: Provisional hypotheses

Why, in the context of local government in South Africa, has the 'dedicated desires' scenario become increasingly hazy and out of reach, while the 'destructive disasters' scenario has moved to centre stage? Schwella applied a systems-thinking approach to address this question.[19]

Systems thinking is defined by the World Health Organization (WHO) as:

> ... an approach to problem-solving that views problems as part of a wider dynamic system. It recognizes and prioritizes the understanding of linkages, relationships, interactions, and interdependencies among the components of a system that give rise to the system's observed behaviour. Systems thinking is a philosophical frame, and it can also be considered a method with its own tools.[20]

Schwella specifically assessed current local government performance and the likelihood of it improving by asking the following reflective–practice questions:
- What happened?
  (This provided an evidence-based assessment of performance and performance trends, based on measured evidence.)
- Why did this happen?
  (This formed the basis of a diagnostic probability performance analysis looking at those actions that led to increased or decreased performance.)
- What lessons can be learnt?
  (This should contribute to personal mastery, individual and team learning, systems thinking and improved mental models through learning.)
- How can the learning be built back into the system for systemic quality and performance improvement?
  (This should enhance prognostic institutional capacity-building

with a view to encouraging continuous improvement in governance.)

In dealing with complex adaptive problems, systems thinking requires a specific epistemology and ontology, on the basis of which valid and reliable hypotheses can be formulated. When following a systems-thinking approach, it needs to be borne in mind that easily observable symptoms are often insufficient for explaining the nature of the problem, its causes, impact and possible solutions. Two techniques can be used to overcome this problem: the iceberg metaphor and the 5 Why?s method.

The iceberg metaphor, explained by Evbuoma et al.,[21] is a classic metaphor used in many disciplines applying systems thinking. It postulates that what is visible at the tip of the iceberg (which helps to answer the question 'What happened?') is only a small observable portion of a much larger, hidden mass beneath the surface (which is heavily linked to 'Why did this happen?'). The metaphor is used to systematically probe and systemically expose the underlying forces that are driving the observable actions.

The 5 Why?s method starts with a grounded problem definition and then proceeds to ask and answer the first Why? question. This generates a realistic and valid (on face value) answer. This answer is then interrogated with the second Why? question. The answer is dealt with in the same way as in the previous round, and so the process continues. After a few rounds, the root causes start to emerge – in contrast to the superficial generalised observation arrived at initially (which may, in fact, be confirmed as correct after all, after a more probing analysis). The 5 Why?s method is valuable in uncovering the deeper, systemic structural issues (influenced, for example, by conflicting mindsets and goals) that are impacting the system at a fundamental level.

The iceberg metaphor and 5 Why?s methods were used to generate empirically sound evidence of why local government systems and municipalities in South Africa are failing. In other words, it was possible to explore beyond what appeared to be obvious causes but were often only superficial symptoms or causes of deep-seated, systemic problems. Superficial findings are not necessarily invalid or untrue, but they grossly oversimplify the complexity and/

or depth of the problems and cannot be relied upon when solutions are being sought.

When a superficial analysis is not accompanied by a more in-depth and systematic probe into the problem, it can lead to distraction or obfuscation and provide a convenient excuse not to dig deeper to expose potential perils below the surface. This is very dangerous, particularly as compromised or corrupt individuals may be unashamedly 'feeding from the trough', but their actions are going unnoticed or being overlooked, and so their toxicity is allowed to spread. The lack of clarity can also encourage blame-shifting and a propensity to do nothing because it is 'someone else's fault' or 'problem'. Blame-shifting and shirking of responsibility can occur in the face of, for example, under-funding, incompetence, lack of commitment, bad leadership, onerous regulatory and compliance requirements, and deliberate sabotage of the operation.

The questions 'What happened?' and 'Why did this happen?' are linked in complex ways. For example, the underperformance of a particular municipality may be plain to see – in its poor service delivery record, in its financial mismanagement, in its disclaimed audit reports and in its dysfunctional council. *Why* this underperformance is allowed to persist might be attributed to various (but not necessarily obvious) factors.

The analysis by Schwella generated some provisional descriptions of South African municipalities, based on their governance and service delivery quality (in other words, 'what happened?'). The evidence points to a dangerous weakening of local government. The performance of most municipalities is exceptionally low and is highly indicative of the 'destructive disasters' scenario. Flowing from the analysis, some reasons (albeit provisional) can be provided for the parlous state of local government (in other words, 'why did this happen?):

- Corruption and other forms of financial malfeasance are alive and well, with some officials being more intent on looting the municipality's coffers than serving the community. This is not helped by the lack of adequate (or any) consequence management. In other words, mismanagement and corruption are actually incentivised.
- The proceeds from corruption typically, and often handsomely,

benefit privileged (but incompetent) insiders who act with impunity. If allegations are made against certain individuals, they usually put on a display of vehement denial and feigned indignation in order to obfuscate and deflect attention. Without a thorough investigation (which may be costly and inconvenient to the implicated parties), the problem often just goes away.
- There is a deeply embedded culture of unprofessionalism, manifesting as a lack of dedication and discipline. In such an environment, committed and selfless leadership and service delivery (with an emphasis on 'service') are foreign concepts. Clearly, too, the concept of *ubuntu* has no place.
- Appointments are often made on the basis of connections and political loyalty rather than skills and merit, which means that incompetence and unprofessionalism become the norm. There is an acute lack of technical and managerial skills, which translates directly into poor service delivery. Yet poor performance (even in the absence of corruption) rarely prompts the provincial administration to act decisively to remedy the situation.
- Municipal councils are often dysfunctional, with council meetings dominated by political posturing and the tabling of spurious votes of no confidence aimed at securing a contrived change of leadership (such as the mayor, deputy mayor, chief whip and municipal manager). In other words, council meetings are often political playgrounds, with inadequate attention being given to the work that needs to be done.
- Although communities across South Africa are growing increasingly unhappy about poor service delivery, evident corruption and a dismissive attitude from municipalities, they often extend the lives of the political parties in charge of the municipalities by voting for them, out of blind loyalty, in successive local elections – or by not voting at all, which may result in the same culpable parties retaining their positions.

These proffered reasons for the parlous state of a large number of municipalities in South Africa have even deeper roots – they are linked to the beliefs, mindsets and goals of many politicians and government officials who are knowingly perpetuating a dire situation. Who, then, put them up to it? Or is there an innate gene that deprives people of conscience and triggers self-seeking behaviour?

The governing party, the African National Congress (ANC), has much to answer for. First, it has a confused ideology. It supports (or pays lip service to?) the Constitution and harks back to the values embodied by Nelson Mandela who envisaged freedom and opportunities for all. However, at the same time, it neglects large swathes of people in favour of keeping the ANC flame alive at all costs and rewarding party loyalists. It has opted for a self-serving definition of 'transformation' rather than a more holistic definition, as set out in section 195 of the Constitution.

The ANC also perpetuates the notion of it being a revolutionary liberation movement, which still needs to 'fight' for freedom from oppression, when it should have adopted the mantle of a mature political party which has the power to bring about considerable change in the country and, moreover, is primarily answerable to the people (and not to itself). The liberation narrative is clear obfuscation, designed to blame the past for the lack of progress to date and to whip up ideological fervour when what is required are practical solutions to serious (but resolvable) problems.

Another area of confusion is that the ANC conveys different attitudes in different contexts, from socialist to populist to capitalist. Also, the well-publicised divisions within the ANC itself, especially in the higher echelons, has a paralysing effect on the effectiveness of the party and its ability to provide leadership in a fast-moving modern world.

The ANC does not run all the municipalities in the country. Some municipalities are run by other political parties or by coalitions of parties. But the ANC sets the tone in national government and most provincial governments, and local government structures inevitably look upwards for guidance. That is how leadership – however good or bad – tends to work.

Conclusion

What lessons can be learnt from the above analysis of the state of South Africa's municipalities? Unfortunately, the most obvious takeaway is that history is repeating itself, again and again, at the local government level, with the very strong likelihood that the 'destructive disasters' scenario will prevail in future. There appears to be insufficient resolve within the municipalities themselves to change the status quo, while the higher powers (at the provincial and national government level) similarly lack the enthusiasm to drive a much-needed turnaround; nor do they see the urgency in doing so.

Those most severely affected are millions of ordinary people in South Africa, from all walks of life, who are entitled to safe and vibrant communities, efficient service delivery from government in exchange for their hard-earned tax contributions, and the comfort of knowing that the country and its provinces, cities and towns are being capably run.

That is why the upcoming 2024 election in South Africa is so important. It puts the power into people's hands to change the unacceptable trajectory onto which the government has allowed the country to stray and which society as a whole appears not to be sufficiently up in arms about. The Preamble to the Constitution is a clear reminder of what the collective vision of South Africans should be:

> We, the people of South Africa, recognise the injustices of our past; honour those who suffered for justice and freedom in our land; respect those who have worked to build and develop our country; and believe that South Africa belongs to all who live in it, united in our diversity.

No one is asking the people of South Africa to forget the past. But the past (especially the recent past) should be full of important lessons that should inform the future. At this juncture, the fat cats appear to be in the lead. But the race isn't over yet.

TWELVE

Finding new, bottom-up solutions to grassroots socioeconomic challenges

Vuyiswa Ramokgopa

Introduction

Thirty years have passed since the advent of democracy in South Africa and the country is at an inflection point. For the first time in our democratic history, there is a broad national consensus that things are not working, and that urgent change is required. Business and civil society leaders are united in their frustrations over the current crisis gripping the country, which has largely been brought about by a failure of political leadership.

Addressing a gathering of over 500 people on the 40th anniversary of the United Democratic Front (UDF), Archbishop Makgoba, the Archbishop of the Anglican Church in Cape Town, lamented: 'We are mired in the mud of corruption. We are a country marred by the most glaring inequality in the world. Services we built for our people have collapsed in some areas, and too many public servants have forgotten they are servants of the public.' He announced a call to action: 'We need to mobilise our energy, our courage, our imagination, our skills and our political will, and channel them into a mighty stream, just as we did against the apartheid state, 40 years ago.'[1]

As the state of crisis deepens and the proverbial cliff edge comes into view, calls to mobilise a mass movement for change have been resonating increasingly among those who might otherwise have considered themselves to be apolitical or outside of the mainstream political discourse. The tragedy of having to watch a once-revered nation descend into chaos and dysfunction at the hands of those who were once hailed as its heroes has become a burden almost too weighty to bear.

In its first decade of democracy, South Africa inspired the world as the miracle country that had transcended its deep historical divisions and a racially oppressive minority government, emerging victorious. We chose peace and unity over hate and divisiveness. We overcame the insurmountable and demonstrated to the world what the power of millions of people, choosing to stand up for what is right, could achieve. Those of us who had the pleasure of experiencing this moment in history will know the overwhelming sense of euphoria and optimism that permeated the air between 1994 and 1998. Our problems were far from over, but we were not consumed by them. Our untreated pain and trauma were concealed by our hope for a brighter and better future. We felt nourished by the belief that anything was possible and that a better life for all awaited us!

The 'rainbow-nation' era defined us and cemented our core values of non-racialism, democracy and constitutionalism. While 1994 saw the official birth of our democracy and the 'new South Africa', as it was known (a simple but effective phrase that was used to describe our infant nation), 2024 marks our move into adulthood. We are now required to take our seat at the adult table and make some tough decisions. Just as most young adults, leaving their childhood behind, experience the thrill of independence for the first time but also trepidation at leaving the comfort of their parents' home, we are filled with both excitement and apprehension. If we seize this moment and fail, what bleak future awaits us? While such concerns are perfectly normal, they are completely inadequate given the magnitude of the crisis that we face, which will undoubtedly worsen if we do not deal with it decisively.

The South African economy has largely stagnated, and real gross domestic product (GDP) has not grown since 2012. In 2018, the World Bank labelled South Africa the 'most unequal country in the world with a consumption per capita Gini coefficient of 67'.[2] This is further exacerbated by the country's staggering youth unemployment which at last count was 60.7 per cent in the 15–24 age range and approaching 40 per cent in the 25–34 age range.

The National Development Plan (NDP) published in 2012 was underpinned by a vision to build a developmental state. The Ten-Year Review of the NDP published in September 2023 clearly illustrates that while there have been successes – such as almost universal access to electricity and water and general improvements in literacy and overall education levels – most measurable economic objectives of the NDP have not been achieved. Instead of a developmental state, the economic policy followed by the African National Congress (ANC) has effectively turned South Africa into a paternalistic welfare state. The adoption of a largely state subsidy-driven approach means that 28 million people now rely on a monthly social grant as a basic means of income. Meanwhile, the black economic empowerment policy has effectively suffocated black industrial development and created a black elite class that is highly dependent on state procurement and public-sector employment.

While the ruling party would have us believe that these examples are signs of success, they in fact highlight a disturbing reality: that society has become increasingly reliant on the welfare of the state, while key indicators of economic progress have all but stagnated – or regressed. As things stand, there are no evident prospects of such a trend being reversed. Put differently, fewer people earn a salary and a greater share of the population, many of whom are young black Africans, are dependent on social grants as their only source of income. This puts additional financial strain on the few who do earn because they have to support unemployed relatives or contribute a greater share of their income in the form of taxes. This situation is obviously not sustainable. If we expect to see a different result from that which the past three decades have delivered, we need to do things differently. For the approximately 8 million unemployed South Africans, we need to offer a new and compelling deal, which will guarantee them and millions of others an equitable stake in the gains from our democracy.

If we are sincere about wanting to turn things around and deliver on the promises made in 1994, the most pressing question is: how do we grow the economy in a manner that is fair, that equitably distributes the gains from that growth, that ensures that more people earn a living wage from the work that they do, and that ensures that citizens are active participants in their own lives rather than mere beneficiaries? Another way to frame this would be: how do we build (in a single generation) an economy that is truly inclusive, modern, identifiably African and globally competitive? The next 30 years *must* be about growth, but they must also be about transforming the structure, nature and focus of the South African economy so that it fosters a common purpose, leverages our natural endowments and strengths, harnesses modern technology and innovation, honours our cultural values, and raises our collective ambitions and capabilities.

In 2020, the World Economic Forum (WEF) popularised the phrase 'the great reset' in response to the global changes in labour markets, global trade, socioeconomic dynamics and global health policies, which had been brought about by the Covid-19 pandemic. As explained by the WEF chairperson, Klaus Schwab, the great reset aims to 'create the conditions for a stakeholder economy ... advance shared goals, such as equality and sustainability and harness the innovations of the Fourth Industrial Revolution to support the public good'.[3]

While the West has largely returned to 'default settings' post Covid, the questions prompted by the great reset remain ever present, if not more urgent, in South Africa. For example, there are questions surrounding the impact of harmful environmental practices on (mostly) rural communities, the role and response of corporates and the private sector in times of political and economic crisis, and the ever-widening chasm between the haves and the have-nots.

This is now also an opportunity to evaluate whether, in the 30 years since the birth of our democracy, we have indeed achieved the 1994 promise of 'a non-racist, non-sexist, democratic South Africa for all' and if not, what needs to be done to enable the fulfilment of this promise for future generations. In attempting to answer this question, we will find a clue in the last two words – 'for all'. The metric that we use to measure our overall success as a country should be our ability to demonstrate socioeconomic progress equitably for all citizens, regardless of the circumstances that they were born into or their place of birth. A promise of social progress or social mobility is a promise that a child born into a low-income family will not be prohibited by the circumstances of their birth from improving their economic circumstances over time. It is also a promise that, all things remaining equal, their children will in turn be born into significantly better economic circumstances.

These promises are not being fulfilled. While the existence of an enabling national industrial policy is important for driving economic growth and large-scale employment, the kind of far-reaching socioeconomic transformation that we desire ultimately needs to be driven from the bottom up, by the people, and must be led and owned by communities and adequately supported at the local level. The next era of development *must*, therefore, be about building self-sustaining, empowered communities and shifting from the current top-down, paternalistic and heavily state-dependent model to a bottom-up, community-led approach where government is a partner and an enabler to local communities rather than simply a provider, funder and employer.

The ups and downs of broad-based black economic empowerment

Black economic empowerment has been one of the flagship economic redistribution policies of the ANC. Since the policy's inception in 2003, its focus has been on creating black wealth through state procurement and transfers of share ownership (private sector), diversifying management and boards of formerly white-owned companies, and procuring goods and services from black suppliers (generally in lower-value segments of the value chain). Another (but less-discussed) area of focus, which has actually been a success, is the transformation of the state and the demographic composition of state-controlled entities and departments. This has been a catalyst for the growth of the black middle class and has provided a launching pad for senior black executives, many of whom have gone on to apply their skills in the private sector.[4]

The Broad-Based Black Economic Empowerment (B-BBEE) Amendment Act, 2013 sought to engineer a shift from a largely equity ownership-focused approach to one that gives greater emphasis to other measures, such as enterprise and supplier development (ESD), corporate social investment and socioeconomic development. However, it is notable that socioeconomic development, which accounts for only 5 points in the 168-point scorecard, contributes the least to the overall score which can be achieved by a 'measured entity'.

Local economic development and localisation

There has also been an increased focus by government over the past decade, through institutions like the South African Local Government Association (SALGA), on local economic development and 'localisation'. The objectives of local economic development are to drive collective decision making, instil a sense of joint ownership and community participation in the local economy, and ensure sustainability. However, the manner in which community development initiatives have been implemented and the current interface with local government have not fostered true public participation, with such initiatives largely remaining state driven (top down).

What is needed, therefore, is an active shift from empowerment of the few to empowerment of the many by investing in the creation of self-sustaining communities who are empowered legislatively and in other ways to drive their own development. This does not mean that everything should be privatised and that the state should be absolved of its responsibilities – quite the contrary, in fact. In empowering communities, we must bring government, state-funded support programmes, business finance and access to credit closer to the people and enable higher levels of accountability and ownership by communities.

A 2022 report published by the B-BBEE Commission, titled 'Measuring the Effective Implementation of Enterprise and Supplier Development Funding', revealed that of the approximately R26 billion spent on small, medium and micro enterprise (SMME) support programmes (covering mentorship, capacity-building and financial support), the provision of loans to small businesses has been the least used of all permissible support mechanisms. This is mainly because it is deemed too difficult to implement and monitor, and therefore often fails to yield the desired outcomes. It has also proven to be challenging to identify and incorporate bona fide small business owners, especially those who operate in the informal sector or in less-accessible locations.

One of the ways in which this problem can be addressed is by localising the disbursement and management of state-sponsored business grant funding as well as private-sector SMME ESD funds. Institutions should be established to facilitate the administration of these grant funds via local credit-granting institutions which can be subsidised via a combination of state grant funding and private-sector contributions. In the United States (US), these are referred to as community development finance institutions. As the name suggests, they perform the very important function of providing different types of development funding to under-resourced communities and communities that cannot be reached with traditional financing.

One of the unique features of the US economy and a notable feature of its banking sector is the decentralisation of banking and the ease of access to credit enabled by community banks. There are approximately 4 500 community banks in the US, which is a dramatic decline since 2008 when there were over 7 000. However, they still make up the majority of retail banks in the country. Defined as banks with less than 'US$10 billion in assets', community banks play a critical role in 'providing traditional banking services in local communities, obtaining deposits locally and providing many of their loans to local businesses'.[5] Unlike mutual banks, which are collectively owned by depositors or a cooperative financial institution that is owned by its members, community banks are usually privately owned but are managed by local residents and have roots in the local community. This makes it easier to conduct risk assessments for lending to small businesses and fosters a sense of ownership, while encouraging reinvestment in the local economy.

Currently, South Africa's financial sector comprises banks, mutual banks, credit providers, short-term insurers, long-term insurers, cooperative banks and registered cooperative financial institutions. Although our traditional financial services sector is internationally recognised for its high levels of sophistication and security, access thereto – and particularly access to credit through traditional secured-lending channels – remains a challenge for most of the population, who are asset-poor. This has resulted in the rapid growth of the microlending industry, which also includes informal, unregulated microlenders. The approximately 810 000 rotational savings groups known as 'stokvels', which have more than 11 million members in South Africa, play an important role in boosting short-term household savings. However, they usually exist for the purpose of funding consumption-related activities as opposed to economic development and income-generating activity.

To catalyse local economic development and the growth of local businesses as well as improve average incomes in under-resourced communities, the growth must be driven by communities themselves. To achieve this, though, there need to be sufficient avenues for locally based small business owners and households to access affordable credit with which to finance their growth.

Active citizenry: From democracy to 'do-ocracy'

In recent months, I had the pleasure of travelling to various towns, cities and communities across all nine provinces in South Africa and speaking both formally and informally with hundreds of people from all walks of life. These conversations were political in nature in that they centred on people's lived experiences and the issues that mattered most to them and how they wished to see these issues resolved. The discussions were never easy. They evoked raw and painful emotions as the people described their daily lives and the specific ways in which they are personally affected by the inadequate provision of government services. One of the most poignant accounts was that of children having to get up very early on winter mornings, while it was still dark, to haul buckets of water from a supply point down the street – just so that they could have warm water to wash in before school, and all because a local energy transformer, which had broken many months before, had not been repaired.

These conversations serve as a daily reminder that the political choices we make are not just ideological in nature; they have real and far-reaching consequences for the daily lived experiences of the people of South Africa. A recurring theme that cropped up in the conversations was the extent to which people felt alienated and distant from the decisions of government and, by extension, from government itself. They reported feeling powerless and deeply angered by the uncaring way in which politicians behave with impunity, accountable only to themselves and their parties. They bemoaned the state of their forgotten communities and the burden of poverty and unemployment on their mental health and well-being. They also cynically described how politicians came and spoke to them every five years (around election time) and then disappeared after that, rarely – if ever – to be seen again.

This is a common refrain that is heard in almost every community throughout the country. What is fascinating is that, despite living under extraordinarily challenging or unbearable conditions, many people have not given up. There are various community-led entities and non-governmental organisations (NGOs) – most of which are small and unfunded – that operate in communities. These organisations are often led by fierce and fearless community leaders who themselves have very little but have taken it upon themselves to shoulder the burden of providing some modicum of relief to the destitute, hungry and hopeless. In many instances, these community leaders are young people who have never had the opportunity to be employed but are bursting with untapped energy and ideas. And most of these leaders are women.

For example, one of the female community figures whom I engaged with was a community organiser named Hilda who was based in Soshanguve, a township about 40 kilometres north-east of Pretoria.[6] She was 38 with three children and had not been in 'formal employment' for 10 years. However, every day she put her considerable reserves of energy to good use by organising activities for the numerous unemployed women who lived in her community, such as community clean-up campaigns, skills workshops, community vegetable gardens and group counselling sessions, which she managed from her backyard. She also recently started a daycare centre, converting a covered driveway and back room into a safe space for children whose mothers were employed in town and were therefore absent for long stretches of the day.

Hilda is what many would describe as an 'active citizen'. She does not receive any fixed remuneration for her efforts; instead, she shares the little that she has with as many people as possible – largely in the form of food and drinks, once the day's activities have come to an end. She has chosen not to be discouraged by her circumstances but rather to activate change in her community. Despite the contention by some leaders in the political establishment that South Africa is a 'passive society' made up of 'people who cannot do anything for themselves ... who sit and wait for service delivery',[7] there is a counter argument – that the spirit of activism and active citizenry is indeed alive and well in South Africa and must be harnessed and unlocked to drive long-term socioeconomic transformation.

The importance of community organising

For active citizenry to thrive, there needs to be a return to community organising. Local communities should proactively and consistently organise, not just to express their discontent through protest but also to drive community action and enable information sharing on an ongoing basis. Community organising can be defined as 'the process by which people come together to identify common problems or goals, mobilise resources, and develop and implement strategies for reaching the objectives they want to accomplish'.[8] It is the seed from which political power is harvested and is one of the most effective ways for marginalised or under-served communities to be heard and have their needs addressed.

What many community organisers lack, but urgently need if they are to deliver impactful results, is ready access to information, resources (financial and non-financial), and state facilities and support programmes. Citizens need a new way of working with (mostly local) government, one that is collaborative and envisions a two-way exchange of value. This is heavily dependent on the quality of the public representatives elected at the local level. Local government is the 'face of our democracy' and the primary delivery vehicle of services to communities all over South Africa. The quality and calibre of leadership at local government level therefore matters – perhaps even more than at the provincial and national levels.

Local (ward) councillors are the primary interface between government and the community and should (in an ideal world) be responsible for keeping residents informed, attending to their grievances and ensuring broad participation in matters of interest to that community. This is the layer of government where, it can be argued, we need the most skilled, competent and selfless leaders who are able to solve problems and ameliorate the daily frustrations experienced by residents.

Instead, local government has become overly politicised and is deemed by many to be of lower standing than provincial and national government, thereby attracting lower-ranking party members and people with limited prospects, outside of political-party deployment, of moving into leadership roles. The proof of this is in the numbers. For example, 31 per cent of municipalities in South Africa are deemed dysfunctional.⁹ On the ground, the community organisers and local leaders who make the mistake of being 'too effective' are often victimised and threatened and their programmes sabotaged by ward councillors and their henchmen. Even the simple act of booking and using a community hall has become politicised, and access to these facilities is limited to those with political proximity and is often subject to 'approval' by the local ward councillors. While ward councillors can be directly elected (as independent candidates), they are generally affiliated with, or they represent, a political party, thus creating an additional layer of accountability between the representative and the residents. Councillors are perceived, first, to represent their party and, second, to represent the ward, which is certainly not how the system was designed.

A paradigm shift is required, which reflects the critical importance of local government. We must all commit to creating an enabling environment for the best and most highly skilled people in society to lead and govern – even at the local/municipal and ward levels. The eligibility requirements for leadership positions in local government should therefore be higher than they currently are, and remuneration policies should be flexible enough to attract and retain top talent from all segments of society.

Furthermore, nowhere is political accountability more critical than in local government. We need to ensure that accountability mechanisms and measures are optimised and actually used. Councillors should be required to host regular community meetings and report back to the appropriate oversight body on key issues arising from those meetings and the progress that has been made towards resolving them. This should be overseen by both the local council and the political party to which the member belongs. Communities also need to ensure that they are better organised and geared for change so that the responsible parties follow through on their commitments.

In rural areas or communities that fall under traditional leadership, much can be learnt from 'the old ways of doing things'. In this context, local tribal councils or '*kgoro*', as they are known in Northern Sotho, would ordinarily play an invaluable role in overseeing the affairs of the community and providing a forum for democratic decision making and consultation. Residents would submit their grievances to the tribal council for deliberation by the Chief and other members of the council. The issues deliberated upon by the tribal council could range from seeking approval for the building of a new highway to mediating a stock-theft dispute between residents. The tribal council has a dual role in that it acts as a town hall and a local court, ensuring that justice is delivered swiftly and transparently, that relevant matters and decisions are communicated widely, and that buy-in is sought from the community on important decisions taken by leaders on their behalf. Although the Chief or King is not a democratically elected official, the practices described above are inherently democratic.

Over time, and with the shift to elected councillors and councils, citizens have become increasingly disconnected from decision making and, in particular, from the individuals who are supposed to be leading and representing them. Other than legal action or rates boycotts, there are few ways to hold elected officials accountable when it is not an election period. This creates distrust and causes a loss of confidence in the system as a whole, while also contributing to the overall dysfunction and decay of communities. Coalition governments comprising a collection of minority parties add an extra layer of complexity, leaving residents confused as to where accountability really lies when it comes to governance and/or the provision of services.

Community empowerment: The key to lasting socioeconomic change in South Africa

If we are to succeed in reversing the current trajectory of economic decline and social fragmentation, we must begin at the level of the community by insisting on greater levels of community participation in the affairs of government. Citizens should be encouraged and enabled to participate in the ongoing 'performance management' of their councillors, and the latter's performance should in turn be overseen by the council. Section 42 of the Municipal Systems Act, 2000 states that 'a municipality must involve the local community in the development, implementation and review of the municipality's performance management system'.[10] However, the lived experience of many residents tells a different tale. Ward committees are the forums where such ongoing engagement is supposed to be taking place. Yet, in many communities, ward committees no longer play the role they were designed to play and have ceased being productive forums.

Community participation forms the bedrock of a functioning society and a resilient democracy. Put differently, democracy is a team sport. As citizens, we must not only reclaim our right to be listened to by our elected representatives, but also be willing to actively participate in the system that has been designed for us. In this way, we will be able to judge our elected officials against higher and more rigorous standards and hold them to account.

Empowerment of the millions of marginalised South Africans begins with the empowerment of communities. The World Health Organization defines community empowerment as 'more than the involvement, participation or engagement of communities. It implies community ownership and action that explicitly aims at social and political change'.[11] It is about enabling communities to design their own futures, build and produce their own goods and collectively make decisions, while also localising development interventions so that the benefits thereof are felt more directly by individuals.

Clearly, empowerment does not equate to an extended period of charity. Rather, it involves communities becoming self-propelled and shaping their own development agenda in partnership with policymakers and other government stakeholders. This will reawaken the spirit of active citizenry, re-instil a sense of ownership and shared purpose in the country, and clear the way for sustainable and shared development.

THIRTEEN

Strengthening the institutions of public accountability in South Africa

Dennis Davis

Introduction

Section 1 (d) of the Constitution of the Republic of South Africa, 1996, proclaims that South Africa is 'one, sovereign, democratic state founded on the following values:

> (d) Universal adult suffrage, a national common voters' roll, regular elections and a multi-party system of democratic government, to ensure accountability, responsiveness and openness.[1]

Given that the Constitution was designed to provide a framework for society that was the antithesis of the apartheid regime, it was understandable that the principles of accountability, responsiveness and openness of government were central ideas that the drafters insisted be included in the vision for a future South Africa.

The concept of accountability employed in the Constitution can be interpreted in at least two ways. First, it has a technical meaning. It refers to the obligation of the head of a department as an accounting officer, as well as their minister, the Auditor-General and the Public Accounts Committee of Parliament, to provide an account of actions or policies that have been adopted by the particular organ of state.

By contrast, accountability in a wider sense means that any person in power needs to explain or justify their decisions or their actions against specified criteria. This in turn may lead to the need to correct any fault or error and prevent a recurrence in the future.[2]

These principles of accountability were placed at the centre of the Constitution precisely because any viable social contract between the citizenry and government does depend on public power being held accountable to the electorate whom it is designed to serve. Similarly, there needs to be the assurance that when there is an abuse of public power, accountability and responsiveness will demand acknowledgement thereof, along with a clear commitment that such abuses will not be repeated in the future.

These promises, as contained in the 1996 Constitution, now appear to be a distant memory. In a recent Afrobarometer survey, only one in every four South Africans expressed satisfaction with South African democracy. Fewer than one in four said that they trusted Parliament, which was designed to be a central institution tasked with preventing the abuse of power by the Executive.[3]

None of these lamentable failures of the key institutions designed by the Constitution to hold public power accountable should be surprising. For example, in 2016, the report by the Public Protector titled 'State of Capture' focused on the relationship between (then) President Jacob Zuma and the notorious Gupta family. The report highlighted three fundamental issues that were eroding the integrity of governance in South Africa: the irregularity in the awarding of public contracts; the illegal appointments of board members and executives to state-owned corporations; and the fundamental repurposing of public institutions such as the South African Revenue Service (SARS) and the National Prosecuting Authority (NPA).

In May 2017, the Public Affairs Research Institute published a report on the condition of state institutions under the Zuma presidency. It claimed that South Africa had experienced a silent coup in which the Zuma-centred power elite had built and consolidated a symbiotic relationship between the constitutional and shadow states in order to construct a rent-seeking enterprise for their own benefit.[4] Shortly thereafter, the so-called 'GuptaLeaks' were released within the media, giving further attention to the widespread corruption of state resources and the destruction of key institutions such as SARS and the NPA. In teasing out this conclusion, Ivor Chipkin and Mark Swilling wrote:

> Corruption normally refers to a condition where public officials pursue private ends using public means. While indeed corruption is widespread at all levels and is undermining development, state capture is a far greater, systemic threat. It is akin to a silent coup and must, therefore, be understood as a political project that is given a cover of legitimacy by the vision of radical economic transformation. The March 2017 Cabinet reshuffle was confirmation of this silent coup; it was the first Cabinet reshuffle that took place without the full prior support of the governing party. This moves the symbolic relationship between the constitutional state and the shadow that emerged after the ANC [African National Congress] Polokwane conference in 2007 into a new phase.[5]

These widespread allegations finally forced the hand of Jacob Zuma, as a result of which the Judicial Commission of Inquiry into Allegations of State Capture, Corruption and Fraud in the Public Sector including Organs of State – which came to be known as the Zondo Commission – was established in January 2018. Nearly four years later, the Commission published a number of definitive findings relating to the lack of accountability and responsiveness of government. These are of great relevance to the formulation of proposals to return the governance of the country to the path that was laid out in the Constitution.

A brief overview of the Zondo Commission recommendations

The first part of the Zondo Commission's overview of state capture concentrated on problems in procurement by the state and its various organs. It noted that the procurement of goods and services that were not actually needed and were not intended to be supplied, as well as the duplication of work already done, were common practice. Deviations from the normal procurement approach involving an open-tender competitive process were frequent occurrences. Also, from time to time, there was a process of confinement where a government department chose to confine the number of businesses eligible for a tender – often to a single bidder.⁶

Coupled with these problems was the lapse of governance of critical state-owned enterprises (SOEs). In particular, the Zondo Commission identified certain patterns of strategic appointments and dismissal – that is, the appointment of compromised individuals to key positions within the SOE, such as the chief executive officer (CEO) or chief financial officer (CFO) or similar positions, particularly those responsible for procurement decisions. In addition, the process of appointing individuals to the boards of SOEs was carefully calibrated to ensure that the boards would not exercise neutral oversight when it came to the running of the SOEs.

The Zondo Commission also found a complete failure of oversight of public institutions, which enabled state capture. In particular, it highlighted the failure of Parliament to exercise any meaningful oversight, the inability of the National Treasury to respond to an ever-increasing pattern of corruption, and the lack of response when a state body was given a qualified audit by the Auditor-General.

Key to the Zuma project was the evisceration of the guardrails of constitutional democracy – in particular, the NPA, the Public Protector and SARS. The extent of state capture at SARS was described against the backdrop of Tom Moyane's (Zuma's Commissioner of SARS) hounding of senior SARS executive Vlok Symington, who had refused to cooperate with Moyane, and Moyane's attempt to construct a criminal case against Pravin Gordhan, as follows:

> The saga illustrates an extreme example of the culture of fear and bullying which characterised Mr Moyane's tenure at SARS. It also illustrates the lengths that he went to [to] have certain people who were obstacles to state capture removed. Mr Symington described this time as a 'nightmare' time at SARS and to visibly see the efficiency rate dropping during Mr Moyane's tenure was something he hoped would never happen again.⁷

Recommendations of the Zondo Commission: A brief examination

The Zondo Commission was particularly and understandably concerned about the abuse of the system of public procurement. It recommended the publication of a national charter against corruption of procurement, with a binding code of conduct; the creation of an independent agency tasked with stamping out corruption in procurement, which would include a council, an inspectorate to police practices, a litigation unit and a bespoke tribunal subject to the scrutiny of a court; the creation of a procurement officer professional body; and various other significant changes to public procurement legislation and regulations.

The litigation unit would be the effective investigative body that would refer cases to the tribunal or a court, depending on the nature of the case. The tribunal would be the body that received applications from the litigation unit, which it would then act on by granting search warrants to the litigation unit or granting applications from the litigation unit to debar people from participating in applications for procurement. The court would determine and judge the case brought by the litigation unit where it concerned civil action relating to the accruement of funds and would also act as the court of appeal in respect of any decision that had been taken by the tribunal. The Commission also recommended amendments to the Political Party Funding Act, 2018 to criminalise the making of donations to political parties in the expectation of, or with a view to, being granted procurement tenders or contracts as a reward for or in recognition of such donations.

The Zondo Commission estimated that the total amount of money spent by the state that was tainted by state capture was approximately R57 billion, of which more than 97 per cent effectively had been stolen from Transnet and Eskom. The notorious Gupta family was said to have received at least R15 billion, although this is probably a significant underestimation of what this family of carpet baggers extracted from state coffers.[8]

Unsurprisingly, the Zondo Commission paid considerable attention to SOEs, which fell under the authority of the Department of Public Enterprises. The central finding was that some members of the boards of these SOEs – particularly the chairperson, the group CEO and the CFO – were people without the integrity, knowledge and expertise required for their positions. Even if they did have the requisite knowledge, they were devoid of any integrity. To this end, therefore, the Zondo Commission recommended that legislation be promulgated to create a Standing Appointment and Oversight

Committee, which would receive applications and interview candidates and make recommendations to the relevant minister. It would also publish a code of conduct and receive and investigate complaints of wrongdoing. If the minister disagreed with the recommended appointments, they would have 30 days in which to reject the candidate, but they would have to supply written reasons for their decision. A committee would then compile an additional list of candidates, ranked in order of preference. The default position was that if the minister continued to reject the recommendations of the committee, the latter's recommendations would ultimately prevail.

The committee would include a retired judge, nominated by the Chief Justice to act as the chair, the Minister of Finance, a legal practitioner appointed by the Legal Practice Council, a representative appointed by the National Economic Development and Labour Council (Nedlac), a trade union representative selected by Nedlac, an auditor selected by the chairperson of the Independent Regulatory Board for Auditors, an industrial expert selected by the SOE concerned, and a senior representative of an anti-corruption non-profit organisation operating in the private sector.

Even more far reaching were the recommendations pertaining to the constitutional structure of the country. The Commission recommended that Parliament consider passing legislation to introduce a constituency-based system of elections that would still be based on proportional representation. The introduction of mechanisms to prevent members of parliament (MPs) from being fired by their parties when they carried out their duties in good faith was also recommended. This represented an attempt to improve the principle of accountability, where MPs could exercise an independent mind rather than being railroaded by party bosses into slavish obeisance to the party leadership and hence to the Executive. Two recommended measures were the introduction of a special committee to exercise direct oversight over the Presidency and the introduction of amendatory accountability, which would make it a violation to ignore the remedial recommendations of Parliament.

The Commission also recommended that consideration be given to the introduction of a voting system where the President would be directly elected. It made the point that this would ensure that the President was elected on the basis of their own popularity with the electorate rather than with their party. It would give voters greater choice and discretion as to how they cast their vote.

Lessons from and implications of the Zondo Commission reports

The key lessons to be learnt from state capture, now archived in the reports of the Zondo Commission, have been summarised as follows:

> It is now clear that while the ideological focus of the ANC is 'radical economic transformation', in practice, Jacob Zuma's presidency is aimed at repurposing state institutions to consolidate the Zuma-centred power elite. Whereas the former appears to be a legitimate long-term vision to structurally transform South Africa's economy to eradicate poverty and reduce inequality and unemployment, the latter – popularity referred to as 'state capture' – threatens the viability of the state institutions that need to deliver on this long-term vision.[9]

To date, legal initiatives to address the practice of repurposing state institutions when captured by a select group have been limited by conditions that promote the formation of elites. This manifests as government officials and politicians, particularly those elected to Parliament and provincial and local government, being intent on enriching themselves and their families through the diversion of public funds from proclaimed public purpose to private pocket.

There can also be little doubt that the failure to reconfigure the South African economy and thus respond to the resilient legacy of poverty, marginalisation and inequality spawned under apartheid creates conditions for a select, elite group to utilise state institutions and corporations to plunder public resources. Within this context, however, the reconfiguration of the legal foundations of key state institutions can make such practices more difficult and, to some considerable extent, enhance the principles of accountability and responsiveness which are enshrined in the Constitution.

However, law alone cannot fix the problem. As Van der Westhuizen said in *Helen Suzman Foundation v President of the Republic of South Africa and others*:

> Corruption threatens the very existence of our constitutional democracy. Effective laws and institutions to combat the corruption are therefore absolutely essential. It is the task of the courts – and this Court in particular – to ensure that legal mechanisms against corruption are as trustworthy and tight as possible, within the demands and parameters of the Constitution.
>
> But courts can only do so much. The corruption-free society can only develop in the hearts and minds of its people – particularly the ones occupying the positions of political and economic power. We need dedication to the spirit and high aspirations of the Constitution. Institutions are tools designed to help people realise their ambitions. Much dedication is required on the part of those handling the tools ...
>
> But even the most sophisticated institutional design will require the exercise of discretion and therefore integrity on the part of, and trust in, the office bearer. Thoroughly closing all perceived loopholes will guarantee little. Generally abstract institutional designs cannot be corrupt. As we know, people can be.[10]

This perceptive observation presents the instructive qualification to any proposals for legislative change. But there are some that could at least reconstruct the constitutional guardrails to promote the principles of governance which were inserted by the drafters of the 1996 Constitution.

The remainder of this chapter focuses on attainable goals that can begin to restore some adherence to the constitutional promise. Obviously, the Zondo Commission's recommendations in the light of the herculean work done by the Commission should serve as a starting point.

Key discrete moves

1. Presidential powers

In any set of proposals there must be a primary acknowledgement that the powers that were granted to the President in terms of the 1996 Constitution were far too wide and unqualified. It is understandable that when the Constitution was drafted in 1994, the attitude was 'Mandela would never abuse his power'. Sadly, and predictably, after Mandela's departure from the presidency, his successors did not comport themselves with the same careful adherence to the principle of accountability.

Under Jacob Zuma, the extensive powers granted to the President were used primarily to construct and then perpetuate state capture. The President was able to appoint the Commissioner of SARS – in this case, Tom Moyane. Moyane successfully fulfilled his mandate to gut SARS as a viable tax-collection institution. His tenure created massive challenges which in many ways have been successfully navigated by his successor, Edward Kieswetter. In this lies a lesson about appointing people of integrity to head up key institutions and the need for a transparent appointment process (to be discussed later).

The President was entitled to appoint the National Director of Public Prosecutions (NDPP). Jacob Zuma made a decision that was deliberately designed to reduce the efficacy of the prosecuting agency. As the court said in *Corruption Watch NPC and others v President of the Republic of South Africa and others:*

> Former President Zuma appointed Advocate Abrahams following his unlawful removal of Mr Nxasana. That removal was an abuse of power. Advocate Abrahams benefited from the abuse of power. It matters not that he may be unaware of the abuse of power; the rule of law dictates that the officers of NDPP be cleansed of all the ills that plagued it in the past few years.[11]

The record revealed that Mr Abrahams played a not-dissimilar role at the prosecuting agency to that which Mr Moyane played at SARS, thereby radically weakening the ability of the prosecuting agency to fulfil its constitutional mandate. Similarly, the President was able to make a series of significant appointments to boards of SOEs – in particular, Eskom and Transnet, which, as indicated, were the sites of sustained pillage of state coffers. All of these appointments were effectively made by way of unfettered discretion granted to the President.

This history mandates that significant change is required in the area of presidential powers. The Zondo Commission's proposal that members of the boards of SOEs can only be appointed through an independent committee chaired by a retired judge constituted a clearly defined response to a key tool of state capture – one that the government has evidently taken seriously in its consideration of legislation aimed at reconfiguring the governance of SOEs.[12] The draft State-Owned Enterprise Bill provides that appointments to the proposed holding company for key SOEs can only be populated from a list provided to the President, as the shareholder of SOEs, by an independent committee chaired by a retired judge and comprising members drawn from interest groups, as proposed by the Zondo Commission.

A similar procedure is required for the appointment of the Commissioner and Deputy Commissioners of SARS and the National Director and Deputy Directors of Public Prosecutions. In this way, the unfettered powers of the President can be contained to ensure that people of talent, expertise and integrity are appointed. It may not be a perfect solution since, as Justice Van der Westhuizen warned, people and not institutions are inherently corrupt. A corrupt president will seek to circumvent the most well-intentioned institutional safeguards, but the more calibrated the safeguard, the greater the possibility of improved transparency and accountability.

2. Election reform

The Zondo Commission made recommendations for electoral reform on the basis that the existing system of proportional representation gave party bosses immense power over public representatives. The threat of being removed from a party's electoral list for a new election or being recalled from a sitting Parliament in the event of a member voting against the wishes of the party were viewed as major obstacles to the legislature holding the Executive accountable, thereby eroding the doctrine of separation of powers.

The Commission's proposal to move to a constituency-based system of elections partly replicated the need for electoral reform demanded by the Constitutional Court following its judgment in *New Nation Movement NPC v President of the Republic of South Africa*.[13] The majority of the court held that a constitutionally compliant electoral system had to allow for individuals to be eligible to stand for election for the National Assembly without the requirement that a candidate be a member of a political party.

This judgment necessitated changes to the relevant electoral laws. The Minister of Home Affairs commissioned a panel of experts, the Ministerial Advisory Committee, to provide technical proposals to give effect to the court order. The Committee consisted of eight members who subsequently submitted a report to the Minister. The Committee was divided on the advice to be given to the Minister. Four members of the Committee proposed a combination of a single-member constituency and a proportional representation system. This was the majority option. Three members proposed a modification of the existing system to permit independent candidates to contest the elections. This was the minority option. One member of the Committee chose not to state a preferred option.

In summary, the Committee offered two options. The minority option entailed modifying the existing multi-member electoral system to accommodate independent candidates in the national and provincial elections, with the minimum of changes to existing legislation. Those in favour of this option believed that it would not interfere with the constitutionally required general proportionality and was the best way to ensure inclusiveness, gender representation, simplicity and fairness for independents. By contrast, the majority option combined the first-past-the-post approach and proportional representation, making it a mixed-member proportional (MMP) system that resembled the current local government electoral system, albeit with some improvements. It proposed the election of MPs from 200 single-member constituencies and the remainder from a single national multi-member constituency. Thus, voters would vote for a single MP to represent them in single-member constituencies (their first vote) and for a party to represent them in the single national multi-member constituency, based on competing for closed-party lists (their second vote).

The government adopted the minority report when it introduced and subsequently ensured the passing into law of the Electoral Law Amendment Act, 2024. This has resulted in the unwieldy compromise of enabling individuals to stand for Parliament while ensuring that the list system continues to dominate the electoral process. Whatever the limitations of the majority report, the system to be adopted for the 2024 election provides no basis for a change that will prompt a more independent level of scrutiny of the Executive by Parliament than has been the case under the previous system. The overwhelming number of MPs will remain beholden to the party line, thereby ensuring a lack of accountability.

3. An anti-corruption agency

While a government that commands a small majority in Parliament may be more vulnerable to parliamentary accountability, it is to other institutions that advocates of accountable government must turn for a more consistent commitment to the principles of accountability and responsiveness. In this regard, the establishment of an anti-corruption agency has been mooted, particularly by the Zondo Commission.

The history of anti-corruption agencies in South Africa provides a cautionary tale. Since the disbanding in 2008 of the Directorate of Special Operations (known as the Scorpions) and its replacement by the Directorate for Priority Crime Investigation (or Hawks), South Africa has witnessed an exponential rise in impunity among the architects of corruption. In 2008, the ANC proposed that the Scorpions be disbanded and become a part of the South African Police Service (SAPS). An opinion poll revealed that the majority of South Africans agreed that the Scorpions should be separate from the SAPS.

South Africa's controversial former president, Jacob Zuma, and his allies believed that the Scorpions were being used to fight political opponents of Zuma's predecessor, Thabo Mbeki. Those opponents included Zuma, who was challenging Mbeki for the presidency while facing a vast array of criminal charges, including corruption, racketeering and money laundering. The charges were part of various investigations conducted by the Scorpions. The ANC's decision ultimately resulted in the Scorpions being disbanded, notwithstanding that they had a conviction rate of between 82 per cent and 94 per cent. By 2018, its replacement – the Hawks – had detection rates of around 50 per cent and court-ready percentages that were even lower.[14]

The effect of the disbandment of the Scorpions was luminously captured by Chief Justice Raymond Zondo as follows:

> One of the worst decisions we've ever taken as a country in our fight against corruption was the disbandment of the Scorpions.

> The Scorpions were said to have a very high conviction rate and were very effective, but we allowed them to be disbanded. Maybe we as citizens did not stand up and fight. I have a sense that if the Scorpions had not been disbanded, we would not have the levels of corruption that we have right now.[15]

The lesson that must be learnt from the manner in which a key institution that was designed to counter corruption and was replaced by a more executively compliant body is this: a fully independent institution that is ideally placed beyond the reach of the ruling party and the Executive is essential if there is to be an effective deterrent against corruption and other nefarious forms of governance. Paul Hoffman, in a commendably tenacious campaign conducted on behalf of such an independent entity, correctly set out the minimum requirements for an effective anti-corruption body:

> The anti-corruption entity must be STIRS compliant. This acronym denotes specialists who are appropriately trained, independent in their structure and operational capacities and fully resourced in guaranteed fashion. Importantly, the entity should enjoy secure tenure of office, the last 'S' in STIRS.[16]

4. State-owned enterprises

The greatest site of corrupt and unaccountable government was the SOEs. As noted, the government has agreed to introduce a State-Owned Enterprise Bill in Parliament. It has responded to the Zondo Commission by providing safeguards to ensure that cadre deployment will not be the basis for the constitution of the board of the proposed holding company, which is designed to hold the shares of key SOEs. The Bill opens up the possibility of private investment through shareholding in SOEs and of the latter being governed by company law rules directed at promoting greater transparency in the performance of such entities.

Legislation alone will not, however, provide a watertight safeguard. Take Singapore's Temasek model, which (as a form of corporate structure) has influenced South African ideas for the draft Bill. Its success has been due to the government's ability to restrain itself from interfering in the affairs of the SOEs.[17] Such 'a strong convention built up over many years' is not a product of law but rather the product of the government's political willpower. One of the significant drivers of the incorporation of Temasek at inception was the government's intention to separate the government from business management.[18]

The importance of the practice and culture of the state and its understanding of its core role have proved to be the critical determinants of the success of the Temasek model. And this insight compels a focus on the nature of the state and politics in South Africa if the country is to vindicate the constitutional mandate about accountable and responsive government.

Conclusion

The original sin after the proclamation of democracy in 1994, which heralded the start of a widening gap between the constitutional commitment to accountable government and the practice thereof, was to be found in the events surrounding the so-called Arms Deal. As Karl von Holdt observed in an analysis of state capture:

> ... [the] first significant scandal to gain public attention was the Arms Deal under Mbeki which involved many big and small kickbacks. The key aim of this appears to have been to secure substantial funding for the ANC. Still, in the process, several ANC-linked businesspeople, front men and political figures – including allegedly Zuma – were able to enrich themselves.[19]

Patronage networks throughout the country were spawned thereafter, with the corruption documented by Crispian Olver in the Port Elizabeth [now Gqeberha] municipality providing a chilling example.[20] The revelations of the activities of the Watson brothers and Bosasa and the VBS Bank are further evidence of the manner in which politicians and business were inextricably linked to ever-increasing levels of corruption. And then came the Guptas, and out of state coffers went billions of rands.

The upshot was the subversion of formal legal structures and institutions to extend rent-seeking practices at the expense of the citizenry and substantive democracy. As Justice Van der Westhuizen noted in his judgment in the *Helen Suzman Foundation* case cited earlier legal institutions in particular and the rule of law in general provide no bulwark against corrupt, unaccountable government when individuals who form part of an archipelago of predatory elites are determined to enrich themselves.

That changes to the electoral system, a circumscription of the powers of the President and the creation of an independent anti-corruption agency can contribute to improved public governance is to be welcomed. But constitutions and institutions created in their image cannot lift themselves into legal reality. A social practice that promotes open and accountable government is the key to the success thereof. In the South African context, that practice is absent – an unsurprising conclusion given the centuries of authoritarian racist rule in the country.

In the absence of a civil society that is committed thereto and thus a reconfigured practice of governance that is focused on the needs of more than 60 million people, no range of legal proposals – however imaginative – is likely to succeed on its own.

FOURTEEN

South Africa: Grappling with the 'age of uncertainty'

Raymond Parsons

'Among the fundamental structural reform items is policy certainty. Simple but fundamental to the investor community. Remember that you cannot force people to invest, but you can create an environment which makes it easier to invest, create jobs and, hey presto, develop the country.' – Former Minister of Finance, Tito Mboweni[1]

'The most distinctive characteristic of the businessman – the thing that most sharply distinguishes him from the lawyer, college professor or, generally speaking, the civil servant – is his capacity for decision.' – Prof John K. Galbraith[2]

Is policy uncertainty the 'new normal' in South Africa?

Against the backdrop of the previous chapters in this volume, it is evident that South Africa has reached a 'tipping point' in its political economy and that a much clearer sense of economic direction will be needed in the aftermath of the 2024 election. A successful macroeconomic framework that enables the country to take a 'high road' instead of a 'low road' in future should ideally be based on three key elements: efficiency, stability and consistency. The overall message of this book is that South Africa has fallen far short, even with the best of intentions at times, in ensuring that these vital elements are placed at the core of its domestic policies. Much of what is being suggested here should not again become a casualty of previously flawed processes and decision making.

South Africa has not lacked for commendable plans of one kind or another over the years to boost its economic performance. In fact, the list seems endless: the Reconstruction and Development Plan (RDP), the Growth, Employment and Redistribution (GEAR) strategy, the Accelerated and Shared Growth Initiative for South Africa (AsgiSA), the New Growth Path (NGP), the National Development Plan (NDP), the Economic Reconstruction and Recovery Plan (ERRP), the Joint Initiative on Priority Skills Acquisition (Jipsa), and several 'job summits'. With all these plans, strategies and blueprints, why have we not yet been able to create an economy that is bigger, stronger and better?

In rounding up the usual suspects, one dominant theme has been persistent policy uncertainty. A government must be willing and able to *implement* what it plans to do in ways that create an acceptable level of predictability. Furthermore, an investment-friendly business environment relies on knowledge of how the strategies emanating from official policies will unfold as time goes by.

Uncertainty, of course, has had a long history in economics – almost as long as the economics discipline has been in existence. And there is always a degree of economic uncertainty in business and individual decision making. That nothing is certain may be the only certainty that many decision makers have to face! Economists, however, do not believe that *all* economic life is uncertain. Uncertainty becomes an issue for the economy only when our livelihoods or prosperity depends on our taking a view of the future. Or when firms and individuals respond to high levels of uncertainty by adopting a precautionary stance. This feeling of uncertainty also waxes and wanes as confidence levels fluctuate. Uncertainty therefore coincides with both optimistic and pessimistic beliefs about the future.

We should note in passing that Prof Daniel Kahneman, who was awarded the Nobel Memorial Prize in Economic Sciences for his wide-ranging work on behavioural economics, also delved into the role of 'optimism' in decision making.[3] 'The optimistic risk-taking of entrepreneurs,' he said, 'surely contributes to the economic dynamism of a capitalistic society, even if most risk takers end up disappointed.' However, he worried about the negative outcomes of what he described as 'overconfident optimism'. 'Extreme uncertainty is paralyzing under dangerous circumstances, and the admission that one is only guessing is especially unacceptable when the stakes are high.' Kahneman concluded that 'the effects of optimism on decision making are, at best, a mixed blessing, but the contribution of optimism to good implementation is certainly positive. The main benefit of optimism is resilience in the face of setbacks.'

Despite the upside potential of 'optimism', the reality is that economic uncertainty has become much worse in recent years, as policymakers constantly send mixed signals about their plans or otherwise deliver shocks or surprises to market participants, with negative consequences for macroeconomic performance. Businesspersons' 'animal spirits' are then steadily dampened. It is now well known that uncertainty reduces the willingness of firms to hire and invest and of consumers to spend, as opposed to reflecting an 'irrational exuberance'. Hence, the increasingly complex policy environment and the ever-rising costs of policy mistakes, especially for an emerging economy like South Africa's, elevate uncertainty cumulatively.

As we interrogate the diagnostics and recommendations for a post-election national agenda for South Africa, the extent to which policy uncertainty again permeates the prospects for success is striking. It is noteworthy that, in recent years, hardly any economic assessment or media release from international or local financial institutions, business lobbies, economic analysts, financial journalists or credit rating agencies has appeared without the words 'policy uncertainty' featuring in them. Elevated policy uncertainty has been the common factor that has badly undermined *all* three desirable pillars of efficiency, stability and consistency in South Africa's macroeconomic policy.

Because the role of policy uncertainty has loomed so large in the economic debate in South Africa over several years, the North-West University Business School decided in 2016 to create a quarterly Policy Uncertainty Index (PUI) to calibrate policy uncertainty levels in South Africa. The design of the PUI was, however, spurred not only by local economic circumstances but also by the increasing interest among academics and policymakers around the world in the cause, effect, measurement and definition of policy uncertainty. It has therefore been possible to draw on global best practice.

There is now also a 'World Uncertainty Index' (WUI), developed by the International Monetary Fund (IMF) and Stanford University, which measures levels of uncertainty in the global economy. It recently highlighted the extent to which Covid-19 and its economic aftermath as well as new geopolitical conflicts had elevated the levels of world economic uncertainty. There are also increasing concerns about the new challenges being posed to the existing 'rules-based' world order, in which smaller economies in particular have a vested interest. 'If I had to identify a theme at the outset of the new decade,' said IMF Managing Director, Kristalina Georgieva, 'it would be increasing uncertainty.'[4]

In addition, the latest World Economic Forum (WEF) Global Risks Report (2024) explores the global risk landscape in all its various forms, ranging from climate change to the emergence of a global multipolar world over the next decade.[5] As a small open economy, South Africa cannot do much about external forces over which it has little or no control. But it can finesse these global realities. Options include engaging in sensible economic diversification, following a prudent foreign policy, strengthening its economic buffers, and building resilience by successfully mobilising the internal factors that *are* under its control – such as keeping domestic policy uncertainty to a minimum.[6]

As mentioned earlier, both global and national empirical evidence overwhelmingly shows that when policy uncertainty is very prevalent in an economy, it has the effect of reducing investment, employment and output. High levels of policy uncertainty are therefore often described as a 'tax' on investment and hence contribute to sluggish growth. Elevated policy uncertainty has been shown to be a strong deterrent to both local and foreign investment, from which South Africa has not been immune in its attempts to be a preferred investment destination.

It is also customary for observers to see the highly variable and volatile behaviour of the rand as mainly the outcome of external economic circumstances in general and the strong US dollar in particular. Yet the reality is that nearly half the forces accounting for the inconsistency in the South African currency are driven by domestic factors. Elevated policy uncertainty, therefore, also significantly influences trends in the rand. 'The government's job is not only to shoot fewer own goals but to convince through positive and coordinated action that South Africa is not riskier than other emerging markets.'[7]

Therefore, the more uncertainty there is in South Africa about anything – such as 'the rules of the game', logistics and transport, energy policy, the regulatory framework, foreign policy, crime levels, corruption, taxes and so forth – the more difficult it becomes from an economic and business perspective. The uncertainties around the energy crisis, for example, have become the Achilles heel of the South African economy. These uncertainties and costs then have to be priced in by firms and consumers in one way or another and eventually have a detrimental impact on economic performance.

The PUI in South Africa has generally been well into negative territory since it was launched in 2016. The latest Nedbank Expenditure Project Listing for 2023 showed a dramatic decline in fixed investment activity 'as persistent power outages, rising interest rates and cost pressures weighed on profitability and eroded business confidence. The weakness in capital spending is expected to continue into 2024. Gross fixed capital formation (GFCF) is expected to grow by about 0.5 per cent, down from a forecasted 4.2 per cent in 2023.'[8] It does not require a profound grasp of economics to know that there must be a close interconnection between growth in capital and growth in population and employment, especially in a developing economy. The persistence of elevated policy uncertainty helps to explain why total private and public investment as a percentage of gross domestic product (GDP) is presently only about 15 per cent – half the 30 per cent target for 2030 originally outlined in the National Development Plan (NDP), which was needed for high levels of job-rich growth. The Ten-Year Review of the NDP recently released by the National Planning Commission (NPC) therefore strongly urged that 'in the immediate term South Africa needs to deal with policy uncertainty, and significantly enhance policy coordination and coherence'.[9] The NPC further pleaded for 'consistency in government policy and engagement with stakeholders'.

This theme of policy uncertainty was also given prominence by Business Leadership South Africa (BLSA) in its extended response to the original NDP released in 2012.¹⁰ Emphasising that perhaps the greatest obstacle to investment in any country is policy uncertainty, BLSA went on to say that 'the NDP highlights policy uncertainty as a concern, but this is mainly in relation to mining. It also rightly identifies providing policy certainty over property rights as a key imperative'. BLSA added that 'indeed, the lack of policy certainty in the agricultural, tourism and mining sectors (all areas where the NDP highlights the potential for significant employment of the unskilled unemployed), is in our opinion a key reason for the lack of investment in them, in spite of the potentially lucrative rewards'.

Of course, there may well also be other factors explaining the weak performance of private fixed investment in recent years. Yet it is difficult to overlook the unequivocal evidence of policy uncertainty playing a major role. For example, the accumulation of corporate cash reserves to what might appear to be excessive levels is not, as critics often say, a sign that South African investors are 'on strike'. There are several reasons why corporates may prefer to hold cash on their balance sheets, including for precautionary and transactional purposes. This 'liquidity preference' should be viewed as one persuasive barometer of reactions to excessive policy uncertainty. 'For as long as you have that heightened policy uncertainty, you will have companies sitting on cash and not investing,' cautioned the South African Reserve Bank (SARB) Governor, Lesetja Kganyago.¹¹

Policy uncertainty and the pending 2024 election

Now, looming over the calibration of policy uncertainty in South Africa are the additional uncertainties arising from the forthcoming election. Towards the end of 2023, Governor Kganyago had already highlighted the 2024 election as being among the key risks facing South Africa's economy. 'Politicians adopting a populist tone ahead of the presidential and legislative vote may create uncertainty among foreign investors, undermining the case for investing in South Africa,' Governor Kganyago said in an interview with *City Press* newspaper.¹²

While policy uncertainty ultimately affects domestic and foreign investment alike, it is instructive to cite a study that examined its impact on foreign direct investment (FDI) in 126 countries from 1996 to 2015.¹³ Using the timing of national elections as a proxy for policy uncertainty, the study found that FDI dropped significantly during election years, when policy uncertainty rose. The research confirmed that policy uncertainty generated by elections encourages private actions to delay (in particular) investments that entail high costs of reversal.

Global research has thus shown that, in many countries, policy uncertainty indices tend to spike when elections are due. Volatility and uncertainty are regular hallmarks of such periods. National elections usually convey one of the clearest signals about the future direction of a country's economic policy. A 2020 study by Stanford University researchers, Nicholas Bloom and Jonathan Rodden, not only confirmed the extent to which an electoral business cycle interacted with policy uncertainty, but also that 'uncertainty is even higher when a national election is a close race and the electorate is especially polarized'.[14]

There are several important elements that will determine the impact of the 2024 election on the uncertainty profile of the South African economy. Of course, this is now relatively new terrain for South Africa, and it remains to be seen to what extent global experience will eventually be reflected in South Africa's current election cycle. However, 'for nearly 30 years,' said Pranish Desai, 'the ANC [African National Congress] claimed dominant party status, as South African national and local politics entirely revolves around the party's dynamics. While the ruling party remains, by a significant margin, the "largest fish" in South Africa's political pond, these waters are murkier than ever.'[15]

As outlined in some of the earlier chapters in this book, the prospect of political shifts after nearly three decades of dominance by the ANC governing party opens up new areas of uncertainty not experienced in South Africa since the first democratic election in 1994. The results of elections in South Africa up until now have been largely foreseeable and predictable, with the ANC regularly securing convincing majorities at most levels of government. The extremely wide range of election outcomes being suggested by political pundits is a clear testament of the elevated level of uncertainty that currently exists.

Five specific factors have converged to raise the level of uncertainty surrounding the 2024 election outcomes:

- Support for the ANC governing party has dipped below the 50 per cent threshold since the local elections in 2021, as is evident in several recent authoritative, opinion-based surveys.
- Individual candidates may now participate in the proportional electoral system without belonging to a political party.
- The political environment is generally more competitive and volatile due to new opposition formations.
- Current support patterns suggest a governance shift into coalition territory, which has so far brought much unpredictability and instability to local government and metro politics.
- Recent authoritative opinion surveys suggest that coalition governance could emerge in three key provincial economies – Gauteng, KwaZulu-Natal and the Western Cape. These three provinces account for a significant 63 per cent of South Africa's GDP, with Gauteng contributing 33 per cent, KwaZulu-Natal contributing 16 per cent and the Western Cape contributing 14 per cent.

Understanding the norms and conditions for successful and stable (new) coalition configurations in South Africa at all levels of government will involve a steep learning curve. It is, though, possible to tap into global best practice in this regard. Various scenarios have been presented on what might happen if the ANC does not win an outright national majority. However, 'the analysis does not exclude the possibility that the ANC maintains its majority in 2024 by the skin of its teeth,' argues Old Mutual investment analyst, Jason Swartz. 'South Africa is deep into uncharted waters and, whichever way we look at it, uncertainty remains the most damaging factor for markets.'[16]

Understandably, therefore, there are still widespread concerns about uncertainty and instability accompanying the emergence of national and provincial 'coalition governance' in South Africa – especially given the poor record so far of coalition arrangements in local and metro municipalities. However, the duration and impact of policy uncertainty will depend on whether any possible future coalition arrangements are 'growth pains' or persistent 'pains of disease'.

If they are 'growth pains', they are positive in the sense that they can eventually lead to the consolidation of democracy in this country. They reflect the ongoing search for good governance and stability, with policy positions that interact with each other, laying the foundation for real consensus in decision making. But if they are ongoing 'pains of disease', as experienced to date at other levels of government in South Africa, then they are negative. They merely aggravate the formation of factions, intensify the preoccupation with office-seeking, and prompt unstable and poor decision making, which also weakens service delivery. 'Growth pains' will require patience, tolerance, accommodation, accountability and other accepted norms for effective coalition governance. This is certainly the option that most stakeholders, especially business, would prefer if coalition governance becomes a reality. Chronic 'pains of disease' in coalition politics will simply perpetuate current elevated levels of policy uncertainty, at great economic cost.

Moreover, it is necessary to highlight the South African economy's chronic vulnerability to policy uncertainty over a long period. The PUI has been extremely elevated for some time and has been in negative territory for an extended period, mainly due to previously recorded domestic and global factors. It is nevertheless important to retain perspective. The preceding analysis does not mean that all economic and business activity comes to a standstill when there is anxiety about increased policy uncertainty, for whatever reasons.

While elevated policy uncertainty has imposed heavy costs on the South African economy, it would be wrong to suggest that business can only thrive if the policy, regulatory and political environment is 'just right' – or when all the obstacles to trade and investment have been cleared away. 'Waiting for this to happen will largely be an exercise in futility because there will never be perfect conditions for business ... Even in the face of heightened policy uncertainty, positive business decisions are still possible.'[17] In its decision making, the business sector is seldom without offsetting or innovative strategies designed to deal with unexpected circumstances. However, the reality is that, for now, steering the South African economy is like navigating poorly charted waters and avoiding rocks of uncertain location.

That said, what key pieces of advice should be given to future political and business leaders to help them ameliorate policy uncertainty, as calibrated by the PUI, and move it towards positive territory? Is it possible to shift the policy certainty needle in a positive direction at all? Suffice to say that negative trends like excessive policy uncertainty are indeed reversible if the right steps are taken to deal with the factors that *are* under South Africa's control. What then might be the *coping* and *remedial* measures that could be taken to help reduce uncertainty in future?

A 12-point indicative agenda

A 12-point indicative agenda, for both the public and private sectors, to help minimise policy uncertainty in a mixed economy and in a changing political economy environment post-2024, is set out below:

1. *If setting the agenda for a new government is one of the strategic themes of this book, then staying on the right economic track is another crucial one.*
   Successful decision making under uncertainty must be a collaborative process which involves gaining access to the right people and relevant information or data. Where elevated policy uncertainty exists, political leaders need to gain access to important policymakers, including central bankers, for advice. 'When uncertainty is high, policymakers should have three objectives,' said Mark Carney, former Governor of the Bank of England. 'First, conduct a sober, objective assessment of the outlook and the risks to it. Second, develop and communicate a plan to reduce those risks, and third, do no harm by minimising any possible confusion about the commitment to core macroeconomic frameworks themselves.'[18] Furthermore, in South Africa's macroeconomic context, SARB Governor, Lesetja Kganyago, said: 'I think by now we've had enough elections to know that, around this time of the season, there are these kinds of noises.'[19]

2. *There is ultimately no substitute for sustained, disciplined political leadership, even though a tough or negative election campaign may place it in jeopardy as the political stakes rise for the contenders and the election deadline approaches.*
   A former chairman of the President's Council of Economic Advisers in the United States (US) expressed the view: 'For good

economics to be overridden by good politics may sometimes have to be accepted. But for good economics to be overridden by bad politics is a tragedy which should be resisted as far as possible.'[20] Responsible political leadership must eventually promote the policy certainty that 'good economics' needs in the longer run, particularly if future shocks to the South African economy are to be minimised. What the 2024 election creates is a window of opportunity for a reappraisal (prompted by widespread public concern) of crucial issues of governance and administration, from which there now need to be appropriate political outcomes and commitments. And even where a government cannot immediately change the risks or uncertainties faced by households and businesses, it has an important role to play in softening the negative impact through social safety nets and other appropriate forms of assistance.

3. *There is a strong need to enhance interaction with the private sector in ways that build trust and the conviction that consultation is meant to be effective, not merely nominal.*
   While government is accountable to several stakeholders, not just business, efficacious consultation with the business community helps to develop a common understanding of the challenges being addressed and the incentives needed for stakeholders to work together in a productive manner. What empirical evidence has shown is that business *can* adjust, even to weak policies, or it can work around such policies where necessary. Business is usually flexible enough to generate various (albeit less-than-optimal) responses to difficult situations. It can navigate both 'good news' and 'bad news', but *not* if faced with persistent open-ended policy uncertainty or inconsistency. In addition, greater insistence on realistic timelines for policy and project implementation would help to foster more certainty.

4. *The NDP, as recently updated and assessed by the NPC, would have been a major source of policy certainty as a national roadmap over the years had it been properly implemented.*
   BLSA indicated in its response to the NDP as far back as 2013

that 'establishing the primacy of the NDP would go a long way to addressing policy uncertainty ... and to make the NDP *the* central planning document of the state'.[21] As indicated earlier, the NPC has also recently lamented the role of policy uncertainty in obstructing positive NDP outcomes since its inception. A stronger commitment to implement and action relevant components of the updated NDP blueprint in the post-election period would help promote more predictability in the policy arena.

Most of the post-election political configurations would find the updated NDP recommendations valuable for this purpose, assuming that there is still a desire to create a favourable economic environment within which the private sector can flourish.

5. *The role of public–private partnerships needs to be widened and deepened to expedite outcomes, especially on the infrastructure front.*

   The uncertainty surrounding the delivery of infrastructure and other services would be reduced if the National Treasury expedited its overhaul of the public–private sector framework in general and strengthened the role of the existing Operation Vulindlela in particular. The ways in which the private sector can supplement and fill the gaps in state capacity (from repairing potholes to strengthening the energy supply) need to be encouraged, wherever feasible, to enhance service delivery. The demarcation between the public and private sectors must accordingly be driven by new practical tools that create more certainty about successful delivery. In its 2024 Global Risks Report, the World Economic Forum (WEF) states: 'Public and private sectors alone, and in partnership, can play a role in bringing down costs and expanding risk reduction strategies'.[22] Policies do matter, but so do the institutions and mechanisms through which they are approved and implemented.

6. *A potent source of policy certainty, if properly used, is the instrument of socioeconomic assessments. Yet this policy tool, originally accepted by Cabinet in 2007, has been largely neglected and overlooked over the years.*

   The purpose of socioeconomic assessments is to assess *in*

advance the impact on the economy – in the areas of costs, benefits and risks – of any proposed law or regulation, with a few exceptions. The extensive use of regulatory impact assessments (RIAs), as the process was originally called, was also urged by BLSA in its response to the NDP a decade ago.[23] Had socioeconomic assessments been more widely utilised in shaping policy, many policy shocks and their negative economic fallout could have been avoided. 'The world of second-best policymaking is full of potential collateral damage and unintended consequences.'[24]

Therefore, the motto must be 'prevention is better than cure'. This does not replace decision making, but it puts it on a far better footing, quality wise. If there is one cross-cutting mechanism that would greatly help to minimise policy uncertainty in future, it would be the more effective and more intensive use of socioeconomic assessments. Greater use of this valuable appraisal tool to ensure a rigorous cost-benefit analysis of legislative and policy proposals would go a long way towards promoting certainty and strengthening investor confidence.

7. *Whatever the outcome of the upcoming election in South Africa, it will be necessary for business, though its usual channels, to engage with the new political leadership, especially once the new Cabinet is announced.*

The business–government relationship will need to be reset based on a fresh action-oriented agenda for collaboration, which seeks to reduce policy uncertainty wherever possible. There is an urgent need to overcome a strange and frequent paradox in policymaking in South Africa, which is the extent to which elevated levels of uncertainty have come to prevail amid an absolute plethora of 'advisory' processes and consultative structures over the years. For example, when the President's Economic Advisory Council was appointed in 2019, it too was given the task of 'ensuring greater coherence and consistency in the implementation of economic policy'[25] which, on the face of it, it has not succeeded in doing.

From the business side, it is therefore necessary to reduce policy uncertainty by insisting on much better coordination, consistency, cohesion and consultation in key areas of policy.

Ideally, the relationship between a new government and business should be one of 'creative tension' – in other words, let neither be suspicious of the other, but let both be watchful!

8. *The 'trust' factor is a two-way street with government and is needed to collectively promote policy certainty after the election.*
The prevalence of a 'trust deficit' often inhibits the capacity to reform or change institutions for the better. Policy coordination and coherence at various levels therefore hinge to a large extent on the degree to which the trust deficit can be reduced in future. Trust evolves and is renewed by people and groups working together as stakeholders to resolve problems and issues, because it is in their common interest to do so. This is not merely trite rhetoric or 'nice' to do. It is imperative for building a climate of solidarity with the new political leadership – especially if South Africa is to achieve superior economic outcomes and effective delivery in the years ahead.

9. *Organised business will need to adapt its advocacy and lobbying strategies to strengthen the 'voice of business' in a changed political environment in South Africa.*
If coalition governance indeed emerges after the election, business will need to adapt its strategies accordingly to ensure as stable a macroeconomic environment as possible. Irrespective of who is in power following the election, the business community still needs a *delivery state*. While business does not govern the country, it has already been playing a key supportive role by helping to keep the country governable, including at the local government level. By supplementing the efforts of the public sector, the business sector has been able to offer advice and provide expertise to sustain public services and ameliorate structural impediments to delivery. But business needs to be assured that in the long run the country's policymakers will strengthen basic state capacity to ensure the ability of public agencies to achieve their intended aims. Tanya Cohen, former chief executive officer of Business Unity South Africa (BUSA), reminded us a couple of years ago: 'The key opportunities

facing the business sector are achieving the right degree of independence within partnerships, a strategic focus, and exercising leadership with courage, resilience and integrity …. BUSA has the institutional standing to throw its weight behind a more strident call for policy certainty and coherence.'[26]

Therefore, the challenges for business and other stakeholders in the economy in the aftermath of the 2024 election will be, first, to freshly assess what forces and pressures are at play to change the policy direction; second, to see at what points the existing structures are more malleable or tractable to change; and third, to mobilise and direct these forces and pressures to bring about the changes needed to minimise costly policy failures and improve South Africa's economic performance. For example, the high-level President's Investment Conference held annually could be deployed more strategically as one future platform for this purpose, as could other points of access to government.

10. *Comprising voluntary-membership, subscription-driven institutions, the organised business sector in South Africa needs the full support of large and small companies in providing the resources needed to carry out its mandate.*
The issue of the proliferation of business structures in South Africa must remain a subject for another day.[27] In the meantime, if organised business in its different configurations is to make an impact, with a proactive agenda, on a new team of political leaders, many more firms should throw their weight behind their representative organisations to help create a more certain economic climate. In difficult times, these apex business structures, local chambers of commerce and other trade associations are indeed 'foul weather friends' to their members. Organised business, for its part, must do everything possible to ensure that there is adequate pooling of resources and technical capacity to push an agreed growth agenda for the country.

South Africa is facing a defining moment in its political and business cycles, when the organised business sector is well poised to collectively contribute to the cause of better delivery in the country.

11. *Firms should formulate risk strategies to minimise their exposure to uncertainty and enhance the stability of their operations.*
While much of South Africa's future may be *unknowable*, it is not *unimaginable*. Firms should formulate appropriate risk strategies to help them navigate new challenges that appear on the horizon. To this end, it is useful to develop (or access) worst-case, best-case and middle-ground scenarios that could offer a road map and some practical solutions. The question is not *whether* the South African economy will adjust to possible shifts in its political economy, but rather *how quickly* and *how well* it will do so, aided by informed and flexible business decision making.

12. *Firms should implement strategies that increase their knowledge and grasp of – and control over – factors that are potentially new sources of serious disturbances in an 'age of uncertainty'.*
Bloom et al.[28] proposed some basic guidelines to assist firms in dealing with heightened uncertainty, including:
    - It is essential for business to pay increasing attention to global economics and politics (especially in a small open economy like South Africa's).
    - The reality of elevated policy uncertainty puts a premium on business flexibility.
    - It is essential for firms to follow a contingency planning approach to enable them to act quickly and minimise the risk of costly mistakes.

In short, firms should organise their operations (perhaps even in unconventional ways) to ensure flexibility and adaptability. That way, uncontrollable variables or uncertainties cannot have too damaging an effect. Firms that are best able to anticipate and manage the relevant risks and opportunities will secure a competitive advantage. Moreover, if their best forecasts turn out to be quite wrong, they need adequate fall-back options. 'Adaptation is above all about survival. Survival involves finding not the best solution, but one that is good enough.'[29] Indeed, *coping* is an entirely rational response in the face of the accepted reality that the South African economy is presently in highly uncertain territory.

A final word

Given the exposition above, what must South Africa broadly aspire to in the face of its pressing challenges of unemployment, poverty and inequality? What South Africa's leadership in both the public and private sectors need to ensure over the longer term is best captured in the original NDP:

> Successful countries have what is called a 'future orientation'. Their policy bias is to take decisions that lead to long-term benefits, as opposed to short-run solutions that could have negative effects later. Such countries generally prefer investment over consumption, have high savings rates, sound fiscal policy, high levels of fixed investment, a high degree of policy certainty, and clear rules of engagement for the private sector. A clear and predictable policy environment enables business to take a long-term perspective on growth and development.[30]

Coda and recapitulation

Chapter 1 – Unpacking political-party dynamics in post-apartheid South Africa *(Anthony Butler)*
- The role of political parties in a democracy
- South Africa's dominant-party system
- The ANC, non-voters and opposition impotence
- Why opposition parties do not attract ANC deserters
- What can opposition parties do?

Chapter 2 – Coalition politics: Is this the way? *(Ralph Mathekga)*
- Electoral systems and newer democracies
- Why the electoral system matters
- South Africa's anxiety about coalitions as the 2024 election approaches
- Multiparty democracy – towards consensus-driven politics
- Multi-party democracy, coalition politics and fragmentation in a historical context
- The real issue with coalitions – fear of the unknown?

Chapter 3 – The economy, business and reform *(Cas Coovadia)*
- The (sorry) state of the nation
- Anticipating the economic future
- On the edge of the precipice – which way now?
- Intensified collaboration between business and government in the priority areas of:
  - energy
  - logistics and transportation

- o crime and corruption
- Stepping stones to South Africa's future

Chapter 4 – Power struggles: Shedding light on South Africa's enduring energy challenges *(Rod Crompton and Bruce Young)*
- South Africa's energy challenges and dilemmas
- Profiling the energy transition in South Africa around the current electricity crisis, new technologies and environmental concerns
- Unpacking the key components of electricity policy, and generation and transmission
- When will loadshedding end?
- Exploring energy options such as gas and hydrogen
- Striking a balance between positives and negatives on the energy front

Chapter 5 – Do geopolitics and trade clash? South Africa's foreign and trade policy options *(Anthoni van Nieuwkerk)*
- South Africa – a small, open economy in a global and African context
- South Africa's foreign policy and strategy – an ambivalent middle power?
- Unimaginable shifts in the Western, liberal, rules-based order
- The Global North and the Global South
- South Africa's economic relations with the G7
- South Africa and BRICS
- Potential for a hybrid economic diplomatic strategy

Chapter 6 – Is Africa open for business? *(Daniel Mminele)*
- Africa's overall potential
- South Africa in the African continental context
- The importance of the African Continental Free Trade Area (AfCFTA)
- A reality check – facing up to Africa's polycrises
- Critical success factors for leveraging Africa's potential:
  - o ensuring policy certainty
  - o committing to regional integration
  - o promoting good governance
  - o implementing effective public–private partnerships

- forging strong business and community ties
- mobilising local and international skills

Chapter 7 – South Africa's financial future: Keeping the debt trap at bay *(Isaah Mhlanga)*
- A fiscal crisis on the horizon for South Africa, driven by its 2023 fiscal policy and historical record of overspending
- Profile of unsound fiscal choices made in recent decades
- Consequences of an unsound fiscal policy for South Africa:
  - decline in business confidence
  - crowding out of public and private investment
  - heightened financial stability risks
  - reduced resilience to economic shocks
  - higher costs of funding for the whole economy
  - sudden stop in access to global financial markets
- Keeping the debt trap at bay – necessary remedies and reforms

Chapter 8 – Banking on credibility: The central bank and monetary policy after 2024 *(Hilary Joffe)*
- The SA Reserve Bank – one of South Africa's major institutional success stories
- Succession planning at the SA Reserve Bank
- Nationalisation? Inflation?
- Managing a world of interest rates 'higher for longer'
- Coping with South Africa's public-debt burden
- Monetary policy beyond 2024

Chapter 9 – Broadening farm ownership for successful transformation in South African agriculture *(Johann Kirsten and Wandile Sihlobo)*
- South Africa still discussing (and wrestling with) the issue of land ownership
- The challenge of accelerating land reform in South Africa
- Where are we now with land reform – why are there disappointments?
- What needs to be done to expedite land reform?
  - creation of a Land Reform and Agricultural Development Agency

- development of the Land Reform and Agricultural Development Fund
- implementation of a land-redistribution strategy for underutilised and unproductive land
- enhancement of the beneficiary-selection process
- streamlining of the bureaucratic procedures around the land reform support programme
- Key policy interventions needed to ensure a robust and stable agricultural sector in South Africa

Chapter 10 – Can we conquer corruption in South Africa? *(Jan van Romburgh)*
- The world of pre-crime ('prevention is better than cure'):
  - formulating a clear and transparent economic crime-prevention strategy
  - employing the right people
  - introducing lifestyle audits
  - leveraging the power of AI to detect 'red flags'
- The world of post-crime:
  - mobilising a clear response plan
  - activating public–private partnerships to boost investigative capacity
  - using internal audits as a proactive, investigative tool
  - prioritising training
  - empowering the Auditor-General
- Winning the battle against corruption

Chapter 11 – Local government in South Africa after the 2024 election: Will the desirable or probable outcome prevail? *(Erwin Schwella)*
- Local government in South Africa – setting the scene
- Two possible scenarios for local government:
  - a 'dedicated desires' scenario – pie in the sky?
  - a 'destructive disasters' scenario – the more probable outcome?
- Tracking the decline of local government since 1994:
  - The Auditor-General
  - Organisation Undoing Tax Abuse
  - Corruption Watch

- - Human Sciences Research Council
- Unpacking the failures of local government – some provisional hypotheses
- How can South Africa avoid history repeating itself?

Chapter 12 – Finding new, bottom-up solutions to grassroots socioeconomic challenges *(Vuyiswa Ramokgopa)*
- The need to do things differently in South Africa
- Localising development finance as a catalyst for local economic development
- Active citizenry – from democracy to 'do-ocracy'
- The role of local government – the 'face of democracy' and the primary public service delivery vehicle
- Community empowerment – the key to socioeconomic change

Chapter 13 – Strengthening the institutions of public accountability in South Africa *(Dennis Davis)*
- South Africa's Constitution as a framework to uphold the principles of accountability, responsiveness and openness of government
- A brief review and evaluation of the Zondo Commission recommendations
- How the findings from the Zondo Commission revealed a complete failure of oversight of public institutions
- Lessons from, and implications of, the Zondo Commission reports:
  - presidential powers
  - electoral reform
  - an independent anti-corruption agency
  - state-owned enterprises
- The need for a social practice that promotes open and accountable government

Chapter 14 – South Africa: Grappling with the 'age of uncertainty' *(Raymond Parsons)*
- Is policy uncertainty the 'new normal' in South Africa?
- Elevated policy uncertainty and the economy
- Policy uncertainty and the pending 2024 election

- A 12-point plan of action to enhance policy certainty
- Political leadership and the public sector
- Business leadership and the private sector
- Policy certainty and South Africa's future economic performance

Notes and other references

Overture
1   Nelson Mandela, *Long Walk to Freedom: The Autobiography of Nelson Mandela* (London: Abacus, 1993), p 617.
2   Erich Fromm, in Raymond Parsons (ed.), *Zumanomics – Which Way to Shared Prosperity?* (Johannesburg: Jacana Media, 2009).
3   Henry Kissinger, *Leadership – Six Studies in World Strategy* (UK: Random House, 2022), p 3.
4   Winston Churchill, *Great Contemporaries* (London: Fontana Books, 1972), p 63.
5   Peter Attard Montalto, 'Hard work and calm patience for the long road ahead', *Business Day*, 4 December 2023, https://www.businesslive.co.za/bd/opinion/columnists/2023-12-04-peter-attard-montalto-hard-work-and-calm-patience-for-the-long-road-ahead/

Chapter 1: Unpacking political party dynamics in post-apartheid South Africa
1   Giovanni Sartori, *Parties and Party Systems: A Framework for Analysis* (Cambridge: Cambridge University Press, 1976); Jaimie Bleck and Nicholas van de Walle, *Electoral Politics in Africa Since 1990: Continuity and Change* (Cambridge: Cambridge University Press, 2019).
2   Shauna Mottiar, 'The Democratic Alliance and the role of opposition parties in South Africa', *Journal of African Elections* 14, 1(2015): 106–23; Nic Cheeseman, 'African elections as vehicles for change', *Journal of Democracy* 21, 4(2010): 139–53; Danielle Resnick, 'How Zambia's opposition won', *Journal of Democracy* 33, 1(2022): 70–84.
3   Jean Blondel, 'Political opposition in the contemporary world', *Government and Opposition* 32, 4(1997): 462–86.
4   Sartori, *Parties and Party Systems*; Mottiar, 'The Democratic Alliance'.
5   Hideo Otake, 'Defense controversies and one-party dominance: The opposition in Japan and West Germany', in Theodore J. Pempel (ed.), *Uncommon Democracies: The One-Party Dominant Regimes* (New York: Cornell University Press, 1990), pp 128–61.

6   Pempel (ed.), *Uncommon Democracies: The One-Party Dominant Regimes* (New York: Cornell University Press, 1990).
7   Hermann Giliomee and Charles Simkins (eds), *The Awkward Embrace: One Party Domination and Democracy* (Cape Town: Tafelberg Publishers, 1999); Raymond Suttner, 'Party dominance "theory": Of what value?', *Politikon* 33, 3(2006): 277–97; Renske Doorenspleet and Nia Nijzink (eds), *Party Systems and Democracy in Africa* (Basingstoke: Palgrave Macmillan, 2014). The author has also drawn heavily on Michael Marchant, 'Understanding Opposition Party Failure and Success in Dominant Party Systems: A Literature Review' (Honours project, Faculty of Humanities, University of Cape Town, 2013) and Laurent Balt, 'An Evaluation of Greene's Resource Theory of Party Dominance' (Master's thesis, Faculty of Humanities, University of Cape Town, 2021).
8   Robert Dahl (ed.), *Political Opposition in Western Democracies* (New Haven, CT: Yale University Press, 1966), p 15.
9   Ethan Scheiner, *Democracy Without Competition in Japan: Opposition Failure in a One-Party Dominant State* (New York: Cambridge University Press, 2006).
10 Matthijs Bogaards, 'How to classify hybrid regimes?: Defective democracy and electoral authoritarianism', *Democratization* 16, 2(2009): 399–423.
11 Kenneth Greene, *Why Dominant Parties Lose: Mexico's Democratization in Comparative Perspective* (New York: Cambridge University Press, 2007).
12 Maurice Duverger, *Political Parties: Their Organization and Activity in the Modern State* (Cambridge: Cambridge University Press, 1964), pp 308–9; Giliomee and Simkins (eds), *The Awkward Embrace*, p 4.
13 Carolyn Forestiere and Christopher Allen, 'The formation of cognitive locks in single party dominant regimes', *International Political Science Review* 32, 4(2011): 380–95.
14 Robert Schrire, 'The realities of opposition in South Africa: Legitimacy, strategies and consequences', *Democratization* 8, 1(2001): 135–48.
15 Collette Schulz-Herzenberg, 'The 2019 national election results', in *Election 2019: Change and Stability in South Africa's Democracy* (Johannesburg: Jacana Media, 2019), pp 170–89.
16 Thiven Reddy, 'The Congress Party model: South Africa's African National Congress and India's Indian National Congress as dominant parties', *African and Asian Studies* 4, 3(2005): 271–300; Alan Arian and Samuel H. Barnes, 'The dominant party system: A neglected model of democratic stability', *The Journal of Politics* 36, 3(1974): 592–614; Anthony Butler, 'Considerations on the erosion of one-party dominance', *Representation* 45, 2(2009): 159–71.
17 For a fuller discussion of this issue, see Anthony Butler, *Contemporary South Africa* (New York: Palgrave Macmillan, 2017), Chapter 6.
18 Shane Mac Giollabhuí, 'How things fall apart: Candidate selection and

the cohesion of dominant parties in South Africa and Namibia', *Party Politics* 19, 4(2013): 577–600.
19 Giliomee and Simkins, *The Awkward Embrace*.
20 Giliomee and Simkins, *The Awkward Embrace*, pp 337–40.
21 Butler, 'Considerations'.
22 Fynbos Kapital and Fynbos Ekwitiet, vehicles of billionaire banker Michiel le Roux, each donated the maximum permitted amount of R15 million to the party in the reporting year 2022/23. Members of the Oppenheimer family likewise made substantial donations.
23 These include former leaders Mmusi Maimane and Herman Mashaba, who now head up competing parties, and promising younger activists such as Lindiwe Mazibuko and Phumzile van Damme.
24 The Political Party Funding Act, 2018 (Act 6 of 2018) requires declaration of donations above R100 000 and prohibits donations of more than R15 million from a single donor in a financial year.
25 World Economic Forum, *Global Risks Report 2022*, https://www.weforum.org/reports/global-risks-report-2022
26 South African Institute of Civil Engineers (SAICE), *Infrastructure Report Card for South Africa* (Midrand: SAICE, 2022), pp 8–11.
27 Paul Holden, *Zondo at Your Fingertips* (Johannesburg: Jacana Media, 2023).
28 Ricardo Hausmann, Federico Sturzenegger, Patricio Goldstein, Frank Muci and Douglas Barrios, 'Macroeconomic Risks After a Decade of Microeconomic Turbulence: South Africa (2007–2020)', WIDER Working Paper 2022/3 (Helsinki: UNU-WIDER, 2022).
29 Collette Schulz-Herzenberg and Robert Britt Mattes, 'It takes two to toyi-toyi: One party dominance and opposition party failure in South Africa's 2019 national election', *Democratization* (2023): 1–22. Those people who identify with a party are most likely to vote for it, even when times are tough.
30 Caryn Dolley, Msindisi Fengu, Mark Heywood and Ray Mahlaka, 'SA's delivery of crucial services under threat after Treasury desperately calls for public fiscal consolidation', *Daily Maverick*, 19 August 2023, https://www.dailymaverick.co.za/article/2023-08-19-sas-delivery-of-crucial-services-under-threat-after-treasury-desperately-calls-for-public-fiscal-consolidation/
31 Schulz-Herzenberg and Mattes, 'It takes two to toyi-toyi'.
32 Schulz-Herzenberg and Mattes, 'It takes two to toyi-toyi'.
33 Schulz-Herzenberg and Mattes, 'It takes two to toyi-toyi'.
34 Schulz-Herzenberg and Mattes, 'It takes two to toyi-toyi', pp 4–6.
35 SAICE, *Infrastructure Report Card*, pp 21–2.
36 World Bank, Worldwide Governance Indicators, https://www.govindicators.org/interactive-data-access
37 Karen E. Ferree, 'Explaining South Africa's racial census', *Journal of Politics* 68, 4(2006): 803–15.
38 David Everatt, 'The era of ineluctability? Post-apartheid South Africa

after 20 years of democratic elections', *Journal of Southern African Studies* 42, 1(2016): 49–64.
39   Schulz-Herzenberg and Mattes, 'It takes two to toyi-toyi', p 2.
40   Nicole Beardsworth, Hangala Siachiwena and Sishuwa Sishuwa, 'Autocratisation, electoral politics and the limits of incumbency in African democracies', *Journal of Eastern African Studies* 16, 4(2022): 515–35; Nic Cheeseman, *The Moral Economy of Elections in Africa* (Cambridge: Cambridge University Press, 2020), pp 6–7; Greene, *Why Dominant Parties Lose*, p 41.
41   Anthony Butler, *The Idea of the ANC* (Johannesburg: Jacana Media, 2012), pp 90–1.
42   Greene, *Why Dominant Parties Lose*, pp 52–61; see also Marchant, 'Understanding Opposition Party Failure', Conclusion.
43   Greene, *Why Dominant Parties Lose*, p 182.
44   Greene, *Why Dominant Parties Lose*, pp 221, 228.
45   Coalition politics is addressed in other chapters in this volume.
46   Nic Cheeseman and Brian Klaas, *How to Rig an Election* (New Haven, CT: Yale University Press, 2018).

Chapter 2: Coalition politics: Is this the way?
1   Nicolaus Tideman, 'The single transferable vote', *Journal of Economic Perspectives* 9, 1(1995): 27–38.
2   For an elaborate discussion of different permutations of the proportional electoral system, see Jason Eisner, 'Indirect STV election: A voting system for South Africa', Johns Hopkins University, https://www.cs.jhu.edu/~jason/papers/eisner.istv91.pdf
3   Staff writer, 'Marriages of inconvenience: The fraught politics of coalitions in South Africa', *The Conversation*, 14 September, 2021, https://theconversation.com/marriages-of-inconvenience-the-fraught-politics-of-coalitions-in-south-africa-167517
4   Anthony Downs, *An Economic Theory of Democracy* (New York: Harper and Brothers, 1957).
5   Constitution of the Republic of South Africa, 1993 (Act 200 of 1993), Schedule 4 (VIII).
6   Constitution of the Republic of South Africa, 1996 (Act 108 of 1996), Founding Provisions.
7   Samuel Makinda, 'Democracy and multi-party politics in Africa', *The Journal of Modern African Studies* 34, 4(1996): 555–73.
8   Makinda, 'Democracy and multi-party politics', p 556.
9   *New Nation Movement NPC and Others v President of the Republic of South Africa and Others* (CCT110/19) [2020] ZACC 11.

Other references
Ashworth, John, Benny Geys, Bruno Hyndels and Fanny Wille (eds). 'Political Competition and Local Government Performance: Evidence from Flemish Municipalities'. Paper presented at the European Public

Choice Society annual meeting, Türku, Finland, 20–22 April 2006.

Atkinson, Doreen. 'Taking to the streets: Has developmental local government failed?'. In *State of the Nation: South Africa 2005–2006*, edited by Sakhela Buhlungu, John Daniel, Roger Southall and Jessica Lutchman. Human Sciences Research Council, 2006.

Buček, Ján and Brian Smith. 'New approaches to local democracy: Direct democracy, participation and the "third sector"'. *Environmental and Planning C: Government and Policy* 18, 1(2000): 3–16.

Crook, Richard. 'Decentralisation and poverty reduction in Africa: The politics of local–central relations'. *Public Administration and Development* 23, 1(2003): 77–88.

Downs, Anthony. *An Economic Theory of Democracy*. Harper Brothers, New York, 1957.

Geyer, Yvette. 'Explainer: Can an independent candidate stand in more than one ward?'. *Mail & Guardian*, 3 August 2016, https://mg.co.za/article/2016-08-03-explainer-is-it-possible-for-an-independent-candidate-stand-in-more-than-one-ward/

Heller, Patrick. 'Moving the state: The politics of democratic decentralization in Kerala, South Africa, and Porto Alegre'. *Politics & Society* 29, 1(2001).

Lipset, Seymour and Stein Rokkan (eds). *Party Systems and Voter Alignment: Cross-National Perspectives*. The Free Press, New York, 1967.

Mainwaring, Scott and Timothy Scully. *Building Democratic Institutions: Party Systems in Latin America*. Stanford University Press, California, 1995.

Mainwaring, Scott and Edurne Zoco. 'Political sequences and stabilization of interparty competition: Electoral volatility in old and new democracies'. *Party Politics* 13, 2(2007).

Mataboge, Mmanaledi. 'ANC fears Tlokwe copycats'. *Mail & Guardian*, 5 July 2013, https://mg.co.za/article/2013-07-05-00-anc-fears-tlokwe-copycats/

Powell, Derek and Michael O'Donovan. *Civil Protests Barometer 2007–2014*. Ford Foundation, https://admin.dullahomarinstitute.org.za/acsl/barometers/20150219-civic-protest-barometer-published-dp.pdf

Chapter 3: The economy, business and reform

1 Statistics SA data (various).
2 Statistics SA data (various).
3 World Bank, *Poverty and Equity Brief – South Africa 2023*, https://databankfiles.worldbank.org/public/ddpext_download/poverty/987B9C90-CB9F-4D93-AE8C-750588BF00QA/current/Global_POVEQ_ZAF.pdf
4 SARS, 'Illicit trade – a threat to our people and sovereignty' (media statement), 22 January 2020, https://www.sars.gov.za/media-release/illicit-trade-a-threat-to-our-people-and-sovereignty/https://www.sars.gov.za/media-release/illicit-trade-a-threat-to-our-people-and-sovereignty/

5 World Bank, *The Container Port Performance Index 2022: A Comparable Assessment of Performance Based on Vessel Time in Port*, https://openknowledge.worldbank.org/entities/publication/6a51b12c-77cd-4236-be5b-13e468fe0cca
6 Transparency International, *Corruption Perceptions Index 2022*, https://www.transparency.org/en/cpi/2022?gclid=EAIaIQobChMI393010Pbgw-MVTYlQBh1S0QfjEAAYASAAEgJa8_D_BwE&gad_source=1
7 South African Cities Network, *State of City Finances Report 2022*, https://www.sacities.net/publication/state-of-city-finances-2022/
8 Human Rights Watch, *World Report 2023*, https://www.hrw.org/world-report/2023
9 Indlulamithi South Africa Scenarios 2030, https://indlulamithi.org.za/resources/indlulamithi-scenarios-2035/

Chapter 4: Power struggles: Shedding light on South Africa's enduring energy challenges

1 Hans-Otto Pörtner, Debra Roberts, Melinda Tignor and Elvira-Poloczanska (eds), *Climate Change 2022: Impacts, Adaptation and Vulnerability. Working Group II contribution to the Sixth Assessment Report of the Intergovernmental Panel on Climate Change (IPCC): Summary for Policymakers*, pp 3–33, available at file:///C:/Users/27834/Downloads/IPCC_AR6_WGII_SummaryVolume-compressed.pdf
2 Mekala Krishnan, Hamid Samandari, Jonathan Woetzel, Sven Smit, Daniel Pacthod, Dickon Pinner, Tomas Nauclér, Humayun Tai, Annabel Farr, Weige Wu and Danielle Imperato, *The net-zero transition. What it would cost, what it could bring*, McKinsey Global Institute, 2022, available at https://www.mckinsey.com/capabilities/sustainability/our-insights/the-net-zero-transition-what-it-would-cost-what-it-could-bring
3 Rod Crompton and Ruwadzano Matsika, 'Energy in South Africa', in Arkebe Oqubay, Fiona Tregenna and Imraan Valodia (eds), *The Oxford Handbook of the South African Economy* (Oxford: Oxford University Press, 2021), p 285.
4 BP, *Energy Outlook* 2023, p 6, available at https://www.bp.com/content/dam/bp/business-sites/en/global/corporate/pdfs/energy-economics/energy-outlook/bp-energy-outlook-2023.pdf
5 Simon Flowers, 'Six energy game-changers since 2015', Wood Mackenzie, 11 August 2023, available at https://www.woodmac.com/news/the-edge/six-energy-game-changers-since-2015/?utm_campaign=the-edge&utm_medium=email
6 Flowers, 'Six energy game-changers'.
7 Authors' calculation.
8 The minerals–energy complex was first identified in 1996 by Ben Fine and Zavareh Rustomjee, *The Political Economy of South Africa: From*

Minerals–Energy Complex to Industrialisation (London: Hurst, 1996).

9 Isabel Fick, 'South African power system transition: challenges and state of play' (paper presented at the webinar 'The Future of the Grid: Knowledge exchange with system operators and global experts', University of Cape Town, 13 September 2023).

10 Staff writer, 'South African households are beating Eskom at its own game with rooftop solar', *Businessech*, 27 July 2023, https://businesstech.co.za/news/energy/707210/south-african-households-are-beating-eskom-at-its-own-game-with-rooftop-solar/

11 As utilities lose sales volumes to other technologies, they raise their prices, which in turn leads to lower sales volumes as customers turn to other technologies.

12 South African Government, 'President Cyril Ramaphosa: 2022 State of the Nation Address', available at https://www.gov.za/speeches/president-cyril-ramaphosa-2022-state-nation-address-10-feb-2022-0000

13 Hartmut Winkler, 'South Africa's power crisis will continue until 2025 – and blackouts will take 5 years to phase out', *The Conversation*, 7 June 2023, https://theconversation.com/south-africas-power-crisis-will-continue-until-2025-and-blackouts-will-take-5-years-to-phase-out-206343.

14 Published by EE Business Intelligence using data from Eskom system status reports, https://www.eskom.co.za/eskom-divisions/tx/system-adequacy-reports/

15 Karl von Holdt, 'The political economy of corruption: Elite-formation, factions and violence', Working Paper 10, Society, Work and Politics Institute, University of the Witwatersrand, 2019, https://docs.wixstatic.com/ugd/de7bea_0590611beee14069a0e98f83dd26e9ae.pdf

16 Crompton and Matsika, 'Energy in South Africa', p 292.

17 Terence Creamer, 'Ramaphosa doubles next renewables round, scraps 100MW cap on distributed plant and moots feed-in tariff as he unveils load-shedding crisis response', *Engineering News*, 25 July 2022, https://www.engineeringnews.co.za/article/ramaphosa-doubles-next-renewables-round-to-5-200-mw-scraps-100-mw-cap-on-distributed-plant-and-moots-feed-in-tariff-as-he-unveils-load-shedding-crisis-response-2022-07-25

18 Carol Paton, 'Cabinet approves new SOE plan – which may mean JSE listings, private investments', *News24*, 14 September 2023, https://www.news24.com/fin24/economy/cabinet-approves-new-soe-plan-which-may-mean-jse-listings-private-investments-20230914

19 Mark Swilling, 'After the flip-flops and zig-zags, is a policy coherence emerging to resolve SA's energy crunch?', *Daily Maverick*, 5 May 2023, https://www.dailymaverick.co.za/article/2023-05-05-after-the-flip-flops-and-zig-zags-is-a-policy-coherence-emerging-to-resolve-sas-energy-crunch/

20 Launched by the President in 2022 at COP27.

21. The Presidency, Republic of South Africa, 'Just Energy Transition Implementation Plan 2023–2027', https://www.stateofthenation.gov.za/assets/downloads/JET%20Implementation%20Plan%202023-2027.pdf
22. Charles Hall, Jessica Lambert and Stephen Balogh, 'EROI of different fuels and the implications for society', *Energy Policy* 64(2014): 141–52.
23. Centre for Sustainability Transitions and the Blended Finance Taskforce, *Better Fnance, Better Grid,* Stellenbosch University, 2023, https://www.blendedfinance.earth/better-finance-better-grid
24. Fick, 'South African power system transition', p 2.
25. Personal communication from Gaylor Montmasson-Clair, 26 September 2023, based on SARS data accessed from Quantec and TradeMap.
26. Terence Creamer. 'Embedded generation project pipeline stands at 9 GW – Ramaphosa', *Engineering News*, 28 November 2023, https://www.engineeringnews.co.za/article/embedded-generation-project-pipeline-stands-at-9-gw-ramaphosa-2022-11-28
27. National Treasury, *Annexure W3 2023 Budget Review – Eskom Debt Relief*, p 1, https://www.treasury.gov.za/documents/national%20budget/2023/review/Annexure%20W3.pdf
28. J.P. Landman, 'Neither a one-day, nor a one-person job', JP Landman, 20 September 2023, http://www.jplandman.co.za/Home/Read/605
29. Winkler, 'South Africa's power crisis will continue'.
30. Centre for Sustainability Transitions and the Blended Finance Taskforce, *Better Fnance, Better Grid,* p 4.
31. Denene Erasmus, 'Ramokgopa warns of another electricity crisis ahead', *Business Day*, 21 September 2023, https://www.businesslive.co.za/bd/national/2023-09-21-ramokgopa-warns-of-another-electricity-crisis-ahead/#:~:text=Eskom%20will%20have%20to%20build,4%2C300km%20of%20transmission%20lines
32. Erasmus, 'Ramokgopa warns of another electricity crisis'.
33. Paddy Harper, 'R63 billion municipal debt places Eskom at risk, says minister', *Mail & Guardian*, 20 August 2023, https://mg.co.za/news/2023-08-20-r63-billion-municipal-debt-places-eskom-at-risk-says-minister/#:~:text=The%20metros%20and%20the%20rest,crisis%20were%20to%20be%20addressed.
34. Crompton and Matsika, 'Energy in South Africa', p 287.
35. Trading Economics, South Africa Imports By Category, https://tradingeconomics.com/south-africa-imports-by-category
36. Jan Rosenow, 'Is heating homes with hydrogen all but a pipe dream? An evidence review', *Joule*, 6(10).
37. Casey Crownhart, 'Everything you need to know about the wild world of heat pumps', MIT Technology Review, 2023, https://www.technologyreview.com/2023/02/14/1068582/everything-you-need-to-know-about-heat-pumps/#:~:text=Heat%20pumps%20today%20can%20reach,today%20reach%20around%2095%25%20efficiency

38 The Economist, 'Heat pumps show how hard decarbonisation will be – The row about them portends more backlashes against greenery', 6 September 2023, https://www.economist.com/leaders/2023/09/06/heat-pumps-show-how-hard-decarbonisation-will-be

39 Timothy Moore and Corinne Tynan, 'How much does heat pump installation cost?', *Forbes*, 20 July 2023, https://www.forbes.com/home-improvement/hvac/heat-pump-installation-cost/

40 National Business Initiative, *Decarbonising South Africa's Power System*, National Business Initiative, 2022, https://www.nbi.org.za/focus-areas/environmental-sustainability/climate-pathways-and-a-just-transition-for-south-africa/#reports

41 Lisa Steyn, 'Sasol in hot pursuit of cheap new gas supply to claw back Secunda fuel refinery write-off', *News24*, 24 August 2023, https://www.news24.com/fin24/companies/sasol-in-hot-pursuit-of-cheap-new-gas-supply-to-claw-back-secunda-fuel-refinery-write-off-20230824

42 Cato Koole and Thomas Blank, 'COP26 made clear that the world is ready for green hydrogen', Rocky Mountain Institute (RMI), 23 November 2021, https://rmi.org/cop26-made-clear-that-the-world-is-ready-for-green-hydrogen/

43 Robin Mills, 'Why green hydrogen is shaping the future of oil and gas majors', *The National*, 22 November 2021, https://www.thenationalnews.com/business/energy/2021/11/22/why-green-hydrogen-is-shaping-the-future-of-oil-and-gas-majors/

44 Ugo Bardi, 'A concise history of the concept of "Hydrogen Economy"', *Resilience*, 21 May 2021, https://www.resilience.org/stories/2021-05-21/a-concise-history-of-the-concept-of-hydrogen-economy/

45 Lyse Comins, 'Feasibility of green hydrogen hub in focus', *Southern Africa's freight news*, 20 January 2022, https://www.freightnews.co.za/article/feasibility-green-hydrogen-hub-focus; Terence Creamer, 'Namibia selects preferred bidder for pioneering $9.4bn green hydrogen project', *Engineering News*, 5 November 2021, https://www.engineeringnews.co.za/article/namibia-selects-preferred-bidder-for-pioneering-94bn-green-hydrogen-project-2021-11-05; Michael Mazengarb, 'Massive $15bn Desert Bloom green hydrogen project gets planning fast track', *Renew Economy*, 13 December 2021, https://reneweconomy.com.au/massive-15bn-desert-bloom-green-hydrogen-project-gets-planning-fast-track/

46 Hydrogen is easier to transport as ammonia.

47 Jennifer Bell, 'NEOM's green hydrogen plant will secure Saudi Arabia's clean energy transition: CEO', *Alarabiya News*, 31 May 2023, https://english.alarabiya.net/News/2023/05/25/Saudi-s-green-hydrogen-plant-will-put-Kingdom-on-global-map-for-clean-energy-CEO

48 Vaclav Smil, *Numbers Don't Lie: 71 Things You Need to Know about the World* (UK: Penguin, 2020, Kindle edition).

49 Sonja van Renssen, 'The hydrogen solution?' *Nature Climate Change*,

10(2020): 1–3; James Morris, 'Hydrogen is not a fuel, it's a cult', *Forbes*, 11 December 2021, https://www.forbes.com/sites/jamesmorris/2021/12/11/hydrogen-is-not-a-fuel-its-a-cult/?sh=2a1fb16e6d07

50 Emanuele Taibi, Herib Blanco, Raul Miranda and Marcelo Carmo, *Green Hydrogen Cost Reduction: Scaling Up Electrolysers to Meet the 1.5°C Climate Goal*, International Renewable Energy Agency, 2020, https://www.irena.org/-/media/Files/IRENA/Agency/Publication/2020/Dec/IRENA_Green_hydrogen_cost_2020.pdf

51 Herib Blanco, *Global Hydrogen Trade to Meet the 1.5°C Climate Goal: Part II – Technology Review of Hydrogen Carriers*, International Renewable Energy Agency, 2022, https://www.irena.org/publications/2022/Apr/Global-hydrogen-trade-Part-II#:~:text=ePub-,Global%20Hydrogen%20Trade%20to%20Meet%20the%201.5%C2%B0C%20Climate,carrier%20back%20to%20pure%20hydrogen

Chapter 5: Do geopolitics and trade clash? South Africa's foreign and trade policy options

1 Based on the World Bank's overview of South Africa, https://www.worldbank.org/en/country/southafrica/overview

2 Liesl Louw-Vaudran, 'Who has the power in SADC?', *ISS Today*, 27 August 2018, https://issafrica.org/iss-today/who-has-the-power-in-sadc

3 Academic Accelerator, 'Economy of South Africa', https://academic-accelerator.com/encyclopedia/economy-of-south-africa#

4 Department of Trade and Industry (DTIC), 'Update on South Africa's trade negotiations and trade relations', Presentation to the Portfolio Committee on Trade, Industry and Competition, 14 March, 2023, http://www.thedtic.gov.za/wp-content/uploads/Trade-Relations.pdf

5 Charalampos Efstathopoulos, 'Southern middle powers and the liberal international order: The options for Brazil and South Africa', *International Journal* 76(2021): 384–403.

6 Efstathopoulos, 'Southern middle powers'.

7 Chris Landsberg, 'Toward a developmental foreign policy? Challenges for South Africa's diplomacy in the second decade of liberation', *Social Research: An International Quarterly* 72, 3(2005): 723–56.

8 African National Congress, *Policy Conference 2022 Discussion Documents*, https://docs.google.com/viewerng/viewer?url=https://www.anc1912.org.za/wp-content/uploads/2022/05/Umrabulo-Policy-Document-18th-May-2022.pdf

9 Department of International Relations and Cooperation, *Annual Performance Plan 2023–2024*, https://www.dirco.gov.za/2023-2024-annual-performance-plan-2/

10 Trevor Shaku, 'Old wine, new bottle: The Economic Reconstruction and Recovery Plan', *South African Labour Bulletin*, 6 October 2021, https://www.southafricanlabourbulletin.org.za/old-wine-new-bottle-the-economic-reconstruction-and-recovery-plan/

11 Department of International Relations and Cooperation, *Framework Document on South Africa's National Interest and its Advancement in a Global Environment*, https://www.dirco.gov.za/national-interest-framework-doc/
12 This includes a vast range of capacity constraints: an unproductive and inadequately skilled workforce; weak infrastructure; low levels of investment; underutilisation of resource potential; socioeconomic impediments to productivity; low levels of innovation and technological development; energy and water constraints; land mismanagement; and so on. See also Matthew Stern and Yash Ramkolowan, 'Understanding South Africa's trade policy and performance', South African Reserve Bank, Working Paper Series WP/20/17, 2021, https://www.resbank.co.za/content/dam/sarb/publications/working-papers/2021/WP%202117.pdf
13 Anne Applebaum, 'The impossible suddenly became possible', *The Atlantic*, 1 March 2022, https://www.theatlantic.com/ideas/archive/2022/03/putins-war-dispelled-the-worlds-illusions/623335/
14 Yara Asi, 'A "crisis of relevance": UN failures in the MENA Region', Arab Center Washington DC, 5 October 2021, https://arabcenterdc.org/resource/a-crisis-of-relevance-un-failures-in-the-mena-region/
15 The Organisation for Economic Co-operation and Development, https://www.oecd.org/about/
16 Council on Foreign Relations, 'What does the G7 do?', 28 June 2023, https://www.cfr.org/backgrounder/what-does-g7-do
17 The Group of 77 at the United Nations, https://www.g77.org/doc/
18 BRICS Information Portal, https://infobrics.org/post/39594/
19 Saher Liaqat, 'BRICS and beyond: Shaping a new world order', *Sri Lankan Guardian*, 3 October 2023, https://slguardian.org/brics-and-beyond-shaping-a-new-world-order/
20 Delegation of the European Union to the Republic of South Africa, 'The European Union and South Africa', https://www.eeas.europa.eu/south-africa/european-union-and-south-africa_en?s=120
21 DTIC, 'Update on South Africa's trade negotiations'.
22 Office of the United States Trade Representative. 'South Africa', https://ustr.gov/countries-regions/africa/southern-africa/south-africa
23 Staff writer, 'SA benefits economically from BRICS grouping', *SANews*, 5 September 2023, https://www.sanews.gov.za/south-africa/sa-benefits-economically-brics-grouping
24 Trading Economics, 'South Africa exports to China', https://tradingeconomics.com/south-africa/exports/china
25 Cameron Mackay, 'Patel stresses importance of China–South Africa trade', *Engineering News*, 11 August 2023, https://www.engineeringnews.co.za/article/patel-stresses-importance-of-china-south-africa-trade-2023-08-11
26 Charlotte du Toit, e-mail message to author, 26 October 2023.
27 Department of Trade and Industry (DTIC), 'Driving Competitiveness: An

Integrated Industrial Strategy for Sustainable Employment and Growth', https://static.pmg.org.za/docs/2001/appendices/010529Strategy.htm
28 DTIC, 'Update on South Africa's trade negotiations'.
29 Stern and Ramkolowan, 'Understanding South Africa's trade policy'.
30 Staff writer, 'Free trade deal boosts Africa's economic development', World Bank, 30 June 2022, https://www.worldbank.org/en/topic/trade/publication/free-trade-deal-boosts-africa-economic-development#:~:text=A%20new%20agreement%20creating%20Africa's,people%20out%20of%20extreme%20poverty
31 Victor Mlambo, Xolani Thusi, Sphephelo Zubane and Daniel Mlambo, 'The African Continental Free Trade Area: Challenges and Possible Successes'. *Latin American Journal of Trade Policy* 12(2022).
32 Department of Planning, Monitoring and Evaluation. *Towards a 25-Year Review, 1994–2019*, https://www.dpme.gov.za/news/SiteAssets/Pages/25-Year-Review-Launch/Towards%20A%2025%20Year%20Review.pdf
33 Abel Esterhuyse, 'South Africa's foreign policy: New paper sets the scene, but falls short on specifics', *The Conversation*, 18 August 2022, https://theconversation.com/south-africas-foreign-policy-new-paper-sets-the-scene-but-falls-short-on-specifics-188253
34 Stern and Ramkolowan, 'Understanding South Africa's trade policy', pp 35–6.
35 Tinyiko Maluleke, 'Final push towards the NDP 2030 finish line – a vital call for action', *Daily Maverick*, 6 October 2023, https://www.dailymaverick.co.za/opinionista/2023-10-06-final-push-towards-the-ndp-2030-finish-line-a-vital-call-for-action/; Antony Sguazzin, 'The NDP is failing amid government inaction', *TechCentral*, 27 September 2023, https://techcentral.co.za/national-development-plan-little-to-show/232299/

Chapter 6: Is Africa open for business?
1 World Bank, #Africa Can, 'Overview', 5 October 2023, https://www.worldbank.org/en/region/afr/overview
2 Hicham El Habti, 'Why Africa's youth hold the key to its development', World Economic Forum, 19 September 2022, https://www.weforum.org/agenda/2022/09/why-africa-youth-key-development-potential/
3 Andrea Willige, 'Here's why Africa is world leader in digital and mobile banking', World Economic Forum, 21 November 2023, https://www.weforum.org/agenda/2023/11/africa-digital-mobile-banking-financial-inclusion/
4 tralac, 'South Africa: Intra-African trade and tariff profile 2022', 1 September 2023, https://www.tralac.org/resources/infographic/15181-south-africa-intra-africa-trade-and-tariff-profile.html
5 AfCFTA/WEF, *A New Era for Global Business and Investment in Africa – Insight Report*, January 2023, https://www3.weforum.org/docs/

NOTES AND OTHER REFERENCES

       WEF_Friends_of_the_Africa_Continental_Free_Trade_Area_2023.pdf

6   Calvin Phume, 'The African Continental Free Trade Area (AfCFTA) unveils remarkable benefits for South Africa', Department of Trade, Industry and Competition (DTIC) (media statement), 9 July 2023, http://www.thedtic.gov.za/the-african-continental-free-trade-area-afcfta-unveils-remarkable-benefits-for-south-africa/

7   AfCFTA/WEF, *A New Era for Global Business*.

8   McKinsey Global Institute, *Reimagining Economic Growth in Africa: Turning Diversity into Opportunity* (report), 5 June 2023, https://www.mckinsey.com/mgi/our-research/reimagining-economic-growth-in-africa-turning-diversity-into-opportunity

9   Zivanemoyo Chinzara, Sebastien Dessus and Stephan Dreyhaupt, 'Infrastructure in Africa: How Institutional Reforms can Attract More Private Investment', International Finance Corporation Working Paper, February 2023, https://www.ifc.org/content/dam/ifc/doc/2023/working-paper-infrastructure-in-africa.pdf

10   IMF, *World Economic Outlook (WEO)* (October 2023), https://www.imf.org/external/datamapper/datasets/WEO

11   UNWTO, 'International tourism to end 2023 close to 90% of pre-pandemic levels' (news release), 10 November 2023, https://www.unwto.org/news/international-tourism-to-end-2023-close-to-90-of-pre-pandemic-levels

12   Saifaddin Galal, 'Share of travel and tourism in Africa's gross domestic product (GDP) from 2019 to 2023', *Statista*, 4 December 2023, https://www.statista.com/statistics/1320400/share-of-travel-and-tourism-in-africas-gross-domestic-product/

13   Lumkile Mondi, 'South Africa and African continental economic integration in the 2020s', in Daniel Bradlow and Elizabeth Sidiropoulos (eds), *Values, Interests and Power: South African foreign policy in uncertain times* (Pretoria: Pretoria University Law Press, 2020).

Chapter 7: South Africa's financial future: Keeping the debt trap at bay

1   The figures represent the author's calculations based on the International Monetary Fund's *World Economic Outlook (October 2023)* database.

2   The figures represent the author's calculations based on the International Monetary Fund's *World Economic Outlook (October 2023)* database.

3   The figures represent the author's calculations based on the International Monetary Fund's *World Economic Outlook (October 2023)* database.

4   The graph shows the author's calculations based on the International Monetary Fund's *World Economic Outlook (October 2023)* database.

5   Hamid Davoodi, Paul Elger, Alexandra Fotiou, Daniel Garcia-Macia,

Xuehui Han, Andresa Lagerborg, Waikei Lam and Paulo Medas, 'Fiscal rules and fiscal councils: Recent Trends and Performance during the Covid-19 Pandemic', Working Paper No. 22/11, International Monetary Fund, Washington, DC, 27 January 2022, https://www.imf.org/en/Publications/WP/Issues/2022/01/21/Fiscal-Rules-and-Fiscal-Councils-512128

6   Davoodi et al., 'Fiscal rules and fiscal councils'.
7   The figures represent the author's calculations based on the International Monetary Fund's *World Economic Outlook (October 2023)* database.
8   The figures represent the author's calculations based on the International Monetary Fund's *World Economic Outlook (October 2023)* database.
9   The graph shows the author's calculations based on the International Monetary Fund's *World Economic Outlook (October 2023)* database.
10 National Treasury, 'Presentation to Standing Committee on Public Accounts – briefing on state-owned company (SOC) bailouts and government guarantees', 14 March 2023, https://static.pmg.org.za/230314_NT_-_SCOPA_Presentation_-_13_March_v2_-_SOEs_bailouts_and_guarantees.pdf
11 Author's calculation based on data from National Treasury for 'Presentation to Standing Committee on Public Accounts', 14 March 2023, https://static.pmg.org.za/230314_NT_-_SCOPA_Presentation_-_13_March_v2_-_SOEs_bailouts_and_guarantees.pdf
12 Staff writer, 'Free higher education for poor, working class students', *SANews*, 16 December 2017, https://www.sanews.gov.za/south-africa/free-higher-education-poor-working-class-students
13 South African Government, 'Presidency response on Heher Commission of Inquiry into Higher Education and Training', 16 December 2017, https://www.gov.za/news/media-statements/presidency-response-heher-commission-inquiry-higher-education-and-training-16#:~:text=The%20Commission%20recommended%20that%20all,Loans%20sourced%20from%20commercial%20banks
14 Victor Mlambo, Mduduzi Hlongwa and Mandla Mubecua (2018). 'The Provision of Free Higher Education in South Africa: A Proper Concept or a Parable?' *Journal of Education and Vocational Research* 8, 4(2017).
15 The Social Relief of Distressed Grant (SRD) was first introduced in May 2020, for an initial period of six months. However, given the subsequent waves of Covid-19, the SRD was extended for a further one-year period in 2021, 2022 and 2023. With each extension, the National Treasury has specified an expiry date for the grant.
16 National Treasury, *Medium-Term Budget Policy Statement*, 1 November 2023, p 35, https://www.treasury.gov.za/documents/mtbps/2023/mtbps/FullMTBPS.pdf

17 Quoted in Olivier Blanchard and Lawrence Summers (eds), *Evolution or Revolution? Rethinking Macroeconomic Policy after the Great Recession* (Cambridge, MA: MIT Press, 2019), p 105.
18 National Treasury, Budget Review 2020, p 26, https://www.treasury.gov.za/documents/national%20budget/2020/review/fullbr.pdf
19 Nancy Marion and Robert Flood, 'Getting Shut Out of the International Capital Markets: It Doesn't Take Much', Working Paper No. 06/144 (International Monetary Fund, Washington, DC, 2006), https://www.elibrary.imf.org/view/journals/001/2006/144/001.2006.issue-144-en.xml

Chapter 8: Banking on credibility: The central bank and monetary policy after 2024

1 The distinction between the SARB's monetary policy and balance sheet activities has been made in Stan du Plessis, 'A stone under the ocean: How money did not disappear and what we now need to do about it', Paper presented to the SA Reserve Bank conference, Pretoria, November 2012; also interview with the author, Stellenbosch, 3 November 2023.
2 Republic of South Africa, The Constitution of the Republic of South Africa 1996 (Act 108 of 1996), Chapter 13 (on the central bank); also, the South African Reserve Bank Act, 1989 (Act 90 of 1989), as amended, which establishes this as the primary objective of the Bank and adds: 'In addition, the Bank is responsible for protecting and maintaining financial stability...'
3 This section draws on Hilary Joffe, '"Dovish" deputy governor Kuben Naidoo resigns from Reserve Bank', *Business Day*, 23 October 2023, https://www.businesslive.co.za/bd/national/2023-10-23-dovish-deputy-governor-kuben-naidoo-resigns-from-reserve-bank/; Hilary Joffe, 'The president must act to avert a messy success at Reserve Bank', *Business Day*, 27 October 2023, https://www.businesslive.co.za/bd/opinion/columnists/2023-10-27-hilary-joffe-the-president-must-act-to-avert-a-messy-succession-at-reserve-bank/
4 The MPC has in the past comprised up to seven members, but in recent years the number has dropped to just five. There is a case to be made for a larger committee as it ensures more diversity of opinion and there is less likelihood that it will be dominated by the views of the Governor, who has the casting vote in the event of a tie. It has also been suggested – see, for example, Raymond Parsons, 'The Bank might draw less flak if MPC's dissenting views were aired', *Business Day*, 11 August 2022, https://www.businesslive.co.za/bd/opinion/2022-08-11-raymond-parsons-the-bank-might-draw-less-flak-if-mpcs-dissenting-views-were-aired/ – that outside experts should be invited to join the committee. However, this could raise concerns about consistency in the Bank's monetary policy communications because outside members would not be subject to the same disciplines or the same accountability

as Bank staff.

5. For a useful discussion of how expectations and the central bank's credibility have influenced inflation outcomes over the recent cycle, see Pongpitch Amatyakul, Fiorella De Fiore, Marco Lombardi, Benoit Mojon and Daniel Rees, 'The contribution of monetary policy to disinflation', *BIS Bulletin* no. 82, Bank for International Settlements, December 2023, https://www.bis.org/publ/bisbull82.pdf

6. Economic Freedom Fighters, *Founding Manifesto*, 27 July 2013.

7. S'thembile Cele and Prinesha Naidoo, 'Mantashe: Reserve Bank's mandate must expand to meet SA's needs', *Bloomberg News*, 6 January 2023, https://www.bloomberg.com/news/articles/2023-01-06/south-africa-s-ruling-party-wants-to-change-central-bank-mandate; Natasha Marrian, 'Reserve Bank mandate up for debate — again', *Financial Mail*, 29 July 2022, https://www.businesslive.co.za/fm/fm-fox/2022-07-29-reserve-bank-mandate-up-for-debate-again/

8. Staff writer, 'Ramaphosa: Hands off Reserve Bank, for now', *BusinessTech*, 3 November 2023, https://businesstech.co.za/news/finance/729129/ramaphosa-hands-off-the-reserve-bank-for-now/

9. Jacob Frenkel, Raghuram Rajan and Axel Weber, 'The world needs a humble approach to central banking', On Point, Project Syndicate, December 2023, https://www.project-syndicate.org/onpoint/central-banks-cannot-solve-all-problems-focus-on-core-mandate-by-jacob-frenkel-2-et-al-2023-12

10. Gita Gopinath (International Monetary Fund), 'Charting a course through rough seas: How emerging markets can navigate tougher external conditions', Keynote address at the SARB Biennial Conference, Cape Town, 1 September 2023.

11. See, for example, Institute for International Finance, *Capital Flows Report: The fading COVID inflation shock*, IIF, December 2023.

12. Lesetja Kganyago, 'Statement of the Monetary Policy Committee' (press statement), South African Reserve Bank, 23 November 2023, https://www.resbank.co.za/content/dam/sarb/publications/statements/monetary-policy-statements/2023/november-/Statement%20of%20the%20Monetary%20Policy%20Committee%20November%202023.pdf

13. For a discussion of the case for a lower target and the success in reducing trend inflation after 2017 without any loss in terms of economic output, see Christopher Loewald, Konstantin Makrelov and Ekaterina Pirozhkova, 'The short-term costs of reducing trend inflation in South Africa', SARB Working Paper Series WP/22/08, 2 August 2022, https://www.resbank.co.za/content/dam/sarb/publications/working-papers/2022/WP%202208.pdf

14. Lesetja Kganyago, 'Statement of the Monetary Policy Committee'.

15. South African Reserve Bank, *Monetary Policy Review*, October 2023.

16. See (most recent) South African Reserve Bank, *Financial Stability Review*, May 2023 and *Monetary Policy Review*, October 2023.

17 This section draws on Hilary Joffe, 'No fall off a fiscal cliff, but a slow-burn route to "financial repression"', *Business Day*, 10 November 2023, https://www.businesslive.co.za/bd/opinion/columnists/2023-11-10-hilary-joffe-no-fall-off-a-fiscal-cliff-but-a-slow-burn-route-to-financial-repression/

18 Carmen Reinhart, Jacob Kirkegaard and M. Belen Sbrancia (International Monetary Fund), 'Financial Repression Redux', *Finance & Development* 48, 1(2011), June.

19 Andrew Donaldson, 'Monetary Management, Financial Markets and public debt: Responding to Covid-19 and the Economic Standstill', Policy brief, Southern Africa Labour and Development Research Unit, University of Cape Town, April 2020, https://covid19economicideas.org/wp-content/uploads/2020/04/Monetary-management_in_covid19_Donaldson_09042020.pdf

20 Gilad Isaacs, Zimbali Mncube, Liso Mdutyana and Kamal Ramburuth, 'Is South Africa Heading for a "Fiscal Crisis"?', Policy brief, Institute for Economic Justice, September 2023, https://www.iej.org.za/wp-content/uploads/2023/10/IEJ-fiscal-crisis-policybrief-2023-12-october.pdf; Joseph Cotterill, 'Ramaphosa government faces calls to tap foreign exchange gains to ease debt burden', *Financial Times*, 16 November 2023, https://www.ft.com/content/967fba57-e40a-4b95-8938-abef287772a6

21 Du Plessis, 'A stone under the ocean'.

22 The Economist, '2024 is the biggest election year in history', 13 November 2023, https://www.economist.com/interactive/the-world-ahead/2023/11/13/2024-is-the-biggest-election-year-in-history

Other references

Cassim, Rashad. 'The state of the South African economy and the role of monetary policy'. Presentation at the Central Banking Conference, Cape Town, March 2023.

Gopinath, Gita. 'Three uncomfortable truths for monetary policy', Remarks made at the European Central Bank Forum on Central Banking, 28 August 2023.

Kganyago, Lesetja. 'Keeping it simple: Monetary policy, growth and jobs in South Africa'. Public lecture at the Wits School of Governance, November 2022.

Kganyago, Lesetja. 'South Africa: A road well traveled'. *Finance & Development*, International Monetary Fund, March 2023.

Republic of South Africa. 'Medium Term Budget Policy Statement 2023.' National Treasury, 1 November 2023.

Sachs, Michael. '"Grim Determination": Reflections on the 2023 MTBPS', Public Economy Project, Presentation to Parliament, November 2023 (unpublished).

South African Reserve Bank, *Monetary Policy Review*, May 2023.

Chapter 9: Broadening farm ownership for successful transformation in South African agriculture

1. Johann Kirsten and Ferdi Meyer, 'Agriculture sector progress versus the targets of the NDP', Bureau for Economic Research media release, 27 September 2023, https://www.bfap.co.za/wp-content/uploads/2023/10/Press-release-ag-performance-vs-NDP.pdf
2. Kirsten and Meyer, 'Agriculture sector progress'.
3. Johann Kirsten, Aart-Jan Verschoor and Colleta Gandidzanwa, 'The South African government has been buying farmland for black farmers: It's not gone well', *The Conversation*, 9 January 2023, https://theconversation.com/the-south-african-government-has-been-buying-farmland-for-black-farmers-its-not-gone-well-197201
4. South African Government, *Final Report of the Presidential Advisory Panel on Land Reform and Agriculture*, 4 May 2019, https://www.gov.za/documents/other/final-report-presidential-advisory-panel-land-reform-and-agriculture-28-jul-2019

Chapter 11: Local government in South Africa after the 2024 election: Will the desirable or the probable outcome prevail?

1. Nica Richards, 'ANC members accused of corruption "must change their ways or leave, asserts Ramaphosa', *The Citizen*, 23 August 2020, https://www.citizen.co.za/news/south-africa/politics/anc-members-accused-of-corruption-must-change-their-ways-or-leave-asserts-ramaphosa/
2. Zintle Mahlti, '"Nothing has changed": Zondo fears state will be captured again, and Parliament won't stop it, again', *News24*, 22 June 2023, https://www.news24.com/news24/politics/government/nothing-has-changed-zondo-fears-state-will-be-captured-again-and-parliament-wont-stop-it-again-20230622
3. Charles Dickens, *A Tale of Two Cities* (UK: Penguin Classics, 1859).
4. Ketumile Masire et al., 'Leadership in Africa: The Mombassa Declaration, African Leadership Council', facilitated by Robert Rotberg, Belfer Center, Kennedy School of Government, Harvard University, https://www.belfercenter.org/publication/african-leadership-council
5. J.D. Meier, 'What is strategic foresight?', https://jdmeier.com/what-is-strategic-foresight/
6. South African Government, Constitution of the Republic of South Africa, 1996 (Act 108 of 1996), https://www.gov.za/documents/constitution/constitution-republic-south-africa-1996-04-feb-1997
7. South African Government, Municipal Systems Act, 2000 (Act 32 of 2000), https://www.gov.za/documents/local-government-municipal-systems-act
8. National Planning Commission, *National Development Plan 2030: Our future, make it work*, https://www.nationalplanningcommission.org.za/National_Development_Plan
9. Richard Bolden, '*Ubuntu*', in David Coghlan and Mary Brydon-Miller (eds), *Encyclopedia of Action Research* (Sage, 2014).

10. Londiwe Buthelezi, '"We've got a bunch of thieves ruling us" – Mathews Phosa', *News24*, 20 July 2023, https://www.news24.com/fin24/economy/weve-got-a-bunch-of-thieves-ruling-us-mathews-phosa-20230720
11. Auditor-General South Africa, 'PFMA General Reports', https://www.agsa.co.za/Reporting/PFMAReports.aspx#:~:text=PFMA%20General%20Reports&text=We%20focus%20on%20auditing%20areas,the%20lives%20of%20our%20people
12. Auditor-General South Africa, *Consolidated General Report on Local Government Audit Outcomes, PFMA 2016–17*, https://www.agsa.co.za/Portals/0/Reports/PFMA/201617/GR/AG%20PFMA%202017%20Web%20SMALL.pdf
13. Auditor-General South Africa, *Consolidated General Report on Local Government Audit Outcomes, MFMA 2021–22*, https://www.agsa.co.za/Portals/0/Reports/MFMA/2021-22/MFMA%20Report%202021-22%20FINAL%20-%2031%20May%202023.pdf?ver=2023-05-31-072950-280
14. South African Government, 'President Cyril Ramaphosa focuses Presidential Coordinating Council on service delivery' (media statement), https://www.gov.za/news/media-statements/president-cyril-ramaphosa-focuses-presidential-coordinating-council-service
15. Organisation Undoing Tax Abuse (OUTA), 'Active citizens are needed to stop the financial rot' (blog), https://www.outa.co.za/blog/newsroom-1/post/active-citizens-are-needed-to-help-stop-the-financial-rot-in-municipalities-1161
16. Corruption Watch, *South Africa Needs Clean Hands*, 2021, https://www.corruptionwatch.org.za/wp-content/uploads/2021/08/CW-local-govt-sectoral-report-August2021.pdf
17. Edelman, *2023 Edelman Trust Barometer South Africa*, https://www.africa.edelman.com/sites/g/files/aatuss536/files/2023-03/2023%20Edelman%20Trust%20Barometer_S.%20Africa%20Report-final.pdf
18. Joleen Steyn and Ben Roberts, 'South Africans are fed up with their prospects and their democracy, according to latest social attitudes survey', *The Conversation*, 26 April 2023, https://theconversation.com/south-africans-are-fed-up-with-their-prospects-and-their-democracy-according-to-latest-social-attitudes-survey-204566
19. Erwin Schwella, 'Knowledge based governance: Governance as learning: The leadership implications', *International Journal of Leadership in Public Services* 10, 2(2014): 84–90.
20. World Health Organization, 'Systems thinking', https://ahpsr.who.int/what-we-do/thematic-areas-of-focus/systems-thinking
21. Ebuwa Evbuoma, Min Hu, Allie Farrell, William Liem and Ellis Ballard, 'Systems thinking iceberg: Diving beneath the surface in education systems', Methods Brief Series 1.01, Social System Design Lab, Washington University in St Louis, 4 September 2021, https://doi.org/10.7936/g9eh-8176

Chapter 12: Finding new, bottom-up solutions to grassroots socioeconomic challenges

1. Nivashni Nair, 'SA must reset its moral compass: Archbishop Thabo Makgoba on UDF's 40th anniversary', *TimesLive*, 20 August 2023, https://www.timeslive.co.za/politics/2023-08-20-sa-must-reset-its-moral-compass-archbishop-thabo-makgoba-on-udfs-40th-anniversary/
2. Victor Sulla, Precious Zikhali and Pablo Cuevas, *Inequality in Southern Africa: An assessment of the Southern African Customs Union* (Washington DC: World Bank, 2022), p 11, https://documents1.worldbank.org/curated/en/099125303072236903/pdf/P1649270c02a1f06b0a3ae02e57eadd7a82.pdf
3. Klaus Schwab, 'Now is the time for a "great reset"', World Economic Forum, 3 June 2020, https://www.weforum.org/agenda/2020/06/now-is-the-time-for-a-great-reset/
4. I have used these apartheid-era classifications in this context, not because I believe they are particularly useful but because that is how the policy is framed and it forms the basis of how progress has been measured over the past three decades – in particular, the extent and rate of growth of 'black ownership' in the economy and its key sectors.
5. Ben Gran and Mitch Strohm, 'What is a community bank?', *Forbes Advisor*, 11 August 2021, https://www.forbes.com/advisor/banking/what-is-a-community-bank/
6. Name has been changed.
7. Lizeka Tandwa, 'Mantashe: Don't rely on government to get you out of poverty', *Mail & Guardian*, 22 August 2023, https://mg.co.za/politics/2023-08-22-mantashe-dont-rely-on-government-to-get-you-out-of-poverty/
8. Jeanette Nagy, 'Community Toolbox. Section 1. Strategies for Community Change and Improvement: An Overview', Center for Community Health and Development, University of Kansas, 2017, https://ctb.ku.edu/en/table-of-contents/assessment/promotion-strategies/overview/main
9. Parliament of the Republic of South Africa Research Unit, *Overview Of Municipalities Under Section 139 Intervention As It Relates To Service Delivery*, 31 August 2020, p 2, https://www.parliament.gov.za/storage/app/media/Pages/2020/september/02-09-2020_National_Council_of_Provinces_Local_Government_Week/docs/municipalities_under_Section_139_intervention_as_it_relates_to_service_delivery.pdf
10. Stephen de Vries and Isioma Ile, 'Low hanging fruit for improved Governance through participatory monitoring and evaluation system in South Africa – With specific reference to ward committee's system', *African Journal of Public Affairs* 12, 1(2021).
11. World Health Organization, '7th Global Conference on Health Promotion: Track themes', Nairobi, 2009, https://www.who.int/

teams/health-promotion/enhanced-wellbeing/seventh-global-conference/community-empowerment

Chapter 13: Strengthening the institutions of public accountability in South Africa

1. South African Government, Constitution of the Republic of South Africa, 1996 (Act 108 of 1996), Chapter 1 (Founding Provisions), https://www.gov.za/documents/constitution/constitution-republic-south-africa-1996-chapter-1-founding-provisions-04-feb
2. Hugh Corder, Saras Jagwanth and Fred Soltau, *Report on Parliamentary Oversight and Accountability*, Faculty of Law, University of Cape Town, 1999, https://www.casac.org.za/wp-content/uploads/2015/07/Report-on-Parliamentary-Oversight-and-Accountability.pdf
3. Pranish Desai and Mxolisi Zondo, 'How to resolve SA's accountability crisis', *Mail & Guardian*, 5 July 2023, https://mg.co.za/thought-leader/2023-07-05-how-to-resolve-sas-political-accountability-crisis/
4. Haroon Bhorat, Mbongiseni Buthelezi, Ivor Chipkin, Sikhulekile Duma, Lumkile Mondi, Camaren Peter, Mzukisi Qobo and Mark Swilling, *Betrayal of the Promise: How South Africa is being stolen* (Public Affairs Research Institute, May 2017), https://pari.org.za/betrayal-promise-report/
5. Mbongiseni Buthelezi and Peter Vale (eds), *State Capture in South Africa: How and Why it Happened* (Johannesburg: Wits University Press, 2023).
6. Many of these recommendations are carefully summarised by Paul Holden, *Zondo at your Fingertips* (Johannesburg: Jacana Media, 2023).
7. Holden, Zondo at your Fingertips, p 55.
8. Holden, Zondo at your Fingertips, p 413.
9. 'Politics of Betrayal', in Haroon Bhorat Mbongiseni Buthelezi, Ivor Chipkin, Sikhulekile Duma, Lumkile Mondi, Camaren Peter, Mzukisi Qobo and Mark Swilling, *Betrayal of the Promise: How South Africa is being stolen*, Public Affairs Research Institute, May 2017, p 4, https://pari.org.za/wp-content/uploads/2017/05/Betrayal-of-the-Promise-25052017.pdf
10. Kwazi Dlamini, 'Scorpions' downfall due to political interference', Corruption Watch, 10 October 2018, https://www.corruptionwatch.org.za/political-interference-in-south-africas-elite-anti-corruption-unit-leads-to-impunity/; *Helen Suzman Foundation v President of the Republic of South Africa and others* [2014] ZACC 32 at paras 220–22.
11. *Corruption Watch NPC and others v President of the Republic of South Africa and others* [2018] ZACC 23 at para 188.
12. See the Amended National State Enterprises Bill of 2023 which seeks to implement the Zondo recommendations.
13. *New Nation Movement NPC v President of the Republic of South Africa* [2020] ZACC 1.
14. Dlamini, 'Scorpions' downfall'.

15 Sinosipho Shrieber, 'Zondo says disbanding Scorpions was "the worst decision ever"', *Business Day*, 9 November 2023, https://www.businesslive.co.za/bd/national/2023-11-09-zondo-says-disbanding-scorpions-was-the-worst-decision-ever/
16 Paul Hoffman, 'Avoiding a repeat of the worst excesses of state capture', *BizNews*, 14 February 2023, https://www.biznews.com/global-citizen/2023/02/14/paul-hoffman-avoiding-repeat-worst-excesses-state-capture
17 Christopher Chen, 'Solving the puzzle of corporate governance of state-owned enterprises: The path of Temasek model in Singapore and lessons from China', *Northwestern Journal of International Law and Business* 36, 3(2016): 303–370.
18 Chen, 'Solving the puzzle', p 313.
19 Karl von Holdt, 'Elite formation, factions, and violence in the political economy of corruption', in Mbongiseni Buthelezi and Peter Vale (eds), *State Capture in South Africa: How and Why it Happened* (Johannesburg: Wits University Press, 2023).
20 Crispian Olver, *How to Steal a City: The Battle for Nelson Mandela Bay* (Johannesburg and Cape Town: Jonathan Ball, 2017).

Chapter 14: South Africa: Grappling with the 'age of uncertainty'
1 North-West University Policy Uncertainty Index (PUI) 4Q 2023.
2 Quoted in Raymond Parsons and Waldo Krugell, 'Policy uncertainty, the economy and business', *South African Journal of Economic and Management Sciences* 25, 1(2022): 1–9.
3 Daniel Kahneman, *Thinking, Fast and Slow* (USA: Penguin Books, 2011), pp 256–63.
4 Kristalina Georgieva, 'The financial sector in the 2020s: Building a more inclusive system in the new decade', Speech given at the Peterson Institute for International Economics, Washington DC, 17 January 2020.
5 World Economic Forum, *The Global Risks Report, 19th edition*, https://reliefweb.int/report/world/global-risks-report-2024-19th-edition-insight-report#:~:text=The%20Global%20Risks%20Report%20explores,a%20warming%20planet%20and%20conflict
6 Compelling case studies on how several adroit smaller economies – ranging from Singapore to Botswana – have successfully navigated a volatile and uncertain world in smarter ways than the traditional great powers are well outlined in Armen Sarkissian, *The Small States Club – How Small Smart States Can Save the World* (UK: Hurst & Company, 2023).
7 Brian Kantor and David Holland, 'Dollar-rand exchange rate is not a mystery', *Business Day*, 19 January 2024, https://www.businesslive.co.za/bd/opinion/columnists/2024-01-19-brian-kantor-and-david-holland-the-dollar-rand-exchange-rate-is-not-a-mystery/#google_vignette (in their article, Kantor and Holland assess that domestic

'shocks' explain up to 46 per cent of the movement in the rand relative to other emerging-market currencies).

8   Nedbank, 'Nedbank Capital Expenditure Project Listing: 2023', 12 February 2024, https://www.nedbank.eo.za/content/dam/nedbank/site-assets/AboutUs/Economics_Unit/Research/EconomicResearch/Nedbank%20Capital%20Expenditure%20Project%20Listing%202023.pdf
9   National Planning Commission, *Ten-Year Review of the NDP 2012–2022*, https://www.nationalplanningcommission.org.za/assets/Documents/Ten%20Year%20Review%20of%20the%20National%20Development%20Plan_26%20September%202023.pdf
10 BLSA, 'Building Competitiveness: Business Leadership South Africa's Response to the National Development Plan', 2013, pp 9–10.
11 Quoted in Parsons and Krugell, 'Policy uncertainty'.
12 Staff writer, 'Kganyago sees 2024 elections among top risks for South Africa', *Bloomberg*, 3 December 2023, https://www.bloomberg.com/news/articles/2023-12-03/kganyago-sees-2024-elections-among-top-risks-for-south-africa
13 Kexin Chew, He Kie and Zhenyu Ge, 'Policy uncertainty and FDI: Evidence from national elections', *Journal of International Trade and Economic Development* 28, 4(2019).
14 May Wong, 'A dangerous mix of polarization and uncertainty during election time', Stanford Institute for Economic Policy Research, 15 October 2020, https://siepr.stanford.edu/news/dangerous-mix-polarization-and-uncertainty-during-election-time
15 Pranish Desai, 'South African politics: Uncertainty prevails', Good Governance Africa, 11 November 2022, https://gga.org/south-african-politics-uncertainty-prevails/
16 Jason Swartz, 'How to prepare for the uncertainty of political coalitions in SA', *Business Day*, 21 August 2023, https://www.businesslive.co.za/bd/opinion/2023-08-21-jason-swartz-how-to-prepare-for-the-uncertainty-of-political-coalitions-in-sa/
17 Raymond Parsons, *Good Capitalism, Bad Capitalism* (Johannesburg: Jacana Media, 2018), p 119.
18 Mark Carney, 'Uncertainty, the economy and policy', Speech delivered at the Bank of England, London, 30 June 2016, https://www.bis.org/review/r160704c.pdf
19 Staff writer, 'Kganyago sees 2024 elections among top risks'.
20 Noel Chester, 'The role of economic advisers in government', in Anthony Thirlwall (ed.), *Keynes as a Policy Adviser* (London: Macmillan, 1982).
21 BLSA, 'Building Competitiveness', p 10.
22 World Economic Forum, *The Global Risks Report*, p 87.
23 BLSA, 'Building Competitiveness', p 11.
24 Gordon Brown, Mohamed El-Erian and Michael Spence, *Permacrisis: A Plan to Fix a Fractured World* (London: Simon & Schuster, 2023), p 164.

25 Cyril Ramaphosa, Opening remarks at the meeting of the Presidential Economic Advisory Council, Cape Town, 27 September 2019, https://www.gov.za/news/speeches/president-cyril-ramaphosa-presidential-economic-advisory-council-meeting-09-oct-2019
26 Tanya Cohen, 'The emerging role of business: From outsider to strategic partner', in Raymond Parsons (ed.), *Recession, Recovery and Reform – South Africa after Covid-19* (Johannesburg: Jacana Media, 2020) pp 138–9.
27 Raymond Parsons, *Good Capitalism, Bad Capitalism: The Role of Business in South Africa* (Johannesburg: Jacana Media, 2018), pp 140–54.
28 Nicholas Bloom, Hites Ahir and Davide Furceri, 'Visualizing the rise of global economic uncertainty', *Harvard Business Review*, 29 September 2022, https://hbr.org/2022/09/visualizing-the-rise-of-global-economic-uncertainty
29 John Kay and Mervyn King, *Radical Uncertainty: Decision-making for an Unknowable Future* (UK: Bridge Street Press, 2020).
30 National Planning Commission, *National Development Plan 2030: Our future, make it work*, https://www.nationalplanningcommission.org.za/National_Development_Plan

Other references
Baker, Scott, Aniket Baksy, Nicholas Bloom, Steven Davis and Jonathan Rodden. 'Elections, Political Polarization, and Economic Uncertainty'. National Bureau of Economic Research Working Paper 27961, October 2020, https://www.nber.org/papers/w27961
David, Antonio and Can Sever. 'Unpleasant surprises? Elections and tax news shocks'. International Monetary Fund Working Paper, June 2023, https://www.imf.org/en/Publications/WP/Issues/2023/06/30/Unpleasant-Surprises-Elections-and-Tax-News-Shocks-534334
Galbraith, John Kenneth. *The Age of Uncertainty*. London: BBC/Andre Deutsch, 1977.
Goodell, John, Richard McGee and Frank McGroarty. 'Election uncertainty, economic policy uncertainty and financial market uncertainty: A prediction market analysis'. *Journal of Banking & Finance* 110(2019).
Mordfin, Robin. 'The Price of Policy Uncertainty – what scares investors most is not knowing the government's next move.' *Chicago Booth Review*, 11 September 2014, https://www.chicagobooth.edu/review/price-of-policy-uncertainty
Redl, Chris. 'Uncertainty matters: Evidence from close elections'. *Journal of International Economics* 124(2020).
Stiglitz, Joseph. 'Time for a Victory Lap?' The American Prospect – Ideas, Politics and Power, 4 January 2024, https://prospect.org/topics/joseph-stiglitz/

Index

A

Accelerated and Shared Growth Initiative for South Africa (AsgiSA) 182
Action SA 5
active citizen(ry) 137, 158, 159, 160, 163
advanced economy 72, 90, 96, 101, 102, 103, 108
African Continental Free Trade Area (AfCFTA) 60, 68, 75, 76, 80, 81
African Growth and Opportunity Act (AGOA) 65
African National Congress (ANC) 1, 2, 3, 4, 5, 7, 8, 9, 10, 11, 12, 13, 14, 16, 18, 23, 24, 42, 43, 44, 58, 59, 69, 100, 108, 110, 133, 138, 148, 153, 155, 167, 171, 176, 178, 187, 188
African Union (AU) 74, 78
Agricultural Land Holding Account Trading Entity 112
Agricultural Research Council 114
Airports Company South Africa (ACSA) 88
apartheid 1, 10, 19, 20, 21, 22, 24, 50, 57, 73, 108, 137, 151, 165, 171
Arms Deal 178
artificial intelligence (AI) 73, 126
Association of Southeast Asian Nations (ASEAN) 76
Auditor-General South Africa (AGSA) 50, 129, 130, 139, 140, 165, 168
authoritarianism 2, 4, 179

B

B-BBEE Commission 156
big data analytics 126
black economic empowerment 153
BRICS 38, 63, 64, 65, 67, 68, 74
BRICS Business Council 68
broad-based black economic empowerment (B-BBEE) 116, 117, 155
Broad-Based Black Economic Empowerment (B-BBEE) Amendment Act, 2013 155
Budget Review (2023) 43
Business for South Africa (BSA) 31, 32, 33
Business Leadership South Africa (BLSA) 185, 191, 193
Business Unity South Africa (BUSA) 31, 32, 33, 194

C

cadre deployment 43, 136, 177
capitalism 62, 182
carbon tax 54
central bank 95, 96, 99, 100, 101, 102, 103, 104, 106, 108, 109, 110, 190
climate change 37, 45, 69, 78, 103, 184 (see also 'global warming')
coalition(s) 2, 10, 12, 13, 15, 16, 17, 18, 19, 22, 23, 24, 25, 29, 95, 100, 162, 187, 188, 189, 194
Cohen, Tanya 194
colonialism 20, 22, 138
community empowerment 162, 163
community organising 160, 161
Companies and Intellectual Property Commission (CIPC) 129
Comprehensive Agricultural Support Programme (CASP) 118, 120

Conference of the Parties (COP) 38, 54 (see also 'United Nations Framework Convention on Climate Change Conference of the Parties')
Congress of the People (COPE) 4, 5
constituency electoral system 174, 175 (see also 'electoral system')
Constitution of the Republic of South Africa, 1993 18, 19
Constitution of the Republic of South Africa, 1996 18, 19, 25, 96, 97, 111, 136, 141, 148, 149, 165, 166, 171, 172
constitutionalism 152
Convention for a Democratic South Africa (CODESA) 21, 22
corruption 2, 5, 8, 28, 31, 41, 71, 88, 123, 124, 127, 131, 133, 134, 137, 138, 139, 141, 143, 146, 151, 167, 168, 170, 172, 174, 176, 177, 178, 179
Corruption Perceptions Index 28
Corruption Watch 141
Corruption Watch NPC and others v President of the Republic of South Africa and others 173
Covid-19 pandemic 61, 72, 76, 78, 84, 85, 86, 89, 91, 102, 103, 108, 154, 184

D

debt trap 83, 92, 93
delivery state 194
democracy 1, 2, 3, 4, 5, 15, 16, 18, 19, 20, 21, 22, 24, 62, 71, 73, 80, 110, 111, 136, 142, 143, 151, 152, 153, 154, 158, 160, 163, 166, 172, 178, 188
Democratic Alliance (DA) 3, 6, 11, 12, 13, 87
Denel 88
Department of Agriculture, Land Reform and Rural Development (DALRRD) 117, 119
Department of International Relations and Cooperation (DIRCO) 59, 68
Department of Public Enterprises 169
Department of Trade, Industry and Competition (DTIC) 58, 75
Development Bank of Southern Africa (DBSA) 117
developmental state 153
Directorate for Priority Crime Investigation (aka Hawks) 176
Directorate of Special Operations (aka Scorpions) 176, 177
dominant party system 2, 3, 5, 7, 11, 12, 13, 14, 17, 18, 20, 24, 25, 187
Draft National Policy on Beneficiary Selection and Land Allocation 119

E

economic crime 123, 124, 125, 127, 128, 129, 130, 131 (see also 'corruption')
Economic Freedom Fighters (EFF) 4, 6, 7, 11, 12, 100
Economic Partnership Agreement (EPA) 64
Economic Reconstruction and Recovery Plan (ERRP) 59, 66, 182
Edelman Trust Barometer South Africa 142
election(s) 6, 7, 8, 9, 11, 12, 13, 14, 15, 17, 19, 23, 25, 29, 44, 58, 71, 82, 95, 97, 98, 100, 104, 107, 108, 110, 112, 133, 149, 170, 174, 175, 181, 186, 187, 190, 191, 192, 193, 194, 195
Electoral Law Amendment Act, 2024 175
electoral system 5, 15, 16, 21, 170, 174, 175, 179
electricity 37, 39, 40, 42, 43, 44, 46, 48, 49, 50, 52, 53, 54, 55, 57, 101, 103, 134, 143, 153
Electricity Regulation Act, 2006 43
Electricity Regulation Amendment Bill 48
electricity supply industry (ESI) 40, 42, 44, 46, 50, 51, 55
emerging economy 58, 72, 83, 85, 86, 87, 90, 96, 102, 103, 104, 106, 108 (see also 'Southern middle power')
emerging market (see 'emerging economy')
energy 37, 38, 39, 42, 44, 45, 53, 55, 72, 76, 77, 88, 92, 185
Energy Action Plan 34, 43
energy availability factor (EAF) 41, 48,
energy return on energy invested (EROEI) 45
enterprise and supplier development (ESD) 155, 156
Eskom 8, 28, 39, 40, 41, 42, 43, 44, 45, 46, 47, 48, 49, 50, 88, 169, 173
European Union (EU) 64, 76, 77, 78
expropriation (of land) without compensation 111

F

fossil fuels 38, 39, 45, 52
foreign direct investment (FDI) 64, 65, 186
Fourth Industrial Revolution 37, 55, 154
Freedom Front Plus (FF+) 4, 5

G

Gauteng 17, 87
geopolitics 39, 30, 57, 79, 96
global financial crisis (GFC) 72, 84, 85, 86, 96, 103, 107
Global North 61, 62, 67
Global South 58, 59, 61, 62, 63, 67
global value chain 69, 82
global warming 37 (see also 'climate change')
Gold and Foreign Exchange Contingency Reserve Account (GFECRA) 109
Gordhan, Pravin 168
governance 124, 125, 133, 134, 136, 138, 140, 143, 146, 162, 166, 179, 187, 189, 194
government of national unity 22
greenhouse gas(es) (GHG) 37, 38
gross domestic product (GDP) 27, 28, 32, 38, 51, 57, 63, 64, 73, 75, 77, 78, 83, 85, 86, 92, 106, 152, 185
gross fixed capital formation (GFCF) 185
Group of Seven (G7) 63, 77
Group of Three (G3) 104
Group of 20 (G20) 63
Group of 77 (G77) 63
Growth, Employment and Redistribution (GEAR) strategy 182
Gupta family 166, 169, 178

H

Heher Commission on the Feasibility of Fee-Free Higher Education and Training 88
Helen Suzman Foundation v President of the Republic of South Africa and others 171, 178
Human Rights Watch 29
 World Report 2023 29
Human Sciences Research Council (HSRC) 142
 South African Social Attitudes Survey 142

I

import substitution 51
Independent Power Producer Procurement Programme 88
Independent Regulatory Board for Auditors 170
Independent System and Market Operator Bill (2012) 42
Indlulamithi South Africa Scenarios 2023 29
 Gwara-Gwara scenario 30
 Vulture Culture scenario 30
 Weaver Work scenario 30
information and community technology (ICT) 10, 66
Inkatha Freedom Party (IFP) 4, 5
Integrated Resource Plan (IRP) 43, 46, 48
internal combustion engine (ICE) 51
International Monetary Fund (IMF) 74, 78, 83, 86, 103, 107, 109, 184
 World Economic Outlook October 2023 83
International Renewable Energy Agency (IRENA) 55
internationalism 58, 59

J

Johannesburg Stock Exchange 58
Joint Initiative on Priority Skills Acquisition (Jipsa) 182
Joint Initiative to Fight Crime and Corruption (JICC) 33, 35
Joint Strategic Oversight Committee (JSOC) 33
Judicial Commission of Inquiry into Allegations of State Capture, Corruption and Fraud in the Public Sector including Organs of State (see 'Zondo Commission of Inquiry in Allegations of State Capture')
Just Energy Transition (JET) 45
Just Energy Transition Investment Plan (JET-IP) 43, 44
Just Energy Transition Partnership 77

K

Kahneman, Prof Daniel 182, 183
Kganyago, Governor Lesetja 97, 101, 105, 186, 190

kgoro 161, 162
Kieswetter, Edward 173
Kusile power station 45, 88
KwaZulu-Natal 6, 8

L
Land Bank 115, 118
Land Bank Act, 2002 116
land ownership (title deeds) 111, 118, 121
land reform 111, 112, 113, 115, 116, 117, 118, 119, 120, 121
Land Reform and Agricultural Development Agency 114, 115, 116, 117, 121
Land Reform and Agricultural Development Fund 116, 117, 118, 121
leapfrogging 73
liquefied petroleum gas (LPG) 53, 54
loadshedding 28, 34, 39, 40, 41, 43, 44, 45, 46, 47, 48, 49, 50, 88, 104
local government 133, 134, 135, 136, 137, 138, 139, 140, 141, 143, 144, 145, 148, 149, 156, 160, 161, 175, 187, 194
localisation 60, 156
Low Emissions Development Strategy 43

M
Maimane, Mmusi 12
majoritarianism 22,
Makgoba, Archbishop 151
Malema, Julius 100
Mandela, Nelson 138, 148, 172
Marxist 11
Mbeki, Thabo 138, 139, 176, 178
Medium-Term Budget 106
Medium-Term Expenditure Framework (MTEF) 117
Medupi power station 45, 88
member of parliament (MP) 170, 175, 176
middle-income country(ies) 1, 7, 10, 28
minerals–energy complex 39, 40, 46
mixed-member proportional electoral system 175 (see also 'electoral system')
modernist 11
monetary policy 95, 96, 97, 98, 100, 101, 102, 103, 104, 106, 110
Monetary Policy Committee (MPC) 98, 99, 102, 104, 105, 106
Moyane, Tom 168, 173
multiparty democracy 18, 19, 21, 22, 24, 25

multiparty system 7, 19, 20, 21, 22, 165
Municipal Finance Management Act, 2003 139
Municipal Systems Act, 2000 136, 162
municipalities (see 'local government')

N
National Assembly 111, 174
National Business Initiative 53
National Development Plan (NDP) 60, 69, 112, 115, 136, 137, 153, 185, 191, 192, 193, 196, 197
Ten-Year Review of the NDP 153, 185
National Director of Public Prosecutions (NDPP) 173, 174
National Economic Development and Labour Council (Nedlac) 32, 170
National Energy Act, 2008 46
National Energy Crisis Committee (NECOM) 33, 34, 44, 47
National Energy Regulator of South Africa (NERSA) 48
National Health Insurance (NHI) Bill (2023) 29
National Infrastructure Plan 2030 43
national interest framework document 59, 60
National Logistics Crisis Committee (NLCC) 33, 34
National Party (NP) 5, 18
National Planning Commission 185, 191, 192
National Prosecuting Authority (NPA) 35, 129, 166, 167, 168
National Prosecuting Authority (NPA) Amendment Bill 35
National State Enterprises Bill (2023) 43
National Transmission Company of South Africa (NTCSA) 34, 48, 49, 50
National Treasury 8, 10, 50, 89, 92, 98, 108, 109, 117, 127, 168, 192
nationalisation 6, 100
Nationally Determined Contribution 43
net-zero economy 38
New Development Bank 66 (see also 'BRICS')
New Growth Path (NDP) 182
New Nation Movement NPC v President of the Republic of South Africa 174
New National Party (NNP) 4
non-governmental organisation (NGO)

INDEX

13, 46, 159
North Atlantic Treaty Organization (NATO) 61
North-West University Business School 183 (see also 'Policy Uncertainty Index (PUI)')

O

Operation Vulindlela 192
opposition party(ies) 1, 2, 3, 4, 5, 7, 8, 9, 10, 12, 13, 14, 23
Organisation for Economic Co-operation and Development (OECD) 62, 63
Organisation Undoing Tax Abuse (OUTA) 141
organised business 194, 195
Organization of the Petroleum Exporting Countries (OPEC) 39

P

Pan Africanist Congress (PAC) 5
Paris Agreement (2015) 37
Parliament 15, 22, 35, 44, 100, 134, 143, 165, 166, 168, 170, 171, 174, 175, 176
parliamentary system 2
Patriotic Alliance (PA) 5
patronage 5, 42, 55, 118, 120, 178
Phosa, Mathews 138, 139
policy (un)certainty 44, 79, 90, 181, 182, 183, 184, 185, 186, 187, 188, 189, 190, 191, 192, 193, 194, 196, 197
Policy Uncertainty Index (PUI) 183, 185, 189 (see also 'North-West University Business School')
political faction 8, 11, 42, 55, 100
political party(ies) 1, 2, 10, 11, 16, 17, 19, 22, 23, 25, 29, 111, 169, 174
Political Party Funding Act, 2018 169
political system 15, 17, 18, 19, 20, 21
polycrises 78
post-apartheid 1, 4, 19, 22, 25, 73, 74, 137 (see also 'apartheid')
Preferential Procurement Policy Framework Act, 2000 43
Presidency, The 34, 47, 170
Presidential Advisory Panel on Land Reform and Agriculture 115, 118
presidential electoral system 15, 16 (see also 'electoral system')
President's Economic Advisory Council 193
President's Investment Conference 195

Proactive Land Acquisition Strategy (PLAS) 112, 113, 114, 118
proportional electoral system 5, 15, 16, 17, 18, 19, 170, 174, 175 (see also 'electoral system')
Public Investment Corporation (PIC) 108
public–private partnership 128, 129, 192
Public Protector 166, 168

R

radical economic transformation 167, 171
Ramaphosa, Cyril 10, 31, 32, 34, 40, 43, 46, 47, 66, 96, 97, 98, 100, 110, 114, 115, 133, 134, 138, 139, 140, 141
Rand Merchant Bank (RMB)/Bureau for Economic Research (BER) Business Confidence Index (BCI) 29, 90
Reconstruction and Development Plan (RDP) 182
regional value chain 75, 76, 82
regulatory impact assessment (RIA) 193 (see also 'socioeconomic assessment')
renewable energy 38, 39, 45, 46, 47, 49, 50, 53, 54, 76
Renewable Energy Independent Power Producer Procurement Programme (REIPPPP) 46, 48, 49
Represented Policy Parties Fund (RPPF) 6
Roadmap for Eskom in a Reformed Electricity Supply Industry 42

S

SA Express 88
separate development 20 (see also 'apartheid')
small, medium and micro enterprise (SMME) 156
social compact 32
social contract 166
social grant 143, 153
social relief of distress (SRD) grant 89, 92
socioeconomic assessment 192, 193 (see also 'regulatory impact assessment (RIA)')
solar power 39, 40, 45, 47, 49, 53, 54
South African Airways (SAA) 88
South African Broadcasting Corporation (SABC) 88
South African Chamber of Commerce and Industry (SACCI) Business

Confidence Index (BCI) 28
South African Cities Network 28
 State of City Finances Report 2022 28
South African Local Government
 Association (SALGA) 87, 156
South African National Roads Agency
 Limited (SANRAL) 10, 88
South African Police Service (SAPS) 129, 176
South African Post Office (SAPO) 88
South African Reserve Bank (SARB) 28,
 90, 95, 96, 97, 98, 99, 100, 101, 103,
 104, 106, 107, 108, 109, 110, 186, 190
South African Revenue Service (SARS)
 10, 28, 129, 166, 168, 173, 174
Southern African Customs Union
 (SACU) 68, 74
Southern African Development
 Community (SADC) 57, 74
Southern African Development
 Community (SADC)–EU Economic
 Partnership Agreement (EPA) 64
Southern middle power 58 (see also
 'emerging economy')
Special Investigating Unit (SIU) 129
state capture 8, 41, 42, 43, 88, 123, 133,
 134, 167, 168, 169, 171, 173, 174
State of the Nation Address (SONA) 32,
 74, 114, 115
state-owned company (SOC) 43, 166
state-owned enterprise (SOE) 8, 11, 87,
 88, 89, 91, 116, 117, 127, 168, 169,
 170, 173, 174, 177
State-Owned Enterprise Bill 174, 177
stokvels 157
Stanford University 184, 186, 187
Strategy for BRICS Economic
 Partnership 66
Sustainable Development Goals (SDGs) 77
Symington, Vlok 168

T
Temasek model 177, 178
tipping point 27, 121, 181
trade 57, 58, 60, 62, 64, 65, 66, 67, 68,
 69, 73, 75, 76, 78, 80, 81, 82, 189
trade agreement 60
trade union 13, 89, 99, 170
traditional leader 11, 13, 161
transformation 20, 24, 27, 111, 138, 159
Transnet 8, 34, 43, 88, 169, 173

transparency 2, 96, 119, 126, 137, 140
Transparency International 28 (see also
 'Corruption Perceptions Index')
Treasury (see 'National Treasury')
tribal council (see '*kgoro*')
two-party system 16, 18, 21

U
ubuntu 137
UN World Tourism Organization 78
United Democratic Movement (UDM)
 5, 87, 151
United Nations (UN) 62
United Nations Development
 Organization (UNIDO) 75
United Nations Economic Commission
 for Africa (UNECA) 76
United Nations Framework Convention
 on Climate Change Conference of the
 Parties (UNFCCC COP) 38
universal health coverage 13
upper-middle-income countries 57

V
value-added tax (VAT) 92
van der Westhuizen, Justice 174, 178
volatile, uncertain, complex and
 ambiguous (VUCA) 60

W
welfare state 153
Western Cape 6
White Paper on Energy Policy (1998) 42, 50
World Bank 28, 72, 77, 152
World Economic Forum (WEF) 73, 75,
 138, 154, 184, 192
 Global Risks Report 2024 184, 192
World Health Organization (WHO) 144,
 163
World Uncertainty Index (WUI) 184

Z
Zondo, Chief Justice Raymond 8, 134,
 139, 170, 176
Zondo Commission of Inquiry into
 Allegations of State Capture 123, 131,
 133, 134, 167, 168, 169, 170, 171, 172,
 173, 174, 176, 177
Zuma, Jacob 8, 98, 138, 166, 167, 168,
 171, 173, 176, 178